ANOREXIA NERVOSA AND BULIMIA: HOW TO HELP

ANORECTIC NERVOSA AND BULIMIA: HOW TO HELP

MARILYN DUKER AND
ROGER SLADE

Open University Press
MILTON KEYNES · PHILADELPHIA

Open University Press
Celtic Court
22 Ballmoor
Buckingham MK18 1XW
and
1900 Frost Road, Suite 101
Bristol, PA 19007, USA

First published 1988
Reprinted 1990, 1992, 1994, 1996, 1997

British Library Cataloguing in Publication Data

Duker, Marilyn
Anorexia nervosa and bulimia.
1. Man. Anorexia nervosa & bulimia
I. Title. II. Slade, Roger, 1944–
616.85′2

ISBN 0-335-09836-3
ISBN 0-335-09832-0 Pbk

Library of Congress Cataloging-in-Publication Data

Duker, Marilyn.
Anorexia nervosa and bulimia: how to help/Marilyn Duker and Roger Slade.
p. cm.
Includes index.
ISBN 0-335-09836-3 ISBN 0-335-09832-0 (pbk.)
1. Anorexia nervosa – Treatment. 2. Bulimia – Treatment.
I. Slade, Roger. II. Title.
[DNLM: 1. Anorexia Nervosa – psychology. 2. Anorexia Nervosa – therapy. 3. Behavior Therapy. 4. Bulimia – psychology. 5. Bulimia – therapy. WM 175 D877a]
RC552.A5D85 1988
616.85′2 – dc19
DNLM/DLC
for Library of Congress 88-12435 CIP

Typeset by Vision Typesetting, Manchester
Printed and bound in Great Britain by
Biddles Limited, Guildford and King's Lynn

Contents

*Average expected body weight

With love to our children
Naomi, Raphael, Nathaniel and Morwenna

Acknowledgements

We would like to thank Liz Deeble and Peter Slade for the support they gave this venture in its early stages and for their conviction that such a book was necessary, and Griselda Campbell for her editorial assistance en route.

Our especial thanks are due to Jill Welbourne. The generosity with which she shared her expertise enabled us to present more fully some of the medical aspects of providing help, and the consistent encouragement she gave was invaluable.

We would also like to acknowledge and thank the many sufferers who over the years have shared their problems, their struggles and their recoveries with us. It is their stories that are woven into this book.

Introduction

This book is for anyone who wants to help a person who is anorexic or bulimic, and sufferers will also find it valuable. It is based on the 'starvation whirlpool' theory which we presented first in *The Anorexia Nervosa Reference Book*, and outline here in Chapter 2. We show in detail how this theory applies in the practical task of providing help.

As in *The Anorexia Nervosa Reference Book* we consider anorexia nervosa and bulimia not as separate problems but as different physical and behavioural manifestations of the same 'anorexic' or food-controlling style of thinking. While it is essential to understand the nature of the condition, this on its own is not enough. A helper needs to know how to talk to a sufferer in a way that is likely to be constructive rather than to exacerbate his or her problem, and we illustrate how this may be achieved.

The book as a whole reflects the sea-change that is taking place in the division of responsibility in caring for the anorexia nervosa/bulimia sufferer. Partly this is the result of conceptual developments such as the starvation whirlpool theory, and partly it is the result of growing medical consensus about the physical aspects of the condition. For it is now widely appreciated that anorexia nervosa/bulimia belongs to the same order of problems as drug addiction and alcoholism, and that like these it is a condition in which the individual's actions produce physical and psychological changes that are entrapping.

Here we strike a new balance between the role of medical and other helpers. Unlike those who offer a social analysis and pay scant regard to physical dangers, we insist the helper asks for and responds to medical information, and we indicate where the need for such information and further help will arise. On the other hand it is no longer appropriate for the treatment of anorexia nervosa to be exclusively a medical preserve. Often those who are medically trained have neither the human skills nor the necessary time to address the root of the problem. So we give encouragement and guidance to those who are prepared to take on the main task of providing anorexia nervosa/bulimia sufferers with appropriate help. Thus we move in the direction, long established in the case of alcoholism and drug abuse, of non-medical agencies sustaining a therapeutic role.

It is essential that the helper is attuned to the particular complexities that anorexia nervosa and its counterpart bulimia present. Established psychotherapy techniques can be helpful, but we have not provided a basic account of these. Rather we have indicated when they may profitably be used, and the kind of pitfalls there can be in using them.

The book divides into three parts. Part I is concerned with the nature of the illness and the different forms it takes. It shows the way theories and ideas influence the kinds of treatment that are still used, and the problems inherent in these approaches. In Part II we give a picture of the illness at different stages. We indicate how family circumstances and social and cultural values combine in the development of the condition, and how all of these contribute to its remaining hidden. This part should enable would-be helpers to get to know more fully the people they are aiming to help. In Part III we describe appropriate responses to the particular problems that are likely to arise in each of four weight bands.

Terms and referents

The term 'anorexic' (a misnomer meaning 'without appetite') will be used to refer to the person who is currently of low weight, successfully restricting food intake and usually exercising excessively as a further means of control. The term bulimic will be used to refer to the person whose weight may be normal or near normal, but whose attempts to maintain food and body control recurrently fail; whose hunger cyclicly manifests itself in bulimic ('ox appetite') eating. Where either anorexic or bulimic may apply, the word 'sufferer' will be used.

Girls and women still form the majority of cases of anorexia nervosa/bulimia, so we mainly refer to the sufferer as 'she'. But occasionally we use 'he' to serve as a reminder that there are numbers of male sufferers. The most recent available series give the incidence of men to women sufferers as between 1:20 and 1:10, but there is reason to believe that the latter ratio is the more correct. Without menstruation as an indicator of change men can become very thin without attracting attention, medical or otherwise. So the probability is that the incidence of the illness in males is under-reported. Likewise for clarity we have usually referred to the doctor as male.

The names we have used in all illustrations are fictitious, though each example is a real sufferer in a real situation.

Measuring weight

Information about weight is given in percentages of average expected body weight (AEBW), this being the quickest way of ascertaining the degree of physical and psychological change, and with this the margin of physical safety and likely associated behaviour.

For example, when a person's weight loss reaches the point where they are only 65 per cent of their AEBW, then their condition will be physically dangerous, their behaviour will have become very rigid and communication problems severe. All of these aspects have implications for the way help, as it affects the person as a whole, is best provided in each individual case.

Anyone's weight can be calculated as a percentage of their AEBW by dividing the current weight of a person by his/her AEBW and then multiplying this by 100, as follows:

$$\frac{\text{Current weight}}{\text{AEBW}} \times \frac{100}{1} = n\%$$

The average expected body weight (AEBW) for any individual is calculated on the basis of their age, sex and height. Tables showing average weights for men and for women are given in the Appendix. Also indicated in the tables are the 65-per-cent AEBW levels where weight loss itself is hazardous.

These tables can be used to calculate, for example, that a healthy weight for a 23-year-old woman, who is 5 ft. 6 in. tall, would on average be 9 st. 6 lb. (132 lb.). Should this same young woman currently weigh 7 st. (98 lb.), then, using the above formula it can be calculated that she would, at this point, weigh only 75 per cent of her AEBW:

$$\frac{98\text{ lb}}{132\text{ lb}} \times \frac{100}{1} = 75\%$$

The approach to help we offer here is one that we have developed over the last decade and a half through our academic research, our practical experience of providing therapy, care and counselling for sufferers and their families, and from our contact with a network of professionals and sufferers from whom we have learned a great deal. Our hope is that with this book many more people may be helped.

Roger Slade and Marilyn Duker

PART I

· ONE ·

Beginning to unravel the problem

There can be few conditions which generate as much interest as anorexia nervosa and bulimia, but where so little practical help is available. Over the last few years there has been a dramatic increase in the number of books and articles appearing in the popular press, and academic papers are now numbered in thousands, but very little of this activity has had any practical significance for those who find themselves having to cope, day in and day out, with the relentless stress that these problems create. Increasing numbers of desperate people find there is nowhere to go with their particular difficulty. Self-help groups offer support and information but generally make no claims to be able to intervene therapeutically. Medical centres are extremely overloaded, and information organizations, in common with general practitioners, have very few places to which to refer the people who contact them. There is a great and growing need for skilled help.

The lack of help might seem surprising, since these conditions are ones that usually occur in a section of the community that is not otherwise deprived. Anorexia nervosa and bulimia sufferers typically come from respectable, middle-class and relatively affluent homes, and their parents are responsible and caring people who tend to move in circles where social and professional contacts with the caring agencies are plentiful. But the question of providing help is not exactly straightforward.

There is, to begin with, no consensus over who has the necessary therapeutic expertise. While hospital treatment programmes for low-weight anorexics that involve restoring the emaciated sufferer to normal weight attract criticism from inside and outside the medical profession, there is also reason to be concerned about therapists who insist that keeping track of changes in body weight, and monitoring symptoms such as vomiting, which are used to control ingestion of food, is peripheral to 'real' therapy.

It is also difficult to provide help for people who do not actively seek it. Far from seeing themselves as in need of help, anorexics feel better when they are skinny and losing weight. From their point of view food control is good. For an anorexic it is other people's anxieties that are the problem. So requests for help are more likely to come from relatives and others who are close. When sufferers have become aware that their anorexic way of life is limiting and ultimately destructive, they still feel they ought not to need help. When they have developed bulimia, they are more likely to seek help because of their distress, but they feel their behaviour does not deserve to be helped. Compared with other people's more tangible and more obvious pressing problems they see their own difficulties over food and weight as unreasonable and unjustified. Bulimics usually feel so hopeless and disgusted about the methods they use to control ingestion of food that they shy away from making their problem public. They can feel they are beyond help. It may be only their suicidal despair that eventually brings them to the point of seeking the support they need.

Mysteriousness

Much that has been written on anorexia nervosa and bulimia conveys an air of mystery which is both mistaken and unhelpful, for all the main characteristics of these illnesses have already been investigated in considerable detail, and a great deal of information is available. There is no reason to wait for further basic research before setting about the task of helping the sufferer. Academic disputes will continue, because the condition of anorexia nervosa in particular is remarkable for the way it challenges well-worn ways of thinking. But the disputes are largely the result of the personal and professional reasons which those involved have for disregarding sections of the relevant information. The commitment to 'objective' science, for instance, leads some to ignore the moral aspects of the sufferer's view of food control. Others, convinced they have found the meaning of the symptom, overlook well-established physiological facts about the effects of starvation. Many more who are sure that hard work, competitiveness and willpower are valuable in their own right are unwilling to see that these qualities in an anorexic are part of what has caused her to become ill.

Leaving professional knowledge and differences of opinion aside, it still remains true that, for those meeting anorexia nervosa or bulimia for the first time, the conditions are both baffling and frustrating. It is this that makes it so difficult to channel the interest that there is in the subject of eating disorders towards benefiting either the sufferer or the members of her family who can be stressed almost to breaking point by her illness. However much concern those close to the sufferer might initially feel, this rapidly becomes diffused in the mounting tension that anorexia nervosa or intractable bulimia create. Likewise, though there may be an abundance of goodwill, it sooner or later gives way to a sense of helpless impotence and downright anger. Bulimics perhaps receive more angry responses because of the literal mess they create in others' lives.

It is not hard to find reasons for the bafflement. Academic explanations of an anorexic's behaviour sometimes seem to contain outright contradictions of the everyday experiences of the people who live with her. While there is wide academic agreement that the lack of a clear sense of self is central to anorexia nervosa; that the sufferer has a very fragile notion of her own being,[1] those close to her can experience her as iron-willed and dominating. Certainly this is true where food control and physical exercise regimes are concerned. She is very definite and demanding about what she will or will not tolerate in relation to domestic routines and arrangements; for these must be predictable to support her control. As tension mounts and preoccupation with her refusal to eat grows, those close to her are unlikely to look beyond her intransigence over food-related matters as they judge her as having a 'strong' personality.

The bafflement that anorexia nervosa and bulimia create runs deeper, however, than contradictions between academic explanations and personal experience. Coming across the conditions for the first time, people generally do not know, in a very fundamental sense, what kind of problem they are facing. They often make certain assumptions – ordinary, everyday assumptions that in so many ways seem perfectly reasonable. But it just so happens that these hinder rather than help an understanding of the sufferer's behaviour.

In the case of classical anorexia nervosa the difficulty in understanding usually becomes clear once the individual has developed definite physical symptoms; that is, the key symptoms of extreme weight loss and the cessation of menstrual periods (amenorrhoea) that are usually associated with the use of the term 'anorexia nervosa'. Until this point has been reached, people are generally unaware that there is anything about the person that needs to be explained. There is, on the surface, no reason to worry about her. It is only when she becomes so thin that her emaciation can no longer be ignored that the need for understanding emerges. The tendency is then to assume that her condition must fall into one of two categories. Either it must be the result of something having gone wrong with the way her body is working – as when a person is suffering with tuberculosis, cancer or a gastric ulcer – or it must be the result of something she is doing to herself.

Similarly the family of the person who regularly overeats and vomits may simply see her as over-indulgent and greedy. They may believe that a little self-discipline is all that is needed and totally fail to understand her experience in her battles with bulimia.

The illness as a category problem

Classifying an event is usually the first step in deciding what to do about it – in this case deciding what kind of help is appropriate. The distinction between physical illness and deliberate action is particularly important here because the responses people make are so very different. Generally we do not see ourselves as having the same kind of choice over events such as physical illness as we feel we have over the things we do. So, where something is thought to be the result of an individual's action, ideas of personal responsibility tend to be invoked, and sometimes also blame. But where an event is classified as physical illness, ideas of personal responsibility and blame have usually been considered unwarranted and unnecessary.

The difficulty where anorexia nervosa and bulimia are concerned is that the conditions do not fit straightforwardly into either of the above categories. Rather they are a mixture of both. They are akin to alcoholism and drug addiction in this respect. They belong to a different or third category in which a person's actions are constrained and have progressively become so as a result of physical and psychological changes that are self-induced. There are a number of reasons why bulimia is perhaps more easily recognized as having this kinship, one being that binges are similar to episodic bouts of drunkenness. Anorexia nervosa meanwhile is 'a horribly complicated tangle that people can get themselves into when their behaviour upsets the conditions under which their body and brain usually function.'[2] Those who work with alcoholism can find themselves fending off similar assumptions that alcoholics are either the passive victims of a disease or susceptibility not yet fully understood, or that they are entirely responsible for their own fate. To inhabit the middle ground in these issues takes skill and practice on the part of the helper.

The impossibility of containing anorexia nervosa or bulimia either in the category of physical illness or that of deliberate action is not simply an academic problem. It is something that is lived out painfully by the sufferer's family. It is a common experience for parents to find themselves constantly thrown between irritation and anxiety. Either they get involved in angry scenes at what appears to be a stubborn refusal to eat or to stop eating where she is bingeing, or they are nagged by the fear that she really might be ill, so that, if it is not her fault, they ought to be more caring. Such is the confusion over which position to adopt that they end up completely at a loss to know how to treat her.

> I knew my daughter was getting too thin and I suggested she ought to see the doctor. I was worried about her health. But there again she was very lively and busy. She had a demanding job, and said she felt fine. So I tried not to worry. But I found myself getting very angry when she always refused to eat proper meals. She'd say she wasn't hungry, then I'd find she'd eaten other food I'd planned for another meal. She'd be so convincing if I said anything, I'd end up thinking I was the one who was unreasonable. But she was so thin there was always that worry. You don't know what to think. You end up confused.

A bulimic's flatmate illustrates a similar experience:

> For ages I didn't know what was wrong. Some days she'd be so energetic and organized and helpful. Then she'd disappear into her room and only come out in her dressing gown to snap at us. I didn't realize she was bingeing like mad. It was only when she took an overdose we found out what had been going on. I felt terrible then about all the times I'd been so angry with her for being so inconsiderate.

A difficulty for those close to the anorexic is her total, rigid consistency. (Equally, as long as she is *not* eating, the bulimic's behaviour will be consistent too.) From this there springs another level of confusion, as this anorexic's parent pointed out:

> She is *so* rational. Her opinions seem reasonable, very clearly thought out – you're convinced there can't be anything mentally wrong with her. But then she'll also seem very obsessive. So obsessive, it's hard to believe *that's* quite so rational.

Differing interpretations of her behaviour can frequently be one of the sources of the tensions and conflicts that develop within the family over the anorexic's problem with eating. One father felt very sympathetic and was sure his daughter was ill and needed help and, amongst other things, contacted various helping organizations, but her mother was equally convinced that the daughter was deliberately attempting to break up the parents' marriage. In another case, while the girl's mother felt her daughter was not to blame for her emaciation, her father was sure she was avoiding having to take her final examinations at university. Either parent may take either position. But, embroiled as they are in the day to day task of coping with their daughter's behaviour, they are unlikely to be aware of the extent to which their differences of opinion may be organized around two opposing views of the nature of anorexia nervosa, neither of which is sufficiently elaborate to gain any leverage on the problem.

The physical illness category

Once clear physical symptoms of emaciation and loss of periods (amenorrhoea) develop, the sufferer will usually be obliged by her family to see a doctor. But although the doctor may make sure that anorexia nervosa is correctly diagnosed, and that there is no other physical condition that might have caused her symptoms, the consultation does not usually resolve the confusion over what to do about them. Medical training does not immunize against bafflement in this instance. Biasing doctors in favour of physiological explanations gets in the way of understanding the problem.

The anorexic's physical appearance when she is low-weight can be quite alarming, particularly when she reaches the point where she needs urgent medical care. Many doctors admit they find it hard to believe that such dramatic and life-threatening emaciation, accompanied as it is by the loss of menstruation and other endocrinological changes, does not have a biological cause. It can also seem highly implausible that such a person who comes from a comfortable home and has a good family background should be suffering from something so straightforward as malnutrition. As one general practitioner said:

> I know the family well. Her father's a solicitor, and very well connected. And Elizabeth's a highly intelligent and cultured young woman, and very charming. I can't believe she would be so stupid, or so lacking in common sense as to do this deliberately.

It is as a consequence of this puzzlement that classic low-weight anorexia nervosa has been actively researched now by the medical profession for well over a hundred years. With each new advance in physical medicine the issue is reopened and more research undertaken.

However, the prevailing medical opinion is that the anorexic's physical symptoms at low weight are those of a healthy person whose body is adjusting to the effects of persistent undernutrition. The physiological picture she presents is much the same as that produced by major calorie depletion from any cause. Most people who become anorexic are physically mature, or nearly so, before they begin to restrict their food intake, and they also eat food that is of high nutritional quality, albeit in minimal amounts. Because of this starvation does not usually stunt growth or leave the legacy of physical disorders associated with dietary deficiencies that it can do when it occurs as a result of famine and other disasters. An exception to this statement is the osteoporosis that can occur in thin, chronic anorexia nervosa sufferers who do not menstruate at all for many years.

As with starvation in any other situation the anorexic's physical symptoms also remit when she takes adequate nourishment again. Even osteoporosis can improve with high calcium and vitamin D intake if this is coupled with a nearer normal level of protein in the person's diet. This ability to recover the original healthy state has, from a medical point of view, provided perhaps the strongest evidence that food restriction is the primary cause of the anorexic's weight loss, however drastic this may have been.[3]

The doctor thus finds himself in the same position in relation to the anorexia nervosa sufferer as any other concerned person. All the evidence suggests that her starved state is self-imposed, yet in the absence of political or religious dogma, or any other clear intention, the extremity of her behaviour and her imperviousness to its life-threatening nature, seem odd and unintelligible. Again it is the intellectual discomfort created in the professional observer that remains a powerful stimulus to medical research. Meanwhile investigations into her physical state offer no challenge to the way the anorexic is controlling her food intake. Indeed such investigations can, and often do, draw attention away from the fact that she is starving herself and effectively disguise the significance of her falling weight from the hospital staff attending her.

> I went into hospital about six months after my periods stopped, into a gynaecological ward just to see if there was anything wrong. I wasn't worried myself. I knew I wasn't eating, and all that mattered was to keep that up. They didn't find anything, and no one mentioned anorexia. Then later I went in again for pains in my stomach. Still no one said anything. They said I was OK, and discharged me. Except that time there was one doctor. He was quite young. He saw me afterwards sort of casually on my way out and said had I thought I might have anorexia. I said no, but I knew I did. But if I had check-ups it kept my parents happy. They felt better if they thought I was doing something to help myself.

The deliberate action category

In many ways it seems the most natural thing to extend an ordinary purposive account of human behaviour to anorexia nervosa to explain the sufferer's actions. Many people restrict the amount of food they eat and do so for a variety of reasons without any suggestion that they are ill. So, at an ordinary common-sense level, it seems likely that the anorexic likewise might have a particular aim in mind when she so consistently refuses food. It has been suggested that her self-starvation could be simply a way of either gaining attention for herself, for instance, or objecting to her female role, or committing slow suicide, or getting at her mother.

It is with the idea that there is some underlying purpose to the anorexic's behaviour that, for most people, the whole issue is likely to rest, particularly if they never come face to face with the problem. Those who do meet the condition, however, soon discover that, for all its apparent plausibility, this common-sense approach quickly breaks down. They find that, although the girl seems to be actively and purposefully creating her symptoms by severely restricting her food intake, she is quite at a loss to explain why she is so utterly preoccupied with regulating herself in this way. Where she does offer reasons, these seem wholly inadequate to explain why she should persist in taking this self-regulation to such extremes. The following report made by a student nurse to the ward sister illustrates this.

> It's hopeless. She wouldn't have it. She just went on saying she wasn't going to drink this stuff because she didn't want to get fat. She insists she's fat enough already, and she's really disgusted at being so fat. She pinched together the skinniest bit of flesh on her ribs to show me. You can count every one of her ribs. Her bones are sticking through her skin! She can't be more than four and a half stone, and she's there lying on the bed because she's too weak to sit up. It just doesn't make sense!

The nurse here had been trying to encourage this emaciated sufferer (4 st. and 57-per-cent AEBW) to take the liquid food that had been prescribed for her. As this account shows, the anorexic's behaviour lacks the flexibility that is usually associated with voluntary action. She seems to be choosing to control her food intake. She seems to have strong personal preferences and great determination to act on these. Yet at the same time she appears to be completely unable to alter course, even though her emaciation is upsetting people she would rather not upset, such as her parents, her husband, her children, her friends. She is unable to alter course even when she is so emaciated she is in danger of dying. Thus, although the anorexic's behaviour looks as though it could be understandable, those who come face to face with the problem find that in practice it is totally unintelligible.

Recognizing the condition of anorexia nervosa

The formal medical criteria for recognizing anorexia nervosa contain two kinds of information. On the one hand there is information relating to the physical symptoms of starvation, and on the other hand there are the facts relating to the anorexic's distinctive attitude towards food and body control.

The importance of the 'anorexic attitude'

For a positive diagnosis of anorexia nervosa to be made it is essential for the doctor to detect the presence of this particular attitude; the condition cannot and *must not* be confirmed on the physical picture alone. If the attitude is not present, then the patient's emaciation is not the result of anorexia nervosa, and other causes for her emaciation must be sought and treated.

In the various sets of medical criteria the anorexic's avoidance of food is described as 'studied and purposive',[4] and her attitude to food and body control as steadfast and 'implacable'.[5] She is involved in 'pursuing a low body weight and then maintaining it',[6] or is engaged in an 'active refusal' to eat enough to maintain a normal weight and/or a 'determined sustained effort' to prevent ingested food from being absorbed.[7] Hers is a 'relentless pursuit of thinness.'[8]

These descriptions of the anorexic attitude effectively distinguish anorexia nervosa sufferers from other groups of patients who may have substantial weight loss without organic cause. It differentiates anorexics from those who have become emaciated because they are, for example, profoundly depressed and physically so slowed down that it is too much effort for them to get meals or even to eat when someone prepares and serves meals for them. It differentiates them from anxious people who have a neurotic fear that food will stick in their throat or give them stomach pains, and from schizophrenics who believe falsely that for instance the food they are being offered is poisoned and so avoid it.

There is a problem, however. For words such as 'studied' and 'active' and 'determined' are usually associated with the idea of being completely autonomous and self-directed as a human being. They describe characteristics that are usually attributed to the person who is well integrated and whole. Accurate though these descriptions are therefore, and helpful to the diagnosis of the problem, they are also an important source of confusion. For they underline the persistent uneasiness there is about the justification for saying that the person who is anorexic is ill.

These criteria need to be understood in relation to the context in which they are designed to work. They are practical tools used in a medical setting in which there is an identified patient, usually with clear physical symptoms, and parents and other relatives expecting some action to be taken. In this situation, if the girl looks particularly skeletal or if her emaciation has actually become life-threatening, it seems an academic quibble to point out that the distinguishing characteristics of the anorexic's attitude are not in themselves unusual; that her attitude suggests normality rather than abnormality, certainly in terms of its appearing to lead to self-directed and autonomous behaviour.

The problems of defining the anorexic's attitude in ways that suggest that she is a person who is fully functioning – who can connect the things she thinks and says with subsequent practical decisions about the things she does – become apparent as soon as her physical emaciation becomes less alarming. Once some weight gain has been achieved, the sufferer's attitude is not usually seen as cause for concern. Thus many parents and relatives, and some members of the medical profession too, are erroneously inclined to think that anorexia nervosa is cured as soon as a normal or near normal body weight has been recovered. But weight gain alone does *not* constitute recovery. If weight is all that has changed, then the likelihood is that the sufferer will progress to alternative means of re-establishing control and, when this seems to fail, to finding some means of obliterating the subsequent feelings of despair (see Chapter Three). A change in her attitude, or style of thinking, is essential if a sufferer is to begin to move away from food control.

Specifically, from the point of view of providing appropriate help, there are also two good reasons why it is important to be able to distinguish the sufferer by her attitude, and without relying on the presence of physical symptoms. Firstly, if the sufferer or her therapist make premature assumptions that a recovery has been achieved simply because lost weight has been regained, then support and advice will be abandoned, or treatment broken off at the very point where this continuing help is most needed (see Chapter Thirteen). Secondly, recognizing and confronting the problem at an early stage (i.e. at that point where the person's style of thinking has become classically an anorexic style of thinking, but her changed ideas are only just beginning to result in weight-restricting and body-controlling behaviour) are the most effective ways of shortening the length of time a person will ultimately spend as an anorexic and/or bulimic.

Once any person has been drawn into the condition, it is very difficult for that person to extract him or herself from the way of thinking it generates, and from the consequent self-destructive lifestyle. Since the problem is one that endures for years, the possibility of recognizing attitudinal symptoms early is worth serious consideration.

Distinguishing the food/body control that is characteristically anorexic

Distinguishing the sufferer by her characteristic attitudes, and in the absence of other symptoms, can be achieved informally or formally. Both ways involve a much finer discrimination of her attitudes than appears in the published medical criteria.

Informal observation

Informally the anorexic can be characterized as someone for whom maintaining control over her food intake and her body is the highest priority, a task in her life that takes precedence over every other. The anorexic will succeed in establishing and keeping control; where she becomes bulimic she will try, but fail repeatedly and spectacularly. This will be observable in numbers of ways. In any situation where there is a choice to be made, she will always take the option that involves non-eating. This may for a time be implicit, as, for example, when she appears to prefer to do her homework rather than go with the rest of the family to see her grandmother. What she knows, and what the rest of the family does not know, is that by arranging to do her homework she can avoid having the meal that her grandmother always serves. Later this will become more explicit, as perhaps when tension mounts within the family because she has continually refused to visit her grandmother or insists she'll only go as long as the visit doesn't coincide with a mealtime, or on condition that she only has to have a cup of tea while she is there. It will just happen she is 'never hungry at Grandma's.'

The following conversation with a sufferer, who at the time was 78 per cent of her AEBW, likewise shows the overriding importance that food and weight have over every other issue.

BEA: The trouble with going out with Joe is I drink too much beer.
HELPER: Are you worried you might have a drink problem?

BEA: Oh no! It's not the alcohol that worries me. It's the calories in the stuff. . . .

HELPER: But if you're drinking that much aren't you afraid you might get into a sexual situation you can't handle?

BEA: No, it's not that. I'm not worried about him wanting to sleep with me. Just as long as I don't put on any weight.

Likewise the dedication to the pursuit of thinness is illustrated by the despairing husband who exclaimed of his emaciated wife: 'Oh, yes. If there were low-calorie water, she'd be having that!' Where rigorous routines of physical exercise are essential to a sense of control, these will take precedence over all other considerations.

CAREERS MISTRESS: I'm surprised at the choices you've made. Were those universities the ones that were offering the courses you wanted?

ELLA [who habitually swims at least two miles every day]: I wasn't too concerned about the courses I suppose. I went on what sports facilities they have. The only ones I was interested in were the ones with a swimming pool on the campus, so I can get there between lectures. I've got to have my swim every day.

The advantages of restricting food are illustrated in the following comment made by a young woman who also used swimming as routine exercise: 'Not eating is much more reliable than exercise as a means of keeping control. What happens if my work suddenly takes me to East Germany and there's no swimming pool in the town?'

The food/body control that is specifically anorexic can be further distinguished by the way that it functions in continually creating and establishing a sense of her 'self'. From this springs the characteristic statements she makes such as: 'I'm all right as long as I've got my eating under control. That's just how I am. If I don't manage that, everything goes,' and 'I'm fine when I don't eat. That's when I can get a few things done' (see Chapter Eight).

An anorexic's food control is also distinguished by the strongly polarized perception she has of the consequences of maintaining or not maintaining it. Her entire idea of her 'self' changes according to whether or not it is achieved. This is evident in the above statements, but the consequences are wider still, for a move from not eating to eating, from being in control to being out of control, involves a similar move in relation to every other distinction that is important to her, such as whether she is a success or failure at school, or at work, or a good or bad member of her family. 'I'm disturbing to the whole family when I eat. I'm uncontrolled and horrible, completely self-obsessed, and it upsets them so much. But when I don't eat I can manage all right. Then I can be thoughtful and sensitive, and behave properly.' The anorexic may be able to avoid upsetting people, and keep up with her school work and generally do the things that are normally expected of her, but only if she is able to maintain her starvation. Success or failure at controlling food switches her, so that her whole being is either 'good' or 'bad'. For the bulimic her erratic eating causes her to alternate between 'good self' and her 'horrible, monstrous, greedy self' every time she swings from controlled starving to uncontrolled binge-eating.

Formal measures

The anorexic's attitude can, as we have said, also be differentiated by more formal means. One psychological test that is widely used was created by selecting a series of statements, mostly about food, that were almost always endorsed by a group of anorexia nervosa sufferers but seldom endorsed by members of a non-anorexic control group. When applied to other groups a high score in this test is quite effective in selecting individuals who to this extent think like an anorexic.[9]

Formal measures of this kind make it possible to survey many different groups relatively easily. Results show that a significant proportion of the population as a whole thinks in this way, but that the proportion varies according to the interests and occupation of particular groups. In a British technical college 6.3 per cent of the women were high scorers on this test, but the incidence varied from almost 10 per cent of those on beauty-therapy courses, and 7.2 per cent on secretarial courses to 0 per cent on building and engineering courses.[10] Among half of the total number of pupils in a British ballet school, 16 per cent were high scorers as compared with only 5 per cent in a similarly aged group of girls attending an ordinary private school.[11] Meanwhile, in a highly competitive American dance school, a figure of 37.7 per cent has been recorded.[12]

People who appear from the results of this test as having extreme attitudes to food control form a very mixed group. When those from the above technical college who had high scores were interviewed, for example, it appeared that 17 per cent were 'normal dieters'. The rest revealed abnormal preoccupation with weight and food intake; 39 per cent indulged in self-induced vomiting and 18 per cent in laxative abuse. Only 7 per cent were anorexic according to those medical criteria which require very substantial loss of weight before diagnosis can be made.

It seems therefore that tests which concentrate on attitudes to food and weight are not always accurate in discriminating those with anorexia nervosa. This is especially so in the case of those concerned about their body shape because they are professional dancers, models, actors or actresses or involved in competitive sports. But the distinction can be made in different ways.[13] Other psychological measures reveal that whereas an anorexic is driven to resolve her deep sense of personal inadequacy by rigidly controlling her food and her body, the dancer or athletics enthusiast who is not anorexic will have good things to say about herself or himself that relate to abilities other than the capacity for maintaining various degrees of self-starvation (see Chapter Six). The non-anorexic person is *not* totally dependent for her sense of self-worth on her ability to restrict food intake.

Even allowing for such subtleties, there seems to be little doubt that in the population as a whole there is a large pool of people who are dependent for a sense of self on establishing or maintaining rigid regimes of food control and exercise. Though they do not all have the frank physical symptoms of undernourishment at any one time, they are nevertheless vulnerable to developing eating problems. For anyone who does not have a firm sense of self food and body control is a very potent 'remedy' (see Chapter Eight), but also a hazardous one. It is highly effective in creating a sense of self where this is lacking because it sets in train a series of personality changes that are readily entrapping (see Chapter Two). Furthermore, these changes are likely to go unnoticed because they actually signify success according to prevailing value systems. This is why the early consequences of controlling food intake can be so insidiously dangerous.

The similarities between anorexia nervosa and bulimia

The new helper will find that the bulimic talking about herself will sound surprisingly similar to the anorexic. They make the same kind of statements about themselves and their world because food and weight are the central preoccupations for both. The following comment, for instance, could be said by either of them, at any weight, no matter whether currently five stone or fifteen. 'Oh yes. Even that half pound matters. Not putting it on means everything to me. I'd have felt terrible. It would have been better if I'd lost half a pound, but I'm relieved I haven't put anything on. I was scared. I was sure that I had.' Likewise they express the same fundamental beliefs about themselves. 'I'm just despicable when I go out of control. I'm disgusting. I'm better when I don't eat. Everything would be fine if I never had to look at food, if I never had to eat at all.' The main difference is that while the bulimic is confronted each day with demonstrations of her failure to control herself and her food, the starving anorexic whose weight is falling feels she is succeeding in staying in control.

It is because they are different consequences of the same need to create and maintain a sense of self that it is possible to deal with the task of providing help for both anorexics and bulimics in the same book. The physical hazards are different in each case, and helping strategies will necessarily vary (see Part III). But effective therapy for both is that which carefully attends to the need to create and develop a firmer sense of self and one that is no longer centred on food and body control. Whether they are in an anorexic or a bulimic phase of the illness, this involves creating substantial changes in sufferers' beliefs about themselves.

Some medical and other objections to taking the two conditions as one problem

Not everyone is happy to accept the view that the physical picture presented by starvers and relentless exercisers, binge-vomiters and laxative abusers is simply the consequence of whichever particular kind or kinds of control they are currently subjecting their body to. For this view appears to treat as identical conditions whose consequences result in clients/patients who physically look very different from each other.

Emaciated, non-menstruating anorexics who organize their whole life around non-eating present quite a different physiological picture from normal-weight bulimics. Either instead of, or as well as, periodic self-starving, bulimics attempt to regulate themselves by preventing the absorption of the food they have eaten and use self-induced vomiting or quantities of laxatives as their way of re-establishing a sense of control. Bulimics usually maintain a weight that is nearer an average expected body weight for height, age and sex than the straightforwardly starving anorexic and, if female, will probably be menstruating normally, or at least intermittently. Often there is nothing in bulimics' physical appearance which would give the slightest clue to show that they have a problem with food.

The idea that the sufferer's physical state is simply a consequence of her currently used form of control tends to create uneasiness because amongst other things it involves abandoning the possibility of discovering a specific physical cure for either condition. For it is unlikely that such radically different pictures as presented by the low-weight anorexic and the normal-weight bulimic could have a common organic cause.[14] It is an idea that also creates doubt about the value of sophisticated and expensive in-patient units specifically for anorexics. It indicates that those aspects of the problem that are specifically medically dangerous can be managed adequately by the interested hospital physician in a sympathetically staffed medical ward. Milder levels of biochemical disturbance can be satisfactorily investigated and replacement therapy prescribed by the sufferer's general practitioner (see Part III).

The approach adopted here might also be considered by some to ride roughshod over important psychological differences between anorexics and bulimics. The superior, aloof, austere and rigid anorexic is markedly different from the impulsive, changeable, guilt-ridden and confused bulimic, and it might seem odd to treat such apparently different personalities as stemming from the same problem. In our view, however, many of the apparent differences in the personalities of the sufferers is the effect rather than the cause of the condition. Personality is the dependent rather than the independent variable. With sustained and successful restriction of food intake, as with alcoholism and drug addiction, the individual's personality is changed often beyond recognition. Those close to the sufferer will be aware of this. As one father said bitterly, jerking his head to indicate the emaciated girl who sat looking distant and superior, 'That's not my daughter. I don't known who it is, but it's not my daughter.'

In academic circles the idea of running together such extremes of controlled and impulsive behaviour may meet resistance because it confounds those theories of personality development which are often used to explain the anorexic's behaviour.

Nor is it particularly congenial to sufferers to be grouped together in this way. The concern to maintain control over food and body is central to both anorexia nervosa and bulimia. Anorexics and bulimics share the same preoccupations and the same fears. But from her position the anorexic does not want to countenance the possibility that control might fail. 'I'm never going to get like that. I don't ever want to be like that,' is the starving anorexic's typical shuddering comment about the bulimic. Because the anorexic's success in controlling her food intake is so crucially important to her, she does not want its value diminished by being associated with people who eat uncontrollably and who have such 'unaesthetic' and 'unacceptable' methods of regaining control. For instance, a sufferer who had consistently maintained her anorexic self-starving lifestyle for many years dismissed a then newly published autobiographical account[15] that focused on the bulimic phase of the illness as 'just a dirty story'.

Meanwhile the bulimic who stuffs and starves herself by turns, who purges and/or vomits and/or uses diuretics in her desperation, and who is convinced that, if only she could achieve or regain total control over her food and her weight, then all her problems would be solved, is generally not very happy to be told that her cherished ambition, even if she attained it, is not a viable one.

Put very simply, bulimia is the anorexic's nightmare and anorexia is the bulimic's dream. It is for this reason that the suggestion that anorexia nervosa and bulimia are different stages of the same condition is unwelcome news to all concerned.

References

1 Bruch, H. (1978). *The Golden Cage*, Open Books, 39.
Crisp, A. (1980). *Anorexia Nervosa: Let Me Be*, London, Academic Press, 65.
McLeod, S. (1981), *The Art of Starvation*, London, Virago, 64.
2 Slade, R. (1984). *The Anorexia Nervosa Reference Book*, London, Harper and Row, 83.
3 Isaacs, A.J. in Dally, P. and Gomez, J. (eds.) (1969). *Anorexia Nervosa*, London, Heinemann Medical Books, 202.
4 Russell, G.F.M. (1970). 'Anorexia nervosa: its identity as an illness and its treatment', in J.H. Price (ed.) *Modern Trends in Psychological Medicine*, London, Butterworth.
5 Feighner, J.P., Robins, E. and Guze, S.B. (1972). 'Diagnostic criteria for use in psychiatric research', *Archives of General Psychiatry*, Chicago, 26: 57–63.
6 Crisp, A.H. (1977). 'The differential diagnosis of anorexia nervosa', *Proceedings of the Royal Society of Medicine*, London, 70: 686–90.
7 Dally, P. (1969). *Anorexia Nervosa*, London, Heinemann Medical Books, 11.
8 Bruch, H. (1978), ibid., ix.
9 Garner, D.M. and Garfinkel, P.E. (1979). 'The Eating Attitudes Test: an index of the symptoms of anorexia nervosa', *Psychological Medicine*, Cambridge, 9, 273–9.
10 Button, E.J. and Whitehouse, A. (1981). 'Subclinical anorexia nervosa', *Psychological Medicine*, Cambridge, 11, 509–16.
11 Szmukler, G.I., Eisler, I., Gillies, C. and Hayward, M. (1985). 'The implications of anorexia nervosa in a ballet school', *Journal of Psychiatric Research*, Oxford, vol. 19, no. 2/3, 177–81.
12 Garner, D.M. and Garfinkel, P.E. (1980). 'Socio-cultural factors in the development of anorexia nervosa', *Psychological Medicine*, Cambridge, 10, 647–56.
13 Weeda-Mannak, W.L. and Drop, M.J. (1985). 'The discriminative value of psychological characteristics in anorexia nervosa. Clinical and psychometric comparison between anorexia nervosa patients, ballet dancers and controls', *Journal of Psychiatric Research*, Oxford, vol. 19, 2/3, 285–90.
14 Slade, R. (1984). ibid., 22–8.
15 Roche, L. (1984). *Glutton for Punishment*, London, Pan Books.

· TWO ·

A path through the theories

The way people approach the task of helping the anorexic is inevitably influenced by the theories they hold. There are many theories, each with different implications for the helper and different possible consequences for the sufferer. One person may insist the anorexic's weight must be increased before psychotherapy can be attempted, whilst another may adopt exactly the opposite strategy. Still another may prefer to concentrate on changing the pattern of relationships in the sufferer's family and avoid dealing directly with the anorexic at all. Thus a newcomer to the problem might be forgiven for thinking that almost anything might be tried in the hope of finding or providing help.

Yet while the range of authoritative ideas might seem daunting, only a relatively small number of distinctions need be made to render the whole field manageable and enable the newcomer to weave a path through the theories. Likewise many of these theories can seem awe inspiring in their sweeping analysis of, say, child development, or Western culture or feminist politics. But hardly any provide helpers with information that is sufficiently finely textured to make it possible for them to engage in a practical way with the sufferers they are meeting face to face.

Two types of theory

As we saw in Chapter One the central dispute has in the past been over the physical symptoms of the low-weight anorexic and whether or not these really are the result of self-induced starvation. But more recently the debate has moved to the psychological effects that starvation brings about, and whether and to what extent these effects explain why the anorexic continues to refuse to eat adequate amounts of food. On this issue theories or explanations of the condition tend to fall broadly into two categories, the divide occurring over the question of the significance that is to be given to the psychological effects of consistent undernutrition.

In the one category are those explanations of anorexia nervosa that build on the evidence that undernutrition and low weight themselves produce dramatic psychological changes. For where food intake and body weight are consistently reduced some experiences are removed, others are altered, and certain experiences are induced that are not available to people who are adequately fed. These changes are important and will be considered in some detail later in this chapter.

In the other category are those explanations that ignore the psychological consequences of restricting food intake and rest instead on the idea that there is a coherent pattern in the anorexic's food control which should be interpreted as a whole. The general view here is that her refusal to eat is something she may be carrying out in pursuit of a particular purpose; or it may otherwise be an expression that carries some meaning, but a meaning that is being expressed in terms of a metaphor. Either way these explanations carry the assumption that, if the meaning or purpose that lies behind the behaviour is discovered, then the whole self-starvation episode will be understood.

The kinds of explanation in this second category have great resilience. Ideas of purpose and intention are, after all, a normal part of our understanding of each other's actions and in general they work very well. They have an immediate intelligibility that the idea that psychological change can be induced by food restriction does not. It is not generally known that persistent undernutrition and low weight can create dependence.[1]

Theories and how they relate to what is seen as needing explanation

This distinction between explanations that encompass the psychological consequences of starvation and those that do not has the effect of dividing the theoretical literature because, in a very fundamental way, it influences the interpretations that are placed on the anorexic's actions. It influences what helpers will actually see in the sufferer, and consequently their view about which aspects of her behaviour need explaining, and which do not.

One of the characteristics of anorexia nervosa that can be used to illustrate this is the sufferer's restlessness, or hyperactivity. This bright-eyed, alert, liveliness was the distinctive demeanour that first enabled the discrimination of these particular emaciated patients from others who were suffering from wasting diseases, such as abdominal tuberculosis, that were prevalent in the nineteenth century. These active, alert (i.e. anorexic) patients would survive if they were fed. The others, despite feeding, would succumb to their infectious diseases.

Those whose theoretical position does not acknowledge the effects of starvation may see the anorexic's hyperactivity as the key indicator to the meaning of the whole starvation episode. For instance, where extreme thinness is being construed as her way of achieving freedom from a sexual stereotype,[2] her restlessness may be interpreted as her enjoyment of the activities denied her by the constraints of fashion and convention within the female role. But, where it is acknowledged that hyperactive behaviour is entirely to be expected in people who are underweight and continuing to deprive themselves of food, the situation will tend to be construed differently. A helper who knows that anyone who gets thin and hungry is typically ceaselessly active will see this as a relatively insignificant symptom that will recede with adequate nourishment and an increase in weight.

Another symptom that can be quite differently understood, depending on the perspective from which it is viewed, is the overwhelming and continual preoccupation with food that is found in low-weight anorexia nervosa. In this instance the two different ways of understanding this symptom lead to quite different ideas about the way in which the anorexic's symptoms generally are created.

Some theorists, ignoring starvation effects, are inclined to see the anorexic's preoccupation with food and eating as evidence of her fixation at an earlier stage of development, sometimes referred to as the oral stage, where food and hunger dominate thought processes. This perception has set in train a search through theories of child development to find reasons why she should want, or need, to return or regress to this earlier stage. A view that has been advanced, to take but one example from the many that have sprung from this tradition, is that the anorexic is someone in whom the early experience of mothering engendered both strong positive and strong negative feelings and that, during adolescence, when she is engaged in a struggle for autonomy, these strong feelings re-emerge and she conducts her struggle in the same terms as she did in early childhood, investing food with the same symbolism as it acquired then. It is a symbolism that is inappropriate at this later stage but nevertheless determines her responses.[3] The assumption in this argument is that the regression the anorexic manifests at low weight in her total preoccupation with thoughts of food is achieved entirely through psychological processes. It is assumed that her progressive reduction in food intake is merely a by-product of the way she is confronting the developmental tasks of adolescence.

But the fact is, whatever the series of events, actions or accidents that have brought about their starved state, starvation actively alters people: a total preoccupation with thoughts of food is found in anyone who is starving, and starvation itself is efficacious in bringing about personality change. The end result of the anorexic's food control would be much the same therefore, whether it was the consequence of psychological regression or not.

The practical significance of the theoretical divide

How a helper believes anorexia nervosa works is of great practical importance, for the understanding of the condition determines the kind of help that is provided. The helper whose theoretical view takes into account the psychological effects of starvation will see anorexia nervosa as a gradually intensifying state of incapacity in which different processes are at work at different stages. This is a view that, as we will show, provides the helper with a set of ideas concerning the sufferer that are flexible and differentiated enough to meet her exactly where she happens to be as, in the long course of the illness, her weight, her behaviour and her subjective experiences change.

The approach on the other hand that ignores the inevitable psychological consequences of starvation is likely to be more fixed. For instance, only one interpretation of the symbolic significance of the refusal of food may be permitted. Being limited, it will be less fitted to the considerable variations and changes in experience that can occur within the condition. This is not to doubt that those working with such a psychodynamic model may be highly subtle and sophisticated in their ability to tease out feelings hidden by unconscious defences. But they may not appreciate that it is not so much a problem of unconscious defences that they are meeting in the low-weight anorexic as the characteristic attenuation or blanking out of feelings and emotions that is found in all underweight and starving people.

Those who have a theoretical preference for placing interpretations on the anorexic's behaviour and attributing it with unconscious meaning are usually, and often justifiably, opposed to medical intervention and generally very liberal in their sentiments. Yet, for reasons that will become clear, sufferers are not only characteristically vulnerable to being taken over by other people's views: they can also experience interpretations of their behaviour as very oppressive.[4]

Of the two types of theory broadly outlined we will concentrate on those which recognize the psychological effects of starvation, for in our view they generally provide a better fit with the fine detail of the illness. However, to acknowledge that starvation has psychological as well as physical consequences is not to imply that the anorexic must therefore be made to put on weight before therapy can begin. Her weight is not irrelevant, as will be evident in the chapters that follow. But being able to help her does not depend on weight being immediately restored, unless, of course, the weight loss is severe enough to endanger the sufferer's life. Then some weight gain must be the first goal – even if only enough to make the situation safe (see Chapter Eleven).

The psychological effects of starvation

There is a range of psychological changes that are created by consistent food restriction and weight loss, and we will turn to the detail of these now. Physical hazards will be considered in Part III.

Intellectual change

First, and perhaps most important, is the way starvation restricts thinking. This impairment is progressive, but it is reversible. It disappears when body weight returns to normal.

The more severely malnourished people become, the more altered is their thinking. In the early stages the changes will be quite subtle but will be detectable none the less in certain areas. It is the helper's awareness of the specific deficits that in practice is therapeutically useful, much more than just knowing in general that starvation diminishes mental capacity.

The way that starvation impairs intellectual functioning is by gradually reducing the capacity for complex thought. As undernutrition progresses and weight falls, thinking becomes simple. Starving people have fewer and fewer available categories in which to place their experiences, and these sets of categories are distinct, and highly polarized. There are no moderate positions, no in-between stages. Everything that is perceived is seen as either black or white, good or bad, acceptable or unacceptable. As the shades of grey in situations progressively disappear, so the subtleties and complexities of life disappear too. It is not only the world that is seen this way. People who are low weight and starving understand themselves too from within this 'all or nothing' way of thinking.

When food intake is consistently restricted, the higher mental functions, such as the capacity for abstract thought, are the first to disappear. Case histories of anorexics often reveal that the problem initially became apparent when they found they were unable to cope with mathematical ideas, and this happened long before any of the more obviously anorexic symptoms began to show. As impairment intensifies the ability to engage in other complex activities gradually diminishes. There is no longer any capacity to be imaginative, or creative, or to meet complicated or challenging situations.

For instance, being with even quite a small group of people will be too much to cope with, and a situation the sufferer will increasingly avoid. The number of interactions that take place in a group readily confuses and overwhelms people whose intellectual capacity is impaired by starvation. It becomes impossible for them to follow what is happening. Indeed they may barely manage to cope with the presence of just one other person.

Every aspect of life will need to be totally predictable and organized well in advance. The ability to respond spontaneously to an unforeseen event completely disappears. Relationships which have been difficult become even more problematic. The ability to cope with frustration is reduced. Hence the established anorexic is characteristically very isolated and set in her own precise routines.

As thinking becomes more polarized with persistent starvation, the range of ideas that can be encompassed grows narrower, and the remaining mental capacity is increasingly taken up with thoughts of food. Hunger ensures that food, and all there is to do with it, becomes a total preoccupation. This is normal when people are starving. It need not necessarily involve sensations of hunger, but will certainly be clear in the person's behaviour.

> She's lost a lot of weight, and she won't eat more than a mouthful of anything. She says she's not hungry and spends all her time poring over cookery books. She'll prepare a meal any time I ask, but she won't eat any of it. I even found a scrap book she'd made full of pictures of food cut out of magazines.

The ability to concentrate also diminishes as weight falls. This is a change the sufferer will notice herself as she finds it harder to read, or to centre her thoughts on her job, or studying. Where food restriction persists and the sufferer becomes extremely emaciated, many more brain functions also begin to fail. For example, memory will deteriorate. The capacity to control the movements of the body will also deteriorate. Low-weight anorexics will notice their own clumsiness. Anorexics who become more severely emaciated are more markedly accident prone. The lower a person's weight, the more generally disorientated they will feel, and the more out of touch with reality (see Chapter Five).

Sexuality

Sexual feelings diminish when food intake is consistently reduced over a long period. This reflects the hormonal change that takes place in both males and females as weight falls. After a certain point the secretion of reproductive hormones is inhibited and, from an endocrinological point of view, the starving person is held in the equivalent of a pre-adolescent bodily state. Clear evidence of an endocrine 'shut-down' in women is provided by the fact that they cease to menstruate. In men evidence of this endocrine change is not so obvious, although male sufferers do report that, as they lose weight, they stop having wet dreams. It needs to be acknowledged, of course, that in human beings the relationships between the secretion of reproductive hormones and sexual interest is not a simple one, because cultural and other factors play their part. But nevertheless the inhibition of hormone secretions does have its effect, and, whether they are male or female, starving people typically have very little interest in sexual activity.

Moods and feelings

Feelings and emotions also become attenuated in the person who is undernourished. Whatever is felt – be it anger, love, hate, pleasure, sadness, jealousy – it will be felt less energetically. As weight loss progresses, strong emotions dwindle away still more. This creates a sense of detachment, a feeling of being 'above all the ordinary turmoil of living', of being anaesthetized against it. It is this experience that gives the anorexic her distant, superior, aloof attitude.

Starvation also induces a state of elation, or euphoria. This experience of well-being is sometimes referred to as a 'fasting high'. This is a psychotropic, or mood changing, effect that occurs quite predictably whenever people consistently cut back on the amount of food they eat. Depending upon the individual's weight and the extent to which food is being restricted, such a change can begin to take place quite rapidly. A person whose weight is quite average for his or her age, sex and height can begin to experience a sense of being high or elated within as little as 24–48 hours.

In physiological terms starvation, i.e. going without food for more than half a day, is perceived by the body's internal monitoring system as hunger stress. This results in the secretion of adrenalin which, as well as creating the keyed-up effect noticeable in the starving person's wider open eyes, faster heart rate and deeper breathing, also mobilizes reserves of glycogen in muscle to provide more blood glucose. Where there is the continued presence of adrenalin in the bloodstream, it acts on the brain and causes it to secrete endokinins. These are chemicals closely related to morphine and have similar tranquillizing and euphoric effects. At the same time, metabolites (such as ketones) which are produced by the breaking down or metabolism of fat also act on the brain and can create an odd and lightheaded experience.

The brain has receptors for morphine-like substances (endomorphins) which are also produced by the body when it is stressed by vigorous exercise. (It is the presence of these receptors which makes human being susceptible to chemicals of this kind when they are administered as a drug or as medical pain relievers.) This is how an individual can come to derive a particular pleasure, or sense of well-being, from strenuous exercise. It is also how, by further stimulating the body's production of endomorphins, hyperactivity itself acts as its own spur in the anorexic, as it does in any person who is excessively dedicated to running, gymnastics or other activity.

It is thus that chronic low-weight anorexia nervosa can be viewed as an addiction to starvation. Occasionally anorexics refer to themselves as starvation junkies, and some psychiatrists now have come to see the low-weight anorexic as being dependent on the biological states that result from starvation, as 'hooked' on recurrent fixes of internally generated brain chemicals.[5]

When she is in this state, the anorexic experiences hyperacuity, which is an enhanced sensitivity to light, sound, colour and other external stimuli that occurs with increasing hunger. Birdsong is louder; the grass is greener; light more intense – and she will be hyperactive. Not only will her hyperactivity be clear from her extreme restlessness and need to be constantly 'on the go', it will also be evident in her disturbed sleep patterns. Far more movements have been recorded during sleep in underweight anorexia nervosa sufferers than in people who are normal weight.[6] Because they are so thin, they do not have the normal muscle bulk to prevent blood vessels being pinched between, say, the hip bone and the bed; as cramp persistently sets in, so they change the position of their body. Anorexics also typically get up very early and may routinely go for a three-mile run at five o'clock in the morning.

The way the anorexic experiences these psychotropic effects as pleasing and as validating her food restriction is clear in the following account.

> Fanny became more and more preoccupied with her inner experiences, the delight over the new intense sensations which seemed to prove she was on the right road. Her hyperacuity to sound led to continuous arguments with her brother for playing records too loud, and she felt that people were shouting at her. Her hypersensitivity to light was so severe that she wore sunglasses all the time, even inside the house.[7]

'Positive' experiences like these are further validated for the sufferer by other intense and highly valued physical sensations such as being completely empty of food and being actually physically lighter. This body awareness also provides her with evidence that she is still in her 'good' category and 'on the right road' (see Chapter Nine).

Theories that build on the psychological effects of starvation

In considering the ways in which the psychological effects of starvation are used theoretically, it becomes immediately apparent that sometimes, and in some places, the changes that starvation creates are construed as highly desirable and good, and at other times, and in other places, these same changes are construed as destructive and bad.

Those who try to work with anorexia nervosa/bulimia sufferers meet distraught families and increasingly incapacitated clients/patients. Anorexics become less and less able to function because of their increasing emaciation, while bulimics become more and more disturbed by the severity and violence of the swings they experience themselves going through – from controlling food and 'non-eating', to chaotic, non-stop bingeing and back again. Constantly faced with the amount of visible distress this creates, these helpers unsurprisingly employ theories that focus on the hazardous aspects of food restriction. They use theories that acknowledge the compulsive quality of starving or bingeing and the natural tendency of these activities to intensify.

Many other groups of people meanwhile place a positive value on food restriction. While their ideas may not always have the stature of academic theories, they are often quite sophisticated. They are also widely influential at a popular level. The practical point here is that those helpers who recognize that food restriction and excessive exercise can be hazardous are likely to find that their perceptions run in direct opposition to the very positive views about these activities that are held by others than themselves.

The conflicting values that surround food and body regulation become particularly apparent as soon as the anorexic has regained a small amount of weight. The anxieties of those around her tend to subside and, as this happens, the helper's account of the difficulties created by continued inadequate eating and a persistently maintained low weight often ceases to carry conviction. The support from relatives and friends, which the helper needs to work effectively with the anorexic in continuing to confront the problems that emerge with any weight gain (including feeling safe about further weight gain), begins at this point to ebb away (see Chapter Thirteen).

The theory that starvation is avoidance of sexuality

For those who work with anorexics a theory that has been particularly influential is that which has focused on the loss of sexual interest that accompanies falling body weight. The view is that the adolescent, confronted with the need to establish a sense of self in the face of resurgent sexuality and the social pressures that occur at this time, finds relief in starvation specifically because this switches off sexual feelings. Where there is thus no desire to be involved in sexual relationships, a major component of this identity crisis is removed. At low weight the anorexic is, endocrinologically, in a pre-adolescent state. She has, it is said, regressed – a state which in this case is seen as being achieved by physiological processes. So in the context of this theory the term 'psychobiological regression' is used.[8]

It is further suggested that, when she is low weight, the anorexic may not be aware that this is the reason why it is so important to her not to return to a higher weight level – a level, that is, at which her endocrine system would readjust and her adolescent sex drive return. Because of her lack of awareness she is, within the terms of this theory, described as 'phobic' about eating and weight gain.

The view that the anorexic is using food control to avoid having to come to terms with sexuality and the responsibilities of adulthood has not only been influential, it is also one of the main justifications for beginning therapy by enforcing weight gain. The assumption is that therapy cannot address the 'real' issues until these have been 'switched on' or rekindled as a result of the increase in weight. This is an important issue, certainly from the anorexic's point of view, and will be considered at greater length in Chapter Four. Let it suffice for the present to say that we do not share the conviction that sexuality has such a pivotal role as this theory would suggest, nor believe that engineering immediate or large weight gains is the best way to begin helping an anorexic.

The theory of starvation as a whirlpool

Our alternative theory begins from the evidence that the effects of starvation are wide ranging and affect more than just sexual interest. This approach focuses on the intellectual and emotional changes that occur as starvation develops, and particularly on the way these changes gradually affect both the individual's ability to choose and make decisions, and the nature of the decisions that are made, including the fateful decisions not just to maintain but to intensify food control.

As sustained food restriction progressively constrains the number of categories of ideas the starving person has to work with, varied and graduated responses give way to a few, rigid certainties. Thus increasingly all choices and decisions come to be made between extreme or polarized positions. The lower weight falls, the greater difficulty there is in grasping the possibility of there being any moderate position on any issue. These intellectual changes affect every aspect of the anorexic's experience, and so every aspect of her existence. Any comments made to her, for example, she will inevitably construe in polarized terms. Other people are either doing their best to make her fat, or they are supporting her in her weight control. Either they are entirely for her, or they are entirely against her.

These changes would not help create anorexia nervosa however, if it were not for the way the anorexic values the alternatives facing her. Apart from the respect she earns from others for being seen to be in control, she also experiences a sense of relief at being freed from a profound and overwhelming sense of confusion and ineffectiveness that she previously suffered (see Chapter Eight). She experiences her altered intellectual state as 'being able to think more clearly'. She does not see that she has only two categories to work with but only experiences the ease with which she can now make all judgements, choices and decisions, which she interprets as following from her 'greater clarity of mind'.

Because, like all starving people, she is beset by thoughts of food and eating, gradually everything of importance becomes construed in terms of food, including her idea of her 'self'. This is how, when she is low weight and her thinking polarized, she comes to have a more definite sense of who she is; how her self comes to reside in food control.

The polarized categories she is working with equally affect her values. They become increasingly rigid and absolute. As these absolute values are applied to her self, so she must be utterly certain of her food control. Failure comes to have unbearable implications for her self-respect, and her ability to accept herself. To lose control is to slip from being a person who is absolutely good to a person who is absolutely bad, as those close to her will notice:

> Since she's had this anorexia there seems to be no middle way with her. Either she's absolutely fine, or everything's absolutely terrible. She's so excessively smug and superior at times, she's quite insufferable. Then she'll be disgusted with herself, saying she's worthless, an abject failure. She loathes herself. Says she's no right to be alive.

For the anorexic to eat even the most minute quantity of food that is not part of her control regime is to be catapulted from a position where she can accept herself into a state of total unacceptability. Just the prospect of this happening can cause her extreme panic. The bulimic's feelings of self-worth likewise ride the same switchback as she alternates between stuffing and starving.

The simple style of thinking induced by food restriction together with these particular values thus create a whirlpool. The decision not to eat rebounds on self-starvers as the consequences of undernutrition affect the way they think about eating and not eating, and the way they view themselves. Each series of changes exacerbates the other, and gradually they are drawn in. The more polarized thinking becomes, the more the decision not to eat is reinforced. Weight falls further, and the cycle continues. As anorexics become more emaciated, the easier it is for them to choose not to eat, the more clearly this decision appears to them as being the only decision possible. So they spiral downwards in the way that will eventually bring them to the point of physical collapse.[9]

This whirlpool (see Figure 1) explains how it is that at any present moment self-starvers' decisions to control their food intake may be deliberate and reasoned, and yet how, over time, the dynamic relationship between the decisions they make and the changes these bring about draws them into a situation that runs away with them. The whirlpool effect shows how the decisions to continue starving and exercising are necessarily made from a different position from the decision to begin. In this lies the compulsive quality of the condition, the way that anorexics' choices are no longer entirely free. It also shows how it is that anorexia nervosa becomes life-threatening.

Comparing and contrasting these theories

Both the theories outlined above suggest that starvation is a means of creating a firmer sense of self for someone in whom this is lacking. In the former psychological-regression theory starvation effects are held to be relieving because they remove both the need to adjust to adult sexuality and the specific turmoil that this entails. In the latter whirlpool theory they are held to be relieving because they remove the sense of confusion and ineffectiveness that the person feels generally in every area of her or his life and replace it with calm and a sense of order. In the former the importance of starvation is seen as lying in the way it affects *one* aspect of experience. The importance of starvation in the whirlpool theory is that its effects act directly on the individual's *total* experience to create total change.

In both cases the anorexic is seen as maintaining a sense of self at the cost of blocking out much of her potential. Again the differentiating factor is whether this potential is seen as partial, involving sexuality in particular, or whether it is seen as

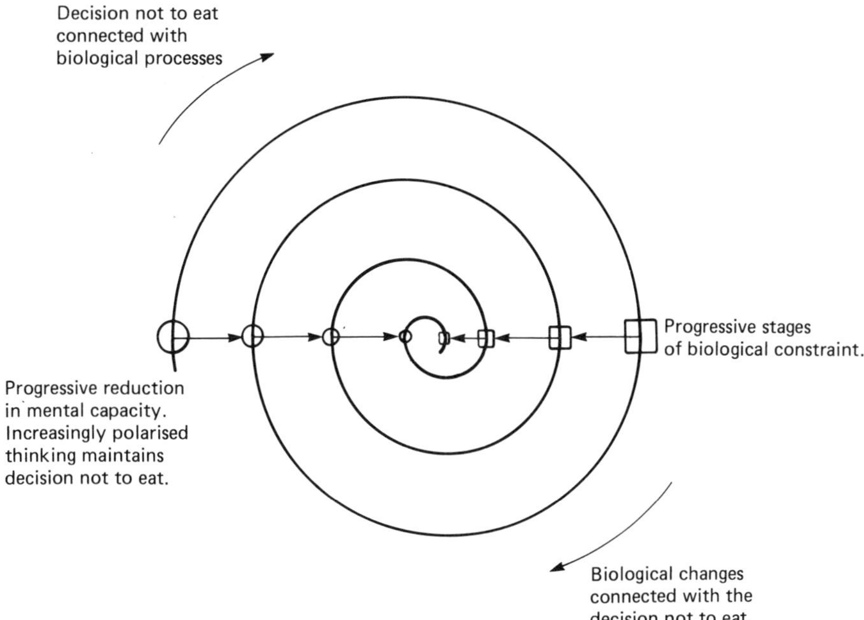

Figure 1: The Whirlpool, showing how the decision to go on self starving/exercising is made from a position that is physically and psychologically different from the position where the decision was made to begin (reproduced from The Anorexia Nervosa Reference Book, *London, Harper and Row, 1984).*

relating to the person as a whole. As we have said, it is also a factor that has important implications for the sufferer in terms of the kind of help she receives, particularly in relation to the problem of her gaining weight.

It is the starvation whirlpool as it affects the person's total experience that is the theoretical basis of the approach to help that will be presented here. It will also become clear in the following chapters how polarized thinking and the personality changes the whirlpool creates play a significant part in confounding so many other treatment approaches.

Positive ideas about food and body regulation

Theorizing about the anorexic's food and body regulation in negative terms can make the sufferer quite angry. As one girl said, 'They all keep on about what I lose by refusing to eat. But they never say anything about what I gain. They just don't know.'

Fasting

The state of altered consciousness that starvation induces can be highly rewarding and in this respect has its place alongside the use of alcohol, street drugs, solvents and so on. There are relatively few people who do not use one or another of these ways of altering experience at some time. Going without food, intentionally or unintentionally, also plays a part in maximizing the desired effects from the alcohol or drugs ingested.

There is a popular and growing literature that extols the use of self-starvation. In this literature first-hand accounts can be found that illustrate the way food restriction is positively interpreted as a way of inducing altered consciousness, though in this context the word 'fasting' is used. In one account, for example, the speaker refers to his 'consciousness fast' and expresses the opinion that:

> Where we are 'now' is a space that is controlled by the ingesting of food. . . . It is a drug. It induces a state of reality which we are prone to call real, simply because this is where we are at. . . . You go into an internal system during a fast which allows for another, and as valid, a reality which is virtually uncharted.[10]

Another describes his fast as taking place in 'a beautiful mountainous area' where there was a 'loose knit, spiritually oriented community' that fasted as part of 'yogic practice or their own interpretation of it'. He describes himself during his fast as:

> Immensely energetic, immensely alert, a very, very high state, very stimulated . . . a sense of being elated by the intellectual context of what you're saying and what you feel. When I say that fasting works as a stimulus I mean that there's a wild euphoria that is continuous and pervasive.[11]

For the helper who is familiar with anorexia nervosa and bulimia this mental state will have a very familiar ring and, contrary to the notion that it is 'virtually uncharted', a very clear map can be drawn of this 'reality', as we will show in Chapter Five.

Dieting, slimming and exercising

Pointing out the way in which food restriction, like excessive exercise, can be used 'for kicks' can serve to marginalize this activity, particularly if it is associated with esoteric subcultures or alternative lifestyles. But the positive evaluation of semi-starvation is much more pervasive than this, and more insidious.

One of our major social values lies in the idea of taking personal responsibility and making something of ourselves (see Chapter Seven). Nor is there a secret about the fact that food and body control is a highly acceptable strategy for achieving this. The message that to feel better about yourself you lose weight is clear in the following 'problem page' reply which, in view of the nature of the starvation whirlpool, is also alarming. (The italics are ours.)

> QUESTION: Where can I find therapy? I've asked my GP but he just smiled and said, 'We all have excesses.' He's not joking. I'm sixteen stone, my nails are bitten to the quick, I drink much too often, can't sleep and cry

endlessly. I've tried hypnotism, acupuncture, pills, potions *et al.*, so therapy seems the only answer.

ANSWER: Start with Weight Watchers. *Success with weight loss will build up your self-esteem, and your self-esteem will help you to have success, and that in turn increases your self-esteem, and hey presto! the vicious cycle is turned into a benevolent one.* You see, therapy only means a kind of help and self-help is one of the best.[12]

Popular magazines available at supermarket checkouts advertize articles with such titles as 'Help a chubby child lose weight and gain confidence'.[13] Thus the message gets through to children too.

There is a vast array of reading material on the topics of fashion and health that encourages people to improve themselves by dieting, slimming, taking an increased amount of exercise, or going on a fast, but the purpose of this is not just cosmetic. It is a way of 'not letting oneself go'; it is a way of meeting the obligation to make something of oneself by one's own personal effort. Hence the idea of self-help can also carry a notion of self-reform. Many of the strategies for this kind of self-improvement are quite extreme, with popular diets suggesting it is 'medically safe' to live on 200 calories a day. The promised result generally is that people who embark on these courses of self-improvement will feel more alive, more finely tuned, cleansed, purified, good, more self-confident and effective. An informed therapist, experienced in working with anorexia nervosa sufferers who are hooked on the psychotropic effects of starvation, described it as 'both eerie and frustrating'[14] to see advertizing slogans stating: 'Fasting is the way to clearer thinking and more energy.'

An activity that embodies some of society's most cherished values acquires a status that makes it difficult to see what is happening. In this case little attention is given to what it is precisely that brings about the sense of self-confidence, well-being and goodness. Many people who rigorously diet and exercise certainly feel better about themselves; but contrary to the way they may judge themselves, their feelings are not entirely a result of their moral goodness. Rather they are the result of these activities setting in train the series of psychological and physical changes described above, changes that in certain circumstances can have very unhappy consequences.

It is the use of two different sets of words for the same actions that ensures that moral values and beliefs are not compromised by the suggestion that the activities might be hazardous. 'Self-starvation' may be dangerous, but a 'fast' is purifying. 'Slimming' has positive ideas associated with it, but to 'maintain a state of semi-starvation' is to present the same activity in a way that is much more negative. The different terms effectively insulate approved activities from valid criticism. It is not easy to suggest that sometimes increased clarity of thought and greater self-confidence might be better described as mental simplicity and restricted choice.

Though they may use medical approval as a marketing strategy, many diets contain no warning at all of possible dangers. When cautions are given, the emphasis is on physical health. There is no information about the nature of the experiential changes these activities can create, or how it is possible to become hooked on feeling 'good' in this way. Hence the dangerously naïve assumption that a person will know when to stop losing weight or be able to stop. People who manage to lose a substantial amount of weight will neither think in the same way, nor have the same emotional state, nor the same perception of their bodies as they did when they started to restrict their food intake.

Not everyone now takes the question of stopping weight loss so lightly, however, as a group of researchers found when studying potential anorexia nervosa in a top London ballet school.

> We were impressed both with the pressures towards maintaining a slim figure and with the forces brought into play to reverse the process of weight loss when this became abnormal. The matron reacted strongly to girls with a marked drop in weight and insisted that it be regained promptly. Friends were similarly concerned. The result, in all the cases we saw, was positive and further deterioration was averted.[15]

There are similarities between the matron's role here and that of the religious superior or novice master or mistress in, for example, a monastic order. In communities like these, which have century-long experience of fasting, it is usually allowed only under the direction of such a supervisor who will ensure the fast has an end and that normal eating is resumed under vows of obedience.

Those who go on from dieting and/or exercising to become anorexic and/or bulimic are generally those who have had difficulty in establishing a sense of who they are and who also believe they ought to make something of themselves through their own personal effort and self-discipline. In these respects they are quite similar to many other people who do not proceed into the starvation whirlpool. But, once established, it is this whirlpool that creates most of the incomprehensible behaviour (psychopathology) that is found in anorexia nervosa. Thus the idea that the rest of the population can be encouraged to diet and exercise with impunity is nothing but a comforting fiction.

Professional objections to the idea of starvation effects

Apart from pervasive ideas and cultural values, the informed helper is likely to meet strong resistance of a different kind to the assertion that the effects of starvation play a crucial part in creating the symptomatology of anorexia nervosa. This resistance exists at a theoretical level and stems from important traditions in psychiatry, the social sciences and feminism. These traditions are not to be dismissed lightly. For apart from their theoretical pedigree, the differences of opinion they create reach right down to the practical discussion, in clinics, hospitals and other therapy centres, of how each particular sufferer might be helped.

People trained in the social sciences tend to find it hard to accept that part of the anorexic's problem has a straightforward basis in the consequences of starvation. They are familiar with the very many occasions when inappropriate and overextended physical explanations have been offered for complex human behaviour, and they are unlikely to change their approach in the particular case of anorexia nervosa unless they have actually had to grapple with the problem. It is usually only then that they become more receptive to other notions.

Those working in a Freudian tradition also have difficulty in recognizing the importance of the biological aspects of starvation. Freud's insights brought about a reallocation of symptoms as between physical and psychological causes. As a result of his ideas, symptoms such as slips of the tongue, for example, and some forms of paralysis which had previously been thought of as having purely physical causes were recognized to be psychological in origin, their reasons and purposes having been repressed. So the suggestion that behaviour which seems meaningful is largely due to physiological change is a backward step for anyone of a Freudian persuasion. Thus those who use this approach tend to offer over-inclusive psychological accounts for some symptoms that are better explained biologically.

Feminists meanwhile are likely to see the problem of helping anorexics in the context of the whole historic struggle of women to regain control over their own bodies. For them it is an example to set alongside the issues of legitimacy, contraception and access to medical care for specifically female complaints. To accept that the effects of starvation play an important part in creating anorexia nervosa too easily seems to allow or condone coercive refeeding programmes, a course which, given the predominance of men in positions of power within the medical profession, tends to take the form of a classic male/female confrontation for control over a woman's body.

Our concern here is not to deny the usefulness or the validity of any of the above views, so much as to question whether they are appropriate or sufficient when applied to anorexia nervosa.

The idea of illness

To acknowledge that starvation itself creates a whirlpool that readily draws in anyone, male or female, who values its effects is to bring theorizing about food control down to an almost prosaic level. It also emphasizes the importance of directing attention in therapy to the detail of the sufferer's experience in the here and now (see Chapters Twelve and Fourteen).

Because of its whirlpool nature the condition must be expected to intensify. There is no need to search for exotic customs, esoteric religious practices or literary analogues to cast some light on the meaning of the anorexic's actions. Starvation creates its own extremes. To explain anorexia nervosa as the struggle of the creative artist, or as the pinnacle of spiritual experience, is not only to be less than honest about the physiological and psychological effects that underlie the process of self-starvation, but also directly to mislead the sufferer. For rather than enabling her to gain the courage to begin the slow process of moving away from her compulsive control, it is likely to reinforce her attachment to her style of thinking by applauding her success (see Chapter Nine).

The fact that the effects of starvation have their own dynamic also gives anorexia nervosa/bulimia some of the characteristics that people usually associate with the idea of illness. It can be identified as a distinct episode in a person's life, although, like alcoholism and drug addiction, an episode of rather a special kind.

There can be objections to calling it an illness, and in particular a mental illness, on the grounds that to do so separates the sufferer from the rest of the population and hides the many similarities that exist between the sufferer's preoccupations and those of others who do not have such distressing symptoms. It can also be argued that to distinguish the sufferer as ill also serves to prevent, or stifle, political action to change the pressures and expectations that are generally experienced by woman in a patriarchal society. But accepting that the extremes which are characteristic of the illness are explained by its process is not so much to separate the sufferer from her environment as to make it easier to see how sufferers' ideas about food and body control grow out of the ordinary beliefs and values they share with their family, colleagues and friends; how they grow out of beliefs and values that are commonly strongly held in the section of the community in which anorexia nervosa/bulimia usually occurs. It makes it easier too, as we shall show in Part II, to see how the everyday ideas concerning the importance of hard work, self-restraint, personal responsibility, commitment and success are swept into the whirlpool of psychological change, and how it is starvation that pushes these ideas to the point where they become unrecognizable in their extremity.

References

1 Slade, R. (1984). *The Anorexia Nervosa Reference Book*, London, Harper and Row, 70–6.
2 Orbach, S. (1978). *Fat is a Feminist Issue*, London, Hamlyn Paperbacks, 166–7.
3 Eichenbaum, L. and Orbach, S. (1982). *Outside In Inside Out*, Harmondsworth, Pelican, 89.
4 Bruch, H. (1961). 'Conceptual confusion in eating disorders', *Journal of Nervous and Mental Diseases*, Baltimore, vol. 133.
McLeod, S. (1981). *The Art of Starvation*, London, Virago, 139–40, 142–3.
5 Szmuckler, G.I. and Tantam, D. (1984). 'Anorexia Nervosa: starvation dependence', *British Journal of Medical Psychology*, Cambridge, 57, 303–10.
6 Crisp, A.H., Stonehill, E. and Fenton, G.W. (1971). 'The relationship between sleep, nutrition and mood: a study of patients with anorexia nervosa', *Postgraduate Medical Journal*, Basingstoke, 47, 207–13.
7 Bruch, H. (1978). *The Golden Cage*, London, Open Books, 14.
8 Crisp, A. (1980). *Anorexia Nervosa: Let Me Be*, London, Academic Press, 86.
9 Slade, R. (1984). ibid., 68–83.
10 Ross, S. (1978). *Fasting*, London, Pan Books, 93–4.
11 Ross, S. (1978). ibid., 5, 24.
12 *Cosmopolitan*, London, April 1981.
13 *Living Magazine*, London, March 1987.
14 Welbourne, J. Personal communication.
15 Szmuckler, G.I., Eisler, I., Gillies, C. and Hayward, M.E. (1985). 'The implications of anorexia nervosa in a ballet school', *Journal of Psychiatric Research*, Oxford, vol. 19, 2/3, 177–81.

· THREE ·

Control by any other name

There are strong pressures in favour of an authoritarian response to the low weight anorexic who continues to refuse food, and an insistance that by whatever means she must gain some weight. Thus strategies to which parents are driven out of desperation will also be put in hand by doctors in the belief that these are the best solutions to an intractable problem. In this chapter we will show how it is that such an approach is unlikely to have the desired effect. Meanwhile the reasons why many medical authorities continue to believe that it is still their best option will be discussed in the final part of Chapter Four.

The suspicion that a person might be anorexic can create an uncomfortable nagging worry in any onlooker. But a definite diagnosis of anorexia nervosa arouses stronger emotions, particularly in the sufferer's parents. Their feelings will range through fear and horror to disbelief and despair, though often their most prominent feelings are ones of anger and betrayal. Anger is often spurred by the realization that the sufferer is as emaciated as she is because she has been deliberately and systematically not eating. As one outraged father said:

> I'm appalled by this! How could she let us down like this? She knows what she's doing. She's said to us straightforwardly that she's quite truthful about everything else . . . but she'll lie her head off over food. How can she behave in this way? How can she go on doing this to herself? It's so stupid!

The situation is not quite so simple, of course, for, as we have seen, the decision to continue cutting down on the amount eaten is influenced by the effect that consistent food restriction itself has upon the person's thinking and experiences. But the idea that anyone can display such remarkable self-control without being truly responsible for it requires a degree of information and understanding about the way anorexia nervosa works that very few people have when they meet the condition for the first time.

The more emaciated the anorexic becomes, the more intense the feelings of those trying to help. As well as worries about her physical health, the sight of her increasingly skeletal body is disturbing. Strong physical revulsion combined with anger and/or fear and the urge that something *must* be done often accompany attempts to reassert authority over the starving anorexic. Asserting authority or moral control is also precisely the kind of action that responsible parents are expected to take. Parents who are seen to behave in this way receive strong social approval, and this is equally matched by the disapproval they can receive when the sufferer's behaviour is considered to be out of hand.

'How could you let her get so thin?' and 'Why don't you stop her?' are simple questions, and ones that friends and neighbours often ask, but in a way that the anorexic's parents sense as blaming. They feel very criticized by such remarks. They also feel the more painfully inadequate as their child's increasingly emaciated appearance proclaims ever more clearly their own incapacity to exercise proper authority, and their failure to care.

> We were worried enough. Carol was looking really awful by then. It'd got to the point where we didn't dare mention food for the row there'd be. But what made it more unbearable was all the criticism. People would just come up and say, 'Why are you letting her do it? You're her mother, aren't you? Surely you've got *some* say? There was no question. I was to blame.

Many young people are legally minors when they first become anorexic, and this can make an authoritarian response to their stubborn refusal to eat seem reasonable. But, where sufferers are legally adult, parents can still actively attempt to influence their behaviour in quite an authoritarian way. Certainly, in the crisis that occurs as the anorexic becomes progressively more emaciated, parents frequently respond to her in a way that would generally be more appropriate for a much younger person. This is how the condition can begin to appear as a form of parent/teenager conflict over autonomy, even though it does not originate in this way.

In the face of what seems to them a wilful disregard either for her own health or for her parents' concern, an authoritarian approach can seem justified. Yet where a sufferer has adult status there is often a different conflict as the following account illustrates.

> This anorexia began when she was fifteen and it was reasonable then to insist she went to the doctor. But she's twenty-two next month, and I don't see I've got the right to insist now. Sometimes I try to encourage her to see the people at the hospital. We might get as far as making an appointment, but she doesn't keep it. She says it's pointless. They were no help before. She'll lie in bed all day drinking nothing but water, or disappear out walking. You don't know what to do for the best. You just – well, you feel hopeless.

Exerting moral control is not a new way of responding to anorexia nervosa sufferers. Over one hundred years ago Sir William Gull, the English physician who first named the condition 'anorexia nervosa', wrote that 'patients should be fed at regular intervals and surrounded by persons who could have moral control over them', and he cited relations and friends as being 'the worst attendants'.[1] When, more than a century later, the same attitudes surface in such remarks as, 'If she were mine I'd give her a damned good thrashing and just make sure she got a few good meals inside her', and 'You've just got to let her know that if she doesn't get a grip on herself you'll do it for her', it seems clear that very little has changed. Those who are professional helpers are not immune from feelings of anger either, as those who have attempted the task may have found. In the current context of scarce resources anorexics have been publicly criticized by members of the medical profession for taking up hospital beds.

The easy assumption that anorexia nervosa stems from the girl's failure to 'get a grip' on herself, or from lack of authority either on the part of her parents, or on the part of professional helpers, rests on a fundamental misunderstanding of the condition. For the sufferer's adamant refusal to eat adequate amounts of food and the emaciation that follows from this grow out of her already excessive commitment to some of society's most cherished moral beliefs (see Chapters Six and Seven). Indeed the sad irony is that the person who becomes anorexic is someone who has more will-power, more determination, a more active conscience than most. Without her characteristic ability to get a grip on herself she would not have become a sufferer in the first place.

The dangers of authoritarian intervention

If alarm over her appearance and physical health were not in themselves reasons enough for suggesting that the anorexic should at least be encouraged, if not explicitly made, to eat and gain weight, then it could be argued that the psychological consequences of her starved state, with the difficulties in communication that these create, should be sufficient justification for adopting a course of immediate weight restoration. It might be seen as a waste of time to attempt to talk to her while she is so constrained. But though it may seem a good idea in face of all these difficulties to respond to her deliberate self-starvation by insisting on refeeding and restoring weight, if this is the first or only response to her behaviour it is unlikely to have the desired effect. This is something that many families learn to their cost. By the time they come to seek help they will often have tried every possible way of persuading the girl to eat, from plying her with tempting food, or offering her rewards such as holidays abroad, to threatening her by refusing such pleasures, all in the hope that this might make her come to her senses.

Not only are such coercive measures unlikely to work. They can also make matters worse. They can assist in her moving from straightforward self-starvation to other forms of food and body regulation. An anorexic who, for whatever reason, fails to maintain her rigid control may turn to making herself vomit, or to dosing herself with laxatives, or both, in her desperation to rid herself of the food she has eaten.

> I was really thin (71-per-cent AEBW) and my A-level exams were coming up, and that was when everyone started getting at me. I had to go and see the headmistress. My mother asked her to talk to me. Then my father put on the pressure. He's a vet. They spelled it out. I *must* put on weight because it would be professionally embarrassing for daddy to have a daughter who was anorexic. It took them a long time to realize I was still avoiding meals. But

> they never stopped pushing. I *must* sort this thing out before university. I did put on weight by the time I took the exams, but after that my eating got more and more odd. I weighed about seven and a half stone (78-per-cent AEBW) by the time I started university in the October. I tried to cut down on my food to get my weight lower. I did a lot of yoga and keep fit and trampolining, but after that first time my weight dropped I could never manage it again. I never seemed to be able to get back to that strict routine. It was when I found I couldn't do it I started to make myself sick. That's got more frequent ever since.

While the anorexic whose weight has been restored may seem to be cured, the reality is that, where she turns to purging and/or vomiting, she is in a worse position than she was before. For these methods of control are from a medical point of view more dangerous than self-starvation. Vomiting that is induced persistently and the continued use of laxatives and/or diuretics, which reduce body fluid and therefore weight, disturb the biochemical balance of the body. Each time an imbalance is created, the body adjusts to achieve the biochemical equilibrium necessary to maintain the functioning of vital tissues, such as conductive tissue in nerve and muscle, and of vital organs such as the heart and the kidneys. The body does this at the cost of losing certain chemicals, particularly potassium. Where such an imbalance is caused regularly, there is gradual adaptation to the constant change. A consequence of the process of adapting to the continual use of laxatives is that progressively greater quantities of laxatives are needed to achieve the same effect. This together with the anorexic's need to be certain not to gain weight can sometimes result in her taking as many as 50–100 Senokot tablets a day.

Although adjustments and adaptations in body chemistry will take place, the position of the sufferer who is regularly eliminating food in these ways is physiologically precarious. For there is a risk that at any time her body may quite suddenly cease to be able to make the necessary adaptations. When this happens, because vital organs are involved, a 'pack of cards effect' is likely to take place so that deterioration is very rapid and can be fatal. A chronic anorexic, for example, who was living at between 65–70-per-cent AEBW and had been a permanent laxative user for seven years, was very efficient at work. Being so efficient she was promoted but felt inadequate to cope with this. Her control tightened, which produced another half-stone weight loss. She caught tonsillitis at this point, after two days suffered kidney failure, and three days after that, in spite of being admitted to an intensive care unit in a teaching hospital, she died.

Strange though it may seem therefore – and particularly perhaps to the anorexic's beleaguered relatives – in its earlier stages pure starvation is to be preferred to the later complications of vomiting and purging. This is so not only from a medical standpoint, but also from the point of view of communicating with the sufferer which is the prerequisite of effective help. Certainly, while a person is low weight, the helper's task in communicating with her can be a difficult one; but even so, talking with someone who is merely suffering the psychological consequences of starvation is far more straightforward than when their thinking, feeling and experiencing is complicated by the biochemical disturbances that are created by persistent vomiting and purging; for where these are occurring, there are more possible variables in moods and feelings, and more variables generally for the helper to take into account in terms of the sufferer's behaviour and judgements of self. The speed of mood changes too can be bewilderingly swift. All of these features ensure a less predictable experience from which the sufferer has to try to learn about herself, and the tangled confusion will be too complex for her to unravel unaided (see Chapter Thirteen).

It is not only as a result of family pressure that an anorexic's eating pattern may change from straightforward starvation to other forms of control. Recourse to vomiting, purging or the use of diuretics, can be a response to being coerced into eating in hospital. Sometimes anorexics have learned alternative ways of controlling food intake directly, from other anorexic patients, for instance, or from nursing staff who are themselves undeclared fellow sufferers.

The anorexia/bulimia board game

Self-starvation, purging and/or vomiting and rigorous exercise are, broadly speaking, the three patterns of behaviour compatible with the ideas of control that are the sufferer's central preoccupation. They give her a range of possibilities for action, and, depending on her previous experience and the circumstances she finds herself in, she moves among them in much the same way as a player moves around squares in a board game (see Figure 2).

When she is low weight or emaciated she will for the most part remain in Square 1 but tend to make routine excursions into Square 2 and be helped on in this by her starvation-induced hyperactivity.

> My aunt made me eat a meal with them. But my sweater had large pockets, so I managed to hide the potatoes and some of the ham, but I had to eat loads. I could feel myself panicking in case they said anything about what I'd left on my plate. I was scared they'd stop me running, but they didn't, and I ran as far as the Toll House which was an extra mile. I felt better then.

Square 4 is where the anorexic lands whenever she eats in a way that she experiences as being out of control. This is the square she tries to avoid at all costs. If she slips or is pushed into Square 4, she will make every effort to escape from it just as soon as she can. It is this that can result in her landing in Square 3.

> I'd managed not to eat anything for five days. I'd kept to black coffee, and fruit juice, but then my control went. I knew I was going to have a binge. The feeling just grew and grew. I couldn't stop it. I'd started stuffing myself before I'd even got through the checkout. Then in the car I just went through the lot. All the biscuits, bread, bars of chocolate, shoving it down as I drove home. Then straight up to the bathroom and got rid of the lot. It was a relief, but I was still angry with myself for giving in. I was determined I wasn't going to eat again.

Anorexics whose starvation regime has crumpled, or been destroyed, move

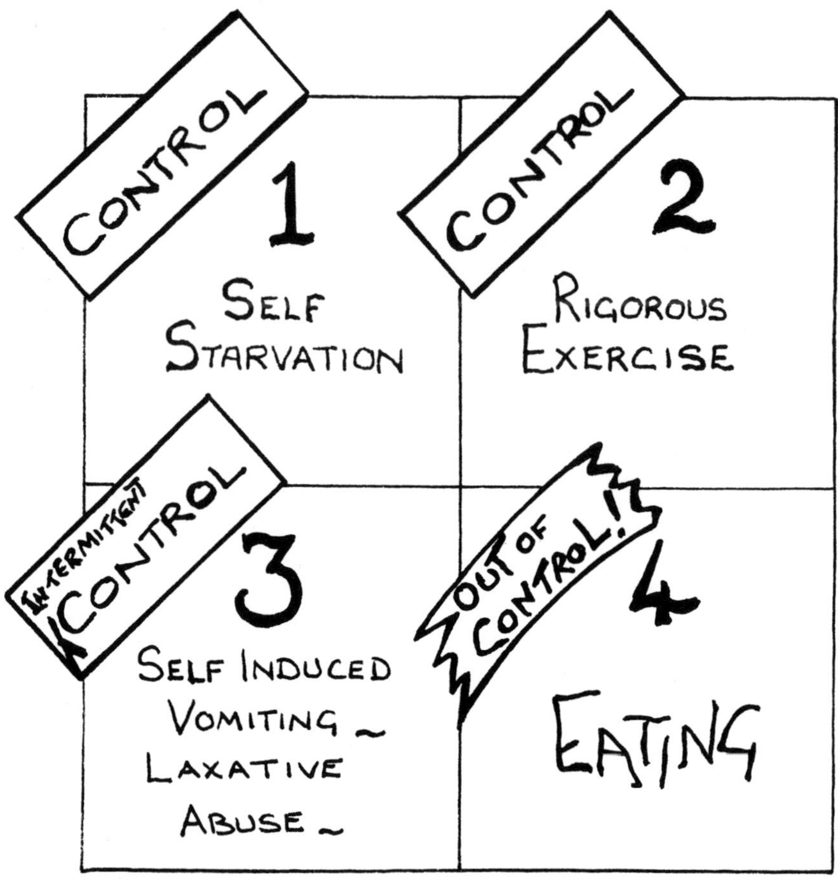

Figure 2: Squares on the board

around the board often quite rapidly using whatever resources are available to regain their preferred position.

> My mother-in-law came over because Derek (the speaker's husband) was coming home. It would have been all right if he'd been there but he wasn't. She made this meal and I had to eat it with her. I tried to get rid of it, but I couldn't bring it all back up, not even with drinking salt water. I panicked. I had to pick Derek up from the station, and there wasn't much time. I could still feel this lump in me. We got back from the station, then I said I had to go out. I had to get to the fitness centre, and I still took a handful of Ducolax when I got back, just to make sure.

Wherever the sufferer moves on the board, her central imperative is the same. Thus, although each pattern of behaviour tends to produce different physical symptoms, they may all be considered as forms of anorexia nervosa (see Chapter

One). Certainly anorexics are by no means always distinguishable by their extreme thinness.

Progression around the board

There is a characteristic progression in the condition that takes place as the sufferer shifts between her restricted options. This progression occurs because some of the moves on the board are difficult to reverse. Classically, though not absolutely invariably, self-starvation and/or excessive exercise mark the beginning of anorexia nervosa. In other words the 'player' will generally join the game in Square 1 and/or Square 2. But sooner in some cases, later in others, the mode of control changes and she/he begins to make moves into Square 3.

> I was (while at boarding school) put back on the diet designed to 'build me up'. This time the supervision was stricter, and it became more difficult for me to pass my butter ration to someone else, to pour Ovaltine down the sink behind the matron's back, or to dispose of extra food by means of the lavatory. But . . . I soon found out that if I swigged a mouthful or two of the laxative *cascara sagrada* from the medicine cupboard, I could get rid of the obnoxious feeling of weight and fullness which had been forced upon me.[2]

It is this move into Square 3 that for many sufferers marks the beginning of the 'bulimic' phase of the illness. The following account describes this point clearly.

> I had resisted for so long and now in the space of about half an hour I had eaten more than I had ever eaten at one time in my life – with no consciousness of what was happening to me. I was just a pig. I hated myself, My stomach was enormous. I got up very painfully and made my way to the toilet. I locked the door and leant over the sink. I wasn't concerned with getting rid of the calories, I just wanted to get rid of the bulk, the swelling and the terrible choking feeling in my throat. I stood over the sink and as quietly as possible made myself vomit. The horror of being out of control faded . . . I didn't realize then that I was forging the first link in an endless chain of starving, bingeing, vomiting and purging. It was the beginning of a new horror.[3]

The move to the bulimic phase in the above account was preceded by a distinct low-weight episode during which the sufferer was re-fed in hospital and subsequently persisted in restricting her food intake and maintaining low weight. In some cases, however, the phase of self-starvation and/or rigorous exercise can be quite short and, given how socially acceptable such behaviour is, it can also go quite unnoticed by relatives and friends.

Whether or not this anorexic phase has been recognized, a substantial majority of those who are seen, or see themselves, as bulimics have been through an initial period in Square 1 and/or Square 2. It is possible to inhabit both of these squares long enough to become entrapped on the board, but without attracting a great deal of attention.

> I had anorexia when I was in my teens. It wasn't for very long, but I did lose quite a bit of weight and they put me in hospital to get my weight up. Afterwards I never used to eat anything during the day. That was when I was still in control. I had to hang on to that. But I'd save everything up for the night time, when my parents had gone to bed. Enormous boxes of chocolate, sweets – I'd save everything for then. I'd hide it in the wardrobe, under lock and key. I'd get excited beforehand, and very irritated if my parents hung around and didn't go to bed. Then all the control would go. I would – well, I behaved just like an animal. Then I had to get rid of it. I'd hate myself. All the excitement would change to fear. I'd have to make myself sick. Really sick. On and on till I'd got rid of it all. I'd be terrified there was still a bit left in me.

'Advantages' of a bulimic pattern of control

Invariably bulimics would like to return to Square 1, but this move is not easy, and for good reasons. Once it has been discovered or learned that, after slipping into Square 4, it is possible to regain a sense of control by vomiting and/or using laxatives, the likelihood is that the sufferer will be unable to resist taking such immediate and visibly effective action again after further episodes of uncontrolled eating. Elimination by whatever means tends to provide swifter reassurance than can be gained by attempting to re-establish a starvation regime.

> I was relieved that the unbearable full feeling was lessened (by vomiting) and that I had undone some of the damage of the last hour. If I could get rid of the food as easily as this . . . I had discovered the answer to all my problems. I could eat what I wanted to without gaining weight and there was a means of easy relief should I ever overeat again.[4]

Controlling food intake by self-starvation can take weeks, or even months, of sustained effort and requires continued surveillance to gain a sense of achievement, with the horizon ever retreating as the effects of starvation themselves increase the imperative for absolutely sure success. But by inducing vomiting or using increasing quantities of laxatives, or both, the loss of control that is so damaging to the sufferer's self-esteem can be 'put right' in the space of about twenty minutes, or at most a few hours, and this in itself can provide a sense of satisfaction and achievement, as this male sufferer describes:

> I'm not going back to that control. I did it. I'm clever [stated with pride and assurance]. I can do that. I lost three stone five by dieting. I feel proud of that. But this way I can have the food. I can eat something really good for me like wholemeal bread with tomatoes and lettuce and salad cream, and then I can get rid of it. That's what I do. And it's quicker. [This speaker's current weight is 74 per cent of his AEBW.]

There are further aspects of food elimination that tend to make it a useful alternative for the sufferer who is desperate to regain the certainty of being in control. She may learn very swiftly that starving herself and becoming emaciated earns her the unwelcome attention of parents and doctors, whereas the effects of vomiting and laxative abuse are generally invisible. She may discover that she can even fool such knowledgeable people as doctors, dieticians, nurses or other professionals. Although her dentist may be aware of the loss of enamel from her teeth as an indication of her persistent vomiting, the condition becomes virtually invisible at this stage, even to those who are medically trained. All that an unsuspecting general practitioner may come across is a somehow inexplicable biochemical imbalance, and this will only be revealed if laboratory tests happen to be carried out. Sufferers who vomit their food generally maintain a lower body weight than those who are primarily laxative users,[4] and neither strategy brings about the weight loss that is achieved by systematic restriction of food intake. So while vomiting and/or purging may not enable them to remain as thin as they would like, at least they have the comfort of knowing they can get rid of the food they have eaten.

These forms of control also enable sufferers to keep up appearances of normal eating, and so to 'manage' on social occasions. It can enable them to join colleagues or workmates for mealbreaks without attracting comment. It means they can eat in front of parents and join family mealtimes. This keeps the family happy, which is an important consideration for the sufferer. Thus, once the transition has been made from straightforward starving to controlling food by attempting to regulate its absorption, the condition can persist completely undetected for many years, or indeed for a lifetime.

> My weight went down to six and a half stone (71-per-cent AEBW) which was low for me because I was quite tall, even at 15. But I started eating because they said they wouldn't let me go to Italy for the summer with my cousin if I didn't put on weight. I put on a bit, and I got my cousin to persuade them I was all right. They let me go, but I wasn't all right. I'd try and keep control, then it would snap and I'd eat and eat and eat. Then I started making myself sick. I wasn't thin, so they carried on thinking I was better. I couldn't tell them. I didn't want to disappoint them. I managed to keep it to myself for nearly seven years.

Though a starver may remain in Square 1 for some time, sooner or later she will be forced out, or her hunger will take over. No position on the 'four square' board is stable. The limited range of options that exists for maintaining control and the tendency there is for there to be a natural progression between them together show up the hazards of authoritarian approaches to weight gain. Coercion may be exercised indirectly, for instance, by playing on the girl's sensitivities to others' needs (see Chapter Six), so she may gain weight to reduce others' worry; or it may be exercised directly, for instance, by insisting on her being re-fed in hospital. Either way she may be brought up to a healthy body weight, but, as we have said, this alone does not switch off her concern with control. She may be heavier, but *her attitude will remain unaltered.*

All too often authoritarian or coercive intervention accelerates the change in the anorexic's pattern of control. Forcing her weight up may simply result in moving her around the board. It will also be the more difficult to create an effective therapeutic relationship with a sufferer after enforcing her weight gain. She does not easily forgive those who crush her control.

Completing the board game

The anorexic who gains weight, or who has her weight restored, but whose feelings and attitudes in relation to food and weight and self-control remain unchanged is emotionally in a highly unstable or chaotic state which causes her enormous and constant distress. The chaos she feels is reflected in her chaotic eating. To reassert food and body control is her one reliable source of reassurance, her one satisfying action. It is the only way she has of redeeming herself.

She may succeed in restricting her food intake and return to a low-weight state. But the greater likelihood is that, as she swings from one extreme to the other, she will move around the board, landing in a disorganized fashion on any square that offers the hope of feeling at least in some measure in control. The nearer her weight is to her AEBW, the more continuously aware she will be of how uncomfortable she is with herself. As her awareness is no longer so narrowed and closed down by the anaesthetizing effects of starvation, the more conscious she is of being totally ineffective, unable to make even the most minor decisions, except the decision to regain control of herself by whatever means. So her entire experience is deeply degrading and humiliating, and highly destructive of self-esteem. Her feelings of failure and hopelessness can become so intense that she becomes desperate to escape, and oblivion can seem to be the only way out.

Thus sufferers may resort to the use of alcohol, legal drugs (either prescribed or obtained over the counter), illegal drugs and in some cases solvents. Any substance, or substances in any combination, is fair means in the attempt to obtain relief from her feelings of panic, confusion, extreme self-hatred and despair.

> It transpired that my patient, a mother with three children, all primary-school age, would, as a normal routine in a seven-day week, have been attending nine one-and-a-half hour aerobics classes and have run twenty-six road miles if she hadn't broken her pelvis. She was in near total panic at not being able to do any exercise at all. That was why she had begun coming to the surgery in tears asking for more and more tranquillizers. Her weight at the time was quite normal (103-per-cent AEBW). But it had previously been much lower.

Overdoses are not unusual at the stage when weight is normal or near normal. They may be suicide bids, but they are not necessarily so. An overdose to many a sufferer is merely a reasonably guaranteed way of obtaining oblivion; as one woman said, 'a way of dealing with a mind that won't shut up.' Even so, actual suicide is always a real possibility.

A small number of sufferers also contrive to deaden or blot out their feelings by physically harming themselves, stubbing lighted cigarettes on their arms, legs and hands, and/or cutting themselves with razor blades, or with fragments of broken glass or china broken for the purpose. Acute physical pain centres awareness.

Nothing else but the pain that is being thus created can be thought about while the sufferer is inducing it, and this is a relief.

To complete the board game then, there are two further squares that need to be added to allow for the possibility of all kinds of self-harm and to admit the possibility of attempted suicide (see Figure 3). Between a quarter and a third of sufferers resort at least once to this latter solution, and almost always after a bout of eating that they have not been able to control. Although only about 2 per cent of sufferers in total actually die, suicide attempts that succeed – or overdoses that go wrong – account for approximately two-thirds of these deaths.

Of all the deaths that result from anorexia nervosa/bulimia the majority occur when the sufferer's weight has increased, or when she has had a bout of eating; in other words when she is in her unacceptable or 'bad' category. This is illustrated in the case of the college student who jumped to her death from a multi-storey car park. Her anorexia nervosa was new. She had lost two and a half stone in the previous four months, a sharp drop in weight that typically marks the 'onset' of the illness in the weight charts of anorexics. In the local newspaper article that referred to her death, and to the fact that she was anorexic, her family was reported as saying that she had not eaten a meal for months. But a few days later, following the post mortem, the same newspaper gave an account of the pathologist's report. The pathologist had found that the girl had eaten a large amount of food shortly before she had died.

The anorexic who continues to starve successfully and maintain herself at a low weight will feel more consistently 'good'. While she is managing this, she will be less at risk of hurting herself in other ways. But because the pattern of 'successful' control of food intake involves compensating strategies such as 'undercutting what I let myself eat just to make sure of not eating too much', and 'keeping a few calories in hand in case I can't get out of being made to eat', the starver runs the risk of spiralling downwards through low weight into a state of dangerous emaciation. But, when her control slips, she may find herself unaccountably accused of shoplifting from foodstores and, when she becomes chaotic, on the uncontrollable switchback of bulimia, she may become explicitly reckless in her behaviour and generally careless of herself. Then she may resort to drink, drugs, become promiscuous in her sexual relationships, be totally spendthrift. Binges can involve vast quantities of food. Thus, as many sufferers and their families are aware, a bulimic's addiction can be as disastrous financially as the addiction of any alcoholic or junkie. As one sufferer explained, 'My marriage broke up. That was because of bulimia. And everything I got, like my share of the house, it all went on food that I vomited. Thousands of pounds, literally – straight down the drain.'

Expressing anorexia nervosa and bulimia as a game that has a limited number of moves also clearly indicates the way the 'players' are trapped within the boundaries of the board. This is the more tragic because those who become anorexia nervosa/bulimia sufferers are typically intelligent and highly sensitive people who have the potential to live and respond in complex and varied ways. As one voluntary worker said of the anorexics she had met in the hospitals she visited, 'It seems so sad. They're such nice girls, all of them. So sensitive and thoughtful, and *very* intelligent.' Yet paradoxically, if they had not been intelligent, and sensitive

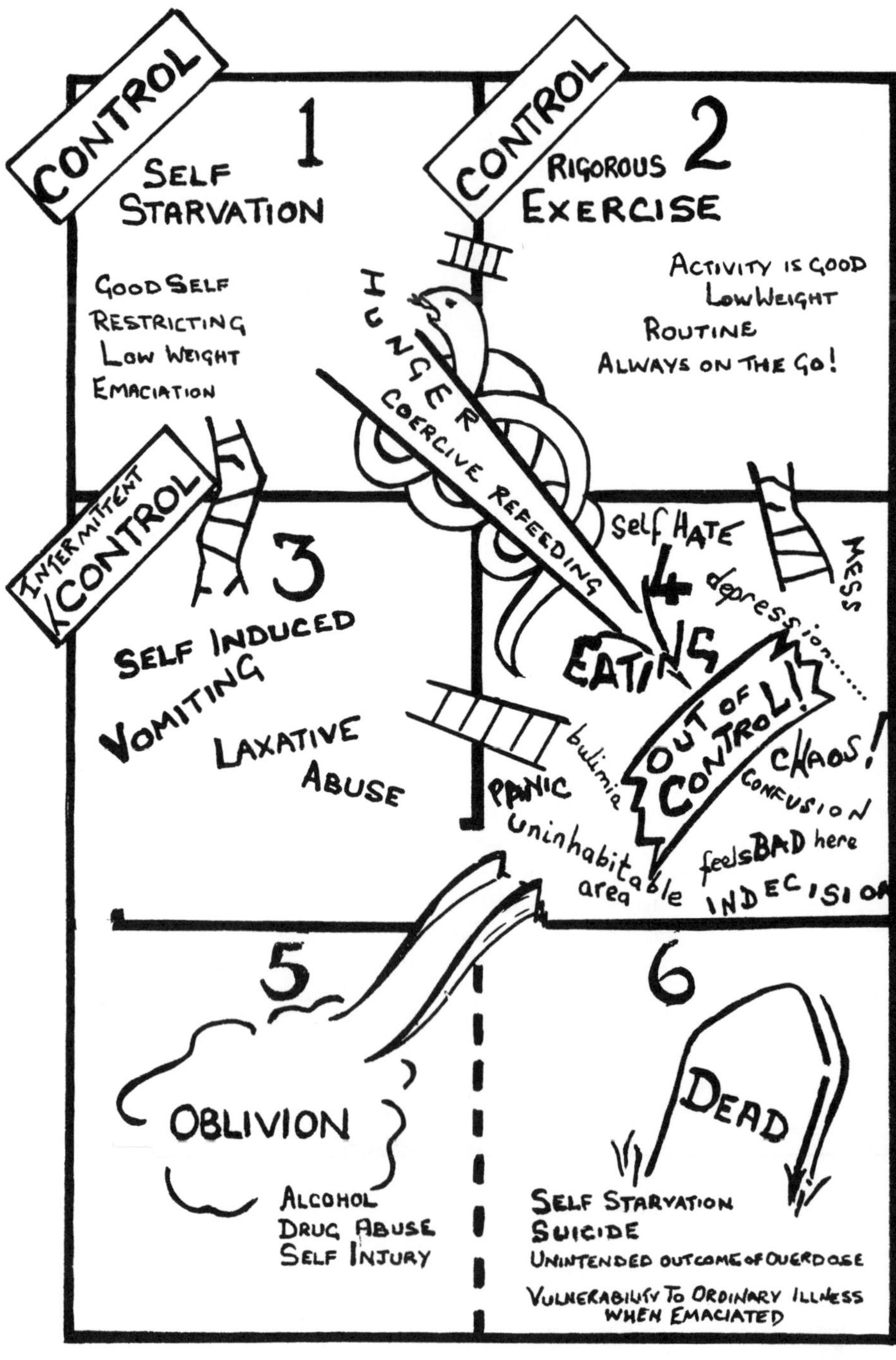

Figure 3: Anorexia nervosa/bulimia: the complete board

and put every effort into being 'nice', they would not have become anorexic in the first place.

It must be emphasized too that this is a game that hardly any of them ever meant to play. Being on some of the squares on the board will provide sufferers with a sense of achievement and security, but it also hides the potential dangers from them and does so to the extent that they have no idea that they are ill, or trapped, or 'playing' this board game. It takes them a long time to perceive there is a problem, to see how they are living with the unanticipated consequences of their actions. The eventual realization of how trapped they are is one of the things that can drive them to despair. Coming to terms with the fact that they have a problem is often the step that brings them face to face with the hopelessness of ever being able to get out of the trap, of ever being able to feel confident, effective, self-directed and real.

It is helpful to be aware of the extent of the despair and the hopelessness the sufferer can experience, and of the way self-harm and oblivion can seem a means of relief. But the helper need not, and indeed must not, share this sense of hopelessness. Many sufferers recover completely, and most improve enough to resume the course of their life, and it is possible to accelerate the process of recovery.

The helper's dilemma

In recognizing the potential hazards of a simple authoritarian response to the anorexic's food restriction, helpers themselves meanwhile come face to face with the dilemma that seems to lie at the heart of any attempt to assist or care for the anorexic who is low weight.

On the one hand, the physical and psychological constraints of starvation have to be reckoned with. This necessarily involves acknowledging the fact that much of her intellectual potential is temporarily unavailable and is so in proportion to the amount of weight she has lost. It also involves being aware that her emotional development has slowed down, or stopped. There is a saying, used in relation to drug abusers and alcoholics, that development ends where addiction begins, and this is no less true for the person who has become hooked on food control. The helper needs to be sensitive to the fact that, not only in terms of body weight but in every respect, the sufferer is someone who is very much less than she could be. She is also in the process of losing years of her youth.

On the other hand, there is an equal and opposite need to be aware that the anorexic is someone who, in being controlled, has discovered a way of feeling positive about herself that is profoundly relieving. It replaces a deep sense of failure and confusion (see Chapters Six and Eight). Food control is not only central to her sense of self; it is all she has to maintain it. If her control goes, she no longer has a self to be.

So the dilemma is that, while the helper would like to lift the constraints and dangers of the effects of starvation by refeeding the low-weight anorexic, to do this without attending to the way she feels is to risk annihilating her sense of self which is already very fragile. On the other hand, while the helper would like to respect the sufferer as a person, since the anorexic's sense of who she is resides in her successful food control, to adopt this course can lead to the helper's allowing her to persist with a lifestyle that can eventually lead to a degree of emaciation that is lethal. Parents, friends and inexperienced helpers who have not been aware of the nature of the anorexic's 'self' not infrequently find themselves confronted with the consequences of their having taken this latter option. Thus occasionally anorexics can die in the bosom of a caring family.[5]

Meanwhile, to look at the dilemma in another way, forcing her weight up risks moving the moderately low-weight anorexic (i.e. the sufferer whose weight is *not* below 65-per-cent AEBW – see Chapter Five) to a position that can be medically more hazardous because of the complications of bingeing and vomiting, and where, because of the nature of her experience when she is using these strategies, the chance of her dying can be doubled. Allowing her to continue to be her 'controlling self' is safer temporarily. But because of the whirlpool that starvation creates, the natural progression is further emaciation.

All too often the cost of solving one problem is to make the other problem worse. Thus those who are looking on from the outside can feel as trapped by the condition as the sufferer is on the inside.

Yet there is no reason why those concerned to help should respond solely to the problem of weight and exclude any consideration of the sufferer's sense of self, or why they should respond solely to her anorexic 'self' and exclude any consideration of weight. It is possible as we will show in Part III to nurture a new sense of self whilst at the same time enabling the slow relaxation of dependence on food control. It is possible for an informed and sympathetic helper to encourage gradual weight gain in a way that is not a total assault on her person.

References

1 Gull, W. (1874). 'Anorexia Nervosa', *Transactions of the Clinical Society*, London, 7, 22–8.
2 McLeod, S. (1981). *The Art of Starvation*, London, Virago, 74.
3 Roche, L. (1984). *Glutton for Punishment*, London, Pan Books, 71–2.
4 Lacey, J.H. and Gibson, E. (1985). 'Controlling weight by purgation and vomiting; a comparative study of bulimics', *Journal of Psychiatric Research*, vol. 19, No. 2/3, 337–41.
5 Dunbar, M. (1986). *Catherine*, London, Viking Books.

· FOUR ·
Bad medicine

When the anorexic's weight continues to fall, and those close to her realize that all their efforts to encourage her to eat are coming to nothing, they generally seek out medical help.

Doctors have a range of sophisticated techniques at their disposal. They may also be able to command greater authority than many a parent or spouse. But, faced with an anorexic's adamant refusal to eat, they are constrained in much the same way as everyone else. There are very few additional responses they can make just because they are medically trained, for there is no cure for anorexia nervosa that is, strictly speaking, medical.

False leads: appetite and mood

The anorexic typically presents a healthy body that is adapting or has adapted to undernutrition as a result of her overriding need to restrict her food intake. Direct manipulation of appetite is of little use because anorexics are not suffering from a loss of appetite. But this is not generally realized. A typical feeling is, 'Of course I'm hungry. I think about food all the time. I can't stop it. I hate it. It's like my enemy. I've got to fight it. I won't let myself give in. I've got to control it.'

In the hope of stimulating her appetite, her family is already likely to have tried to tempt her with food that is especially interesting or that she used to like, but with little success. The problem as the anorexic sees it is to control her hunger: hence her anger and her fear when she is plied with food, and the tension and violent scenes that arise at mealtimes.

There is no reason therefore to prescribe appetite stimulants, although this is unfortunately still done by some practitioners. If they are effective, these drugs merely increase the anorexic's frightened struggle against food. The low-weight anorexic will characteristically allow herself something like a carton of plain yogurt, an apple or tomato, a slice of chicken and a lettuce leaf in one day. But more than this she dare not eat because she is terrified her desire for food will run away with her and she will lose her precious control. This is a terror that can escalate to the point where she stops eating altogether.

In view of her enormous fear of weight gain, the use of appetite suppressants might be considered a more logical approach on the grounds that they might enable her to shift from total starvation to a point where she is eating moderate amounts. This is a move that would certainly need to be achieved as part of a negotiation with the sufferer herself. It may avert an eventual low-weight crisis. But the disadvantage is that the drugs, such as fenfluramine, that are used as appetite suppressants are similar to amphetamines and carry the risk of addiction. Given the frequency of substance abuse in later-stage patterns of behaviour, their introduction would seem to be unwise. Other writers too have pointed out that such drug treatments pose a particular danger for the anorexic or the bulimic.[1] In any case such a strategy can win the medical practitioner at most only a short breathing space. Some bulimics will have attempted to regain their ability to achieve self-starvation with the help of appetite suppressants, for these can be obtained by a determined sufferer from unwary general practitioners, if a good case is made out for chemical assistance to 'start slimming'. Thus: 'I can get anything from my GP. He's so fanatic about the dangers of obesity. That's why I stay with his practice. It's worth the journey, and he never asks too many questions.'

Likewise little can be achieved by prescribing psychotropic – that is, mood-changing – drugs, for the condition is not essentially a mood state. There are some sufferers, more often bulimics than anorexics, who may be clinically depressed as well as being trapped in their food/body-controlling style of thinking. Some may also be anxious, and drugs can be used with profit to alleviate these secondary states of anxiety and depression. But psychotropic drugs will not alter a sufferer's fundamental belief in the importance of food control, and this has been borne out by the experience of those who have used drugs as part of hospital treatment programmes.

The distinction between anorexia nervosa and affective disorders such as depression has, in the past, been a contentious issue. But now it is more widely recognized that the condition is distinguished by the central dynamic that revolves around the idea of control – the dynamic that in conjunction with self-starvation creates the whirlpool described in Chapter Two. Feelings of depression and anxiety in the early stages of anorexia nervosa are directly related to the sufferer's being in control or not. The more control she has over food and eating, the fewer anxious episodes she will have, and she will feel unhappy far less often. This pattern is distinctly different from the pattern that occurs in anxiety states, or with depression that has become an illness in its own right, where it is the persistent disabling and unrelenting mood of hopelessness that is the main problem.

Where people become emaciated as a result of a depressive illness, an increase in their weight will be accompanied by a lessening of their depression. Anorexics/bulimics on the other hand become significantly more depressed with *any* gain in weight, however minimal. For this indicates to them that they are out of control. It is clear evidence of their *total* failure, and feeling a total failure is depressing.

The central role that attitudes and values play, both in the genesis of anorexia nervosa and in its perpetuation, clearly indicates the limitations of medicine in this instance. A person's attitudes, values and beliefs, by their very nature, are not amenable to change by simple drug therapy.

Treatment objectives

Given that physical medicine can provide no cure for anorexia nervosa and that doctors, like anyone else, are constrained by the sufferer's rigid refusal to eat, there are broadly speaking two possibilities. Doctors can either set out to overcome the anorexic's 'wilful' refusal to eat and use whatever medical techniques are necessary to do this. Or they can set about gaining her co-operation, however minimal, in taking part in organizing her own nutritional first aid and eventual recovery.

Of course, the situation a doctor faces with each individual case is more detailed than this dichotomy suggests. However, short-term treatment objectives have a very important influence on outcome. Everyone wants the sufferer to 'get better'. But the more immediate question is how a particular intervention is supposed to bring this about. The question of control is crucial. For it is upon developing a sense of personal autonomy that eventual recovery depends. Even doctors who realize that, beyond the minimum necessary to maintain life, weight gain alone is not a cure may still be tempted to use in the short term methods that will actually frustrate their aim to produce recovery in the long term. The manner in which intervention is taken is often more important than what is actually done, and the question is whether the proposed intervention is designed to overcome the sufferer's food control, or whether it is a step towards helping her gain real autonomy. Some interventions, which we will describe, can only be used for one of these purposes, which is to overcome food control. But with others, particularly drug therapies, the distinction is not so clear.

In addition to the issue of control, the amount of weight gain the doctor is aiming to achieve is also important. Methods which may be justifiable as a lifesaving measure are psychologically destructive when used to return the sufferer to normal weight. Some basic assumptions about the nature of the condition are involved in this objective, and we will return to these later in this chapter.

Confusingly, both the co-operative and coercive approaches are likely to be called 'medical help'. So it is important for the sufferer, and her relatives, to differentiate between the two ways that medicine may be used when she is low weight.

There is a limited number of ways in which any patients who are emaciated can be given the nourishment they need. Intravenous feeding is one of these. Tube feeding into the stomach is another. But a liquid diet of regular, bland nutritional drinks is the mainstay of such help. These are widely used in geriatric wards and for post-operative cases. But an anorexic who feels she is being stripped of her food control will not co-operate. She may be dying of starvation, but she will actively resist by removing the nasogastric tube, or switching off the drip that is supplying her essential nutrition. Chapters Ten and Eleven will be devoted to describing how sufficient co-operation may be achieved in enabling the patient to accept the minimum necessary intervention. In this chapter we will continue to discuss the situation where doctors, willingly or unwillingly, become drawn into using medical techniques to overcome the anorexic's 'wilful refusal' to eat.

The very authority conferred by medical knowledge and the expectations families have of those with medical training tend to push doctors in the direction of coercive intervention before they have elicited even minimal consent. Faced with a stubborn anorexic who is steadfastly refusing to eat, and desperate relatives looking to them for help, they are only too likely to institute a refeeding programme and overcome her resistance rather than undertake the lengthy, time-consuming process of encouraging her gradually to change her attitude.

Additional medical interventions and their limitations

A wide variety of medical techniques has been used in the hospital setting to overcome the low-weight anorexic's refusal to eat and increase her body weight. She generally finds these very alarming, and she is not necessarily alone in this. The techniques described below are being or have been used with the aim of lessening her resistance.

Insulin therapy

Insulin therapy has been used to solve the problem of making the anorexic eat by creating in her an uncontrollable hunger for sugar and carbohydrate that she would relieve – along with the other unpleasant side effects of sweating, dizziness and increased anxiety that this treatment brings about – by taking in food containing these substances.

In an emaciated body, however, there are no reserves of glycogen, and insulin levels may already be very high. So there is considerable risk in using this form of intervention. All anorexics' reactions to insulin are not standard, and it has been found that even a very small, apparently safe dose can prove to be dangerous in some particularly sensitive patients, and deaths have been reported. There has been one instance recorded where the high-carbohydrate breakfast, which is the essential second half of this medical treatment, was forgotten. The insulin injection that had been given caused the girl to go into irreversible coma and suffer lasting brain damage. For these reasons insulin therapy is no longer widely used, but families should be aware of its existence and be forearmed with good reasons why they should decline it for their daughter or son.

Electroconvulsive therapy

Another approach is electroconvulsive therapy (ECT) which has been routinely used by some doctors as a measure of last resort in patients who persist in not eating. It is one psychiatric treatment for conditions that display fixed patterns of thinking and acting that do not change in response to new information or changes in situation.

A small amount of anaesthetic is injected into the vein on the back of the patients' hand or into their arm which quickly puts them to sleep for a few minutes.

Whilst they are asleep a psychiatrist places two electrodes on their head and a small electric current is passed. This causes them to have a very mild fit. The procedure is painless and the patient will not be able to remember the experience of the fit.

It is believed that this treatment temporarily disrupts the neurological basis on which the patient's behaviour depends so that, for a while, patients are unable to return to their usual ways. It is used in the hope that during this interval a more productive style of thinking will develop. ECT is most commonly used for people who are severely depressed.

Although in clinging desperately to her food control the anorexic may appear to be similarly rigid and immovable, her fixed pattern of behaviour is not the result of a mood state. It has a different basis. If ECT has any place, it is for that subcategory of patients with eating disorders who appear to be severely depressed in addition to being anorexic or bulimic.

Surgery

A rather drastic approach is surgery. Leucotomies have occasionally been performed in cases of anorexia nervosa.

A leucotomy is a brain operation in which a portion of nerve fibres (white matter) connecting the two cerebral hemispheres is separated by an incision. Older methods of performing leucotomies produced widely variable physical results in the areas of brain actually cut by the surgeon's knife. Newer stereotactic operative techniques can allow a more precise target to be established and limited cuts to be made; but even so, while the power of the person's beliefs to shape their behaviour is lessened by such an operation, the beliefs themselves remain unchanged. The subsequent psychological results have been generally unhelpful and even disastrous. There has been an instance of an anorexic committing suicide because, following this treatment, her eating changed and she put on weight, but thinness was still her overwhelming desire. There had been no change created in her style of thinking. So it seems doubtful whether such a drastic measure is either appropriate or justified.

Drug therapy

Ways of giving nourishment to a patient are limited, as we have said. Medication may be used in this process, but when, why and how it is used can differ profoundly. It can be used as assistance in a co-operative exercise between a doctor and the anorexic patient who wants to damp down the terrors of the refeeding process (see Chapter Eleven), or it can be used to coerce.

A variety of psychotropic drugs has been used in the treatment of difficult and resistant anorexic patients in hospital. Among these chlorpromazine, which is a major tranquillizer, has a prominent place in the medical literature on anorexia nervosa. It has been described by one authority as 'the drug of choice' and as 'remarkably free of dangers'.[2] But though it may create fewer problems than other drugs of this kind (e.g. thioridazine and trifluoperazine), chlorpromazine is nevertheless epileptogenic. It also depresses bone marrow and stops the production of new blood cells (aplastic anaemia), and it can cause jaundice.

Its main value is in helping the patient to start eating. Furthermore, and unlike the minor tranquillizers that may alternatively be used, it does not disinhibit the patient and so does not create problems with 'management'. (Minor tranquillizers – i.e. benzodiazepines, which include diazepam (Valium), lorazepam (Ativan), chlordiazipoxide (Librium) – carry the danger of releasing more feelings and impulses than both the sufferer and those who care for her can cope with.) But chlopromazine does not bear on the core attitude of the sufferer. Thus, 'One year after admission there is no difference, either physically, emotionally or in attitude towards eating, between those given and those not given the drug'.[2]

Taking control of the anorexic patient

Chlorpromazine does not cure anorexia nervosa, and its effects preclude any alternative therapy that depends on talking to the patient. Thus the purpose of its use lies in the control it gives the doctor. This treatment aim is one that has survived unchanged over a hundred years. In the 1870s it was advocated that the physician should take 'firm moral control'.[2] Today the main advocate of the use of chlorpromazine provides a conspicuous example of the doctor taking control of the patient as a treatment objective.[3] Furthermore he illuminates how the need for the doctor to be in control can take other direct forms and involve actions that make few acknowledgements in the direction of sophisticated medicine.

> We rely mainly on response-prevention for vomiters, but have occasionally employed the technique of telling the patient that she will have to eat anything she vomits. One practical demonstration is usually enough to break the pattern.[4]

Many centres involved in treating anorexia nervosa no longer rely on medical interventions to overcome the sufferer's resistance. They prefer instead the organized and systematic use of the pressures that the hospital as an institution can exert. It is well known that total institutions can change behaviour. Monasteries, prisons, boarding schools and army barracks, as well as hospitals, are total institutions because they regulate all aspects of an individual's life twenty-four hours a day. Those who run them generally have little difficulty in gaining the compliance of members or inmates.

This sort of pressure may be seen by some people as less drastic and therefore more appropriate than some of the medical approaches outlined above. Nevertheless it is important to be aware of the extreme degree of environmental control that is not infrequently used in hospitals in the attempt to change the anorexic's behaviour in relation to eating and weight gain.

The anorexic who undergoes this kind of treatment can find herself separated from her home, family and friends, with her possessions and clothes taken from her, this being a well-known strategy for preventing a person from leaving hospital. She is often confined to bed and may be denied pillows, television, reading materials, visitors and other 'privileges' such as letters and phone calls. These will be rationed according to the extent of her compliance over eating, and here she will certainly be under continual pressure and surveillance.

> I wasn't allowed to go to the lavatory. They told me I'd got to use a commode. They said it would be brought in after meals and that was when I had to use it. I wasn't allowed to have a bath. I said I usually had a bath every day but that made no difference. I would have to make do with a strip-wash, and that meant a bowl and water being brought because the sink in the room had been blocked. That was just in case I had any ideas about getting rid of food down the sink, or being sick down it. The windows were bolted closed for the same reason. It wasn't a hospital. It was a prison.

While undergoing such restrictions and privations the anorexic is required to eat very large quantities of food (see Chapter Five).

Behaviourism: a theoretical rationale for taking control

Behavioural psychology is often used as a theoretical rationale for the above approach in the treatment of low-weight anorexics, although it is doubtful whether it does in fact provide one. There is no doubt that coercive hospital regimes can and do result in anorexics eating and increasing their weight. But whether this outcome is really explained within the concepts of behaviourism is also debatable.

This psychological theory asserts that almost all behaviour is learned and ultimately controlled by the environment within which the organism acts. A person's behaviour is assumed to be a response to stimuli impinging from the environment, or a response to the consequences to a person for having behaved in a particular way. By investigating the relationship between external events and the organism's responses, the psychologist hopes to arrive at laws of behaviour broadly analogous to the laws of natural science. To the extent that anything that can be learned can also, given the appropriate techniques, be unlearned, behaviourism may be seen as a liberating theory and has been the source of many useful therapeutic techniques.

Academically, behaviourism is at its weakest when it attempts to explain the development of morality and higher intellectual functions in human beings. Yet it is precisely these qualities that are so distinctively a part of anorexia nervosa/bulimia, a point that will be elaborated in Part II. It is not surprising, therefore, that those who approach the condition from within this theory make a fundamental mistake about its nature. The sufferers' food and body control is not an isolated item of learned behaviour. It is their sense of who they are. The problem at heart is not about food but about personhood, and autonomy, and that is why the manifestations of the sufferer's need for control can take a variety of forms.

From its philosophical roots, and in the research tradition, behaviourism deals with behaviour in small segments. It is held that links are reinforced between the stimulus properties of particular situations and specific responses by the individual. In therapy undesirable links may be extinguished. Consequently treatment programmes designed under this approach are characteristically very detailed, systematic and structured.

Used correctly, behaviour modification techniques have often proved an effective way of dealing with troublesome symptoms, but symptoms that are limited in their extent. Helping people to stop smoking or to overcome irrational fears are just some of the areas in which they have been successfully used. These problems may make a general mess of a person's life, but the trouble flows from a relatively isolated item of learned behaviour. In these cases individuals feel their symptoms inhibit their capacity to get on with and enjoy life and, since behavioural approaches can have an ameliorating effect, their use seems appropriate here. The behaviour therapist is carrying out these patients' wishes by showing them one way to do what they want to do. In the case of anorexia nervosa, however, it would seem that there are moral and possibly legal objections that might be levelled at the use of the kind of procedures illustrated above, because the patient does not *want* the aim the therapist has in mind.

Although the anorexic's refusal to eat may be construed as a symptom, it is not a limited symptom in the sense that it interferes with her enjoying life. It *is* her way of living. She is a person who has come to understand and experience her enjoyments, her effectiveness, her whole being in terms of her ability to restrict her food intake. For this reason, and unlike the person who has a fear of open spaces or who wants to stop smoking, the anorexic who has been made to eat and gain weight does not feel she has been liberated from a tiresome symptom. Rather she feels she has been destroyed, that her will has been crushed by a superior force.

Legitimating coercion

It is hard to avoid gaining the impression that behaviourism is primarily a convenient language to justify taking control by institutional coercion. What actually happens in wards or units where behaviour modification is used as a policy seems to support this. Behaviour modification does not properly operate by lecturing people about what they ought to be doing, but by changing the reinforcements attendant on what they actually do; in practice, however, the responses of hospital staff are highly moralistic. Comments such as the following are commonplace.

> You told me you'd eaten those sandwiches, and staff nurse discovered you'd hidden them down behind the radiator. You're really deceitful, aren't you! It wasn't a very nice mess for the ward orderly to find. I'm surprised an intelligent girl like you would do such a thing. You know you've got to eat.

Even if staff are instructed not to be judgemental, sufferers are so sensitive they will tune acutely to the real attitude that those around them may attempt to hide (see also Chapter Nine).

Furthermore behavioural techniques, as they are ordinarily employed in psychotherapy, do not usually involve environmental control of the order described above. Indeed it would seem to be questionable whether the behaviour-modification regimes that low-weight anorexics are often subjected to in a hospital context are compatible with behaviour theory at all. When other people take direct and total control over the minutiae of an individual's life – when they take control over their ingesting food, their access to lavatory facilities, their reading material, their contact with the outside world, and so on – it seems doubtful whether a learning theory is needed at all to explain the individual's resulting actions. Much of the original research in behaviour modification was done on the pecking responses of pigeons; but the procedure as it is used in cases of low-weight anorexia nervosa is rather more akin to taking the pigeon by the neck and shoving its beak on to the green button. It is a situation in which the recipient's personal psychology becomes irrelevant.

The apparent success of such programmes in organizing weight gain may have nothing to do with the theory of behaviourism. Looked at from a different perspective, these methods can be seen as creating very stark situations in which communication takes place in a very simple way, with the result that the anorexic patient, quickly receiving the message that is being put across, manoeuvres effectively to extract herself from that situation. Certainly this is the anorexic's experience as typically reported.

> They told me I was going to have to eat 3500 calories a day. The nurses had to sit there till I'd finished everything. If it wasn't food it was thick milky drinks they made me force down. Once I'd put on half a stone they let me walk to the lavatory which was down the corridor, but a nurse always had to come with me to make sure I didn't bring all the food back up. It was so humiliating. Disgusting. And I hated it. Then it began to dawn on me. The way to get out was to go along with what they wanted, and after that it wasn't too bad. I ate to get out. They were all very pleased and said how well I'd done. But as soon as I got out I got back to my routine. I lost all the weight they'd made me put on – and more.

When black-and-white thinkers meet head on

Communications of the above kind may be unambiguous but they are not necessarily productive. In such a situation the rigid polarized thinking of the starving anorexic is being met, quite simply, with a response that is equally and oppositely rigid and polarized. It is a situation that can be parodied thus:

> ANOREXIC: Whatever you say, I *won't* eat, because that's the most important thing for me.
>
> OTHERS: Whatever you say, you *will* eat, because that's the most important thing for us.

Except in the purely physical sense that it will avert a medical crisis, organizing the anorexic's surrender to external control is not the progress it appears. For it represents the shift between the absolute alternatives she faces anyway between total control and total loss of control; extremes that are the more marked the lower the body weight of the sufferer is, and the more polarized in her thinking.

The use of behaviour-modification techniques or any other confrontational approach that sets up a situation in which two wills meet in opposition can effectively allow, and even enable the anorexic to hide from her problem. For it is a situation in which she can direct all her efforts into maintaining or re-establishing her food control in the face of opposition. It provides her with an opportunity to be a success in her own terms; an opportunity to set out once again to win – and win she will. For the anorexic or bulimic, as for many other people, it is easier to be against something or somebody than to confront her own feelings. So she will cling all the more to her own views in opposition to 'these stupid doctors'.

> I was five and a half stone when they made me go into hospital. That was a moment of weakness. But they weren't going to make me eat. That was the one thing I was certain about. They weren't going to make me put on an ounce. They threatened and wheedled, but I knew I was right, and I was going to win . . . and it wasn't till later, a few years later I realized how frightened I was.

Not only is no change created in her situation by establishing external control. As the board game showed, the sufferer will do all she can to revert to her preferred position when these controls are removed.

Anyone who thinks in terms of rigid polarities and who has a poor sense of self typically responds to coercion or persuasion with an attitude of 'no change' or 'total change'. This is a phenomenon that has been well investigated, and is acknowledged as one of the likely processes that underlies the change in attitude that takes place when people undergo dramatic religious conversions and abrupt switches in political allegiance.

Where the anorexic or bulimic is concerned, it would seem that this pattern is reflected in the large numbers of sufferers who, having had their weight restored in hospital, are readmitted after they have successfully starved themselves yet again to the point of being severely emaciated.[5] It would also seem to be reflected in the further numbers who, though they appear to have benefited from such treatment in that they have sustained their higher body weight and have not needed to be readmitted, have in fact slipped into using the other less visible forms of control. These are the so-called 'recovered anorexics', or 'false positives', who may or may not eventually reveal themselves as still suffering. Janet's story is by no means unusual.

> I had anorexia when I was sixteen. I know I lost a lot of weight, but it didn't last long. The doctor was very brusque and I was sent into hospital where I was drugged out of my head and fed till I weighed ten stone four, which is what they said I ought to be. Then they let me out. I think I tried to get back into a routine, but I don't think I managed very well. It was easiest while I was at university. The harder I worked the more I could push it all out of the way. But after that – going without food when I could. Making myself sick. I did that till about two years ago. I just seem to lurch from one mess to another. I thought it was because I couldn't cope, I was so inadequate I couldn't manage like everyone else. I still feel better when I'm thinner. I get nearly suicidal if I put on – well, even just a pound. It's taken me a long time to realize . . . to face the fact that . . . (pausing for some time) the anorexia's still there. I don't want to accept it. But . . . well, it is.

The use of legal powers to detain and treat the anorexic

Most of the procedures described in the present chapter can be backed by legal powers. The criteria and procedures for compulsory admission to hospital and treatment are set out in Part II of the Mental Health Act, 1983.[5]

Although this may be judged to be necessary in the interests of his or her safety, the decision for a patient to be thus detained cannot be made on the judgement of doctors alone. A patient may be detained under section 4 in the case of 'urgent necessity' for admission; under section 2 'for assessment (or for assessment followed by medical treatment)'; under section 3 where it is appropriate for the patient to receive such treatment as is likely to 'alleviate or prevent a deterioration of his condition' and this is necessary for the health and safety of the patient. But in addition to a recommendation by one medical practitioner under section 4, and recommendations by two medical practitioners under sections 2 or 3, there must also be an application by an approved social worker (ASW) or the patient's nearest relative (section 11(1)). Either the social worker or the nearest relative has to agree that, in his or her view too, it is reasonable, given the patient's behaviour and/or circumstances, that he/she should be compulsorily detained.

Usually, where the question arises of admitting a person to hospital against their will the person concerned would rely on the understanding and support of parents, family and such people as his or her social worker or community nurse to provide a balance of opinion and defend her right not to be legally detained. Where the anorexic is concerned however, this issue raises all the difficulties about the nature of her behaviour that were set out in Chapter One. That is, the difficulties over whether, and to what extent, her food and body control is to be considered rational, self-directed and the action of a well-functioning human being; or whether, and to what extent, it is to be considered irrational and actually out of control. As a result of the confusion that exists over these issues, the agreement of all parties that is required under any of the relevant sections of the Mental Health Act to admit and/or treat the sufferer against her will is not in practice always forthcoming.

Meanwhile the anorexic is often left to drift on with her problem, innocent of the possibility that she may find herself in the position where she or her family have to defend her behaviour as rational if she is not to be legally detained in hospital against her will; such is the nature of the condition that, by the time this situation arises, the sufferer may have alienated her family to the extent that they will be unwilling to help her defend this right. Nor does the anorexic usually know that, if the Act is invoked and she is at the same time classically emaciated and has failed to keep a previous undertaking to eat and gain weight, in these circumstances she and her family are unlikely to win an appeal against the decision that has been made.

The sufferer's alienation from the medical profession

Intervention procedures such as those described above ,tend to poison the relationship between the anorexic and members of the medical profession. This can effectively hinder their obtaining medical help, even for minor ailments or injuries.

> I'm afraid Sally won't go near a doctor for anything. She had a very bad gash on her chin when she came off her bike last summer. It really needed a couple of stitches. I suggested she saw our GP, but she got into panic about doctors dragging her into hospital. She ought to have had the right treatment. But I was worried . . . I know she didn't eat at all for several days. I kept finding food in the bin. So she's got a nasty scar, and it needn't have been so bad.

Sometimes their experience of previous 'treatment' can have been so distressing that, combined with the extreme thinking that starvation brings about anyway, they can come to the point where they would rather die than succumb again to medical help. The close friend of one male anorexic gave the following account of such a situation.

> He looks dreadful. His bones are quite clearly visible and his skin is sort of hanging on them. His eyes are sunken too, and of course he's very weak. He can't get out of bed except by rolling on to the floor. He'll crawl across to his chair too, unless he thinks I'm looking, and if he thinks I am then he'll make an enormous effort to stand up first, before sitting in the chair. He absolutely refuses to entertain any idea of going into hospital. I've tried to talk to him about it, and to his mother, but she really doesn't know what to do. You see, he had a terribly bad time when he went in there before. He was sectioned, so he had to stay there. But it was a question of being strapped to a bed in a darkened room, which he found quite . . . horrific. I can understand he doesn't want to go through that again. But what's so worrying is that he's saying he'd rather die than be taken in there again.

Sufferers may not always reach this extreme. This man's weight had fallen to 52-per-cent AEBW, at which level he was indeed dying. But it is by no means unusual to meet higher-weight sufferers who are not only unwilling but absolutely determined to have nothing further to do with the medical profession; as was the woman who visibly shuddered at a counsellor's suggestion that it might be wise if her doctor checked whether the sufferer's physical health had been impaired by her vomiting. Having said very little before this point, the woman remained entirely mute for the rest of their meeting.

In self-help groups it has been found that sufferers simply do not see medical practitioners as a source of support, comfort and caring. There is a real, persistent and universal undercurrent of fear associated with 'medical help'. They talk about 'being locked away and fattened up'. The experience of being processed rather than understood by doctors emerges strongly in their accounts. A recent study has documented the alienation of sufferers from the profession as a whole. Of members of self-help groups in one health region it was found that only one in five of group members were known to medical practitioners as being anorexia nervosa/bulimia sufferers.[6]

The doctor's point of view

Whilst it is possible to appreciate an anorexic's fears and anxieties, doctors can find themselves in a difficult position *vis-à-vis* the anorexia nervosa patient. Medical practitioners are not usually allowed the luxury of inaction. They are conventionally the people who 'do something' about obvious physical symptoms. Therapy that involves a gradual approach to change tends to lack the appearance of doing something. So, as we pointed out earlier, doctors are pushed towards the more confrontational methods of dealing with the anorexic at low weight. Instituting a refeeding programme is at least to be seen to act.

Given the reputation anorexics have for being unrewarding patients, many doctors would rather not get involved. Nor are there any opportunities with anorexia nervosa for using high-technology medicine to achieve a patient's rapid cure, and no kudos to be gained this way either. Hospital physicians will often be more than ready to hand over any anorexic patient whose condition is not yet life-threatening. 'She needs someone to talk to', is the usual dismissive phrase, often accompanied by a sudden concern to know why there is not more help of this kind available. But the problem is that the social worker or psychiatric community nurse who, in a health-service context, might be expected to respond, is unlikely to know much about anorexia nervosa.

Even informed and interested members of the medical profession can still find themselves in a difficult position from which to develop a co-operative approach. Not only is the sufferer likely to be brought or referred for help when her weight loss is quite severe, but she will also frequently come with her resistance to change having been greatly increased by the doctor having been set up as her adversary. Parents often threaten the girl with seeing the doctor. Unless the sufferer has been his patient previously, the doctor is also at a disadvantage in that he does not begin with any kind of relationship with her – and the lower an anorexic's weight is, and the more simple her thinking, the more difficult is the communication that might achieve this.

Doctors can become understandably irritated at having an extremely emaciated anorexic handed on to them only after the best opportunities to build a therapeutic relationship have been allowed to slip by a counsellor who has not been aware of the need to confront the problem of the sufferer's falling weight. It is important for helpers of any persuasion not to have wide-ranging discussions with a sufferer whilst ignoring the fact that her weight is drifting downwards. We would stress that weight is not the only thing the helper will need to talk about; but there is no point in talking exclusively about other things if her weight is falling rapidly to a physically dangerous level. Generally there seems little point in criticizing doctors for using draconian measures to restore the anorexic's weight if they are only called upon to help at the point where urgent life-saving intervention has become necessary. A combination of late referral and high resistance to intervention of any kind can leave the doctor ultimately with no option but to adopt a purely physiological solution to the presented problem.

How much weight gain?

It is not generally realized how much of the conflict that there is between the anorexic and her doctor arises not so much over the necessity of some weight gain, but over the question of the *amount* of weight gain that is to be achieved. Everyone who is aware of the real nature of the condition accepts that the sufferer's weight should, in the end, reach a stable near-normal level for her height and age (90-per-cent AEBW) if recovery is to be achieved. Below this the sufferer's weight level itself indicates that she cannot be counted as recovered. Many doctors, however, feel that this amount of weight restoration has to be the *first* step. Others, including ourselves, believe that the more modest goal of restoring weight to a level that is merely medically safe is the better first option in the long term. This is a level (75-per-cent AEBW) that is considerably lower (see Chapter Eleven).

For a person who is in a starved state, and whose thinking and perceptions are altered because of this, the demand that she should tolerate being re-fed in a short period of time, e.g. ten–twelve weeks, to a normal or near normal weight is extreme and unreasonable. It is a demand that virtually guarantees non-cooperation on the part of the sufferer, for she will understand it as 'having to be made fat'. Although she will often resort to a strategy of compliance to escape from a situation that is so intolerable to her, outright conflict over refeeding is typically any anorexic's first response. It can by contrast sometimes be easier to negotiate or bargain a co-operative agreement with the anorexic, if the aim is only to raise her weight to a medically safe level.

The problem of coping with the danger of a medical emergency at very low weight is quite different from the idea that it is therapeutically necessary to achieve a rapid restoration of weight to a normal, or near normal level. That both may take place in hospital tends to obscure this fact.

Where an anorexic's weight has become dangerously low the immediate and very practical problem will be to prevent her from dying of starvation, and there is no doubt that medical skills can be essential in achieving this. But many doctors again believe that, for their efforts to have any lasting effect, they must increase her weight to a level that is near normal for her height and age. It is this assumption that tends to result in their becoming embroiled in lengthy battles with anorexic patients, and lead to their adopting methods that may be questionable.

There is a direct connection between the theory a doctor has in mind and the amount of conflict he experiences with his patient. The use of the procedures we have described in this chapter is not usually motivated by the desire to be cruel or retributive towards a particularly resistant patient. Rather it is a calculated response to the problem of anorexia nervosa as the doctor has been led to see it.

Relatively few doctors with any experience of dealing with anorexic patients believe that weight gain alone is a cure, and they are aware of the patient's feelings about enforced weight gain. But these doctors continue to insist upon this because they believe effective psychotherapy is not possible unless weight is at a near-normal level. They believe that, despite the unpleasant experience weight gain entails for the sufferer, this is the best approach they have and, as it is the cause of so much trouble, it is important to consider where this conviction comes from.

The tyranny of assumptions

There are two main assumptions that support the idea that rapid weight gain to near normal level is essential. The first involves the theory, outlined in Chapter Two, that the root problem in anorexia nervosa is the sufferer's avoidance of adult sexuality. According to this view weight is important because it is its loss that makes avoidance of sexuality possible, because sexuality is effectively switched off by the biological and emotional changes that are brought about by malnutrition and reduced body weight. The second assumption is that there is a clear threshold at which this avoidance process works, and it is believed the low-weight anorexic will always stop gaining weight as she approaches this level. So the theoretical justification for bringing her rapidly up to this threshold is that this is where the 'real problem' is, and the view is that it cannot be dealt with until it is reached.[7] This theory selectively emphasizes one consequence of starvation and low weight and tends to ignore the many others, even though to do so creates further theoretical problems. The effect of starvation on sexuality is not particularly immediate, so extra arguments are needed to enable this theory to explain why the anorexic's food control actually begins.

It would seem that there is little to justify the selective emphasis that this theory places on sexuality, except the preconceptions of those who adhere to it. Changes in sexuality do not occur until a person has lost approximately 15 per cent of her/his body weight; but as we also saw in Chapter Two, it takes only hours before starvers achieve experiences that they perceive as virtuous, as producing clarity of thought and greater autonomy, and as enhancing their sense of well-being. So rather than just being rewarding indirectly, and solely in terms of removing sexual feelings, acts of self-starvation are rewarding in many direct and more immediate ways.

To focus on sexuality is to draw attention to the one effect of starvation about which it is plausible to think in terms of on/off switches and a single clear threshold, conveniently marked by the cessation of menstruation, rather than to bring into focus, as the whirlpool theory does, those other changes that are gradual and where steps are progressive.

For those who work with the preconception that the feelings that are 'really' troubling the anorexic are sexual feelings, and who emphasize the fact that there is a threshold below which sexual feelings are not experienced, the logical step is to bring the anorexic's weight up to a level where sexual feelings will return. Since the belief is that no 'issues of significance' will emerge until the patient reaches this threshold, near-normal weight might as well be achieved rapidly.

Those who hold this view do not accept that others who provide psychotherapy while the sufferer is still low weight are using a valid alternative approach, and one which has the advantage that it need not be coercive. They believe such helpers will find themselves unwittingly collaborating with the anorexic and perpetuating the illness by thus giving significance to her low-weight condition, and supporting her in it while she has no awareness of the 'real issues'. This illustrates the important connection there is at the level of ideas between the selection of sexuality as the one significant consequence of starvation, and the treatment strategy of engineering very substantial increases in weight in an in-patient context.

The selective emphasis on sexuality follows from the particular theory of personality development that is being used, which is in the Freudian tradition, and therefore lays great emphasis on the role of sexuality in the development of a person's sense of self: particularly during the adolescent stage of development when the resurgence of sexuality and changing social expectations can create an identity crisis.

This stress on sexuality in anorexia nervosa would appear to carry the conviction it does because it is consistent with much more general assumptions about women: particularly that they are primarily nurturers and child-rearers, an assumption that leads to women experiencing great difficulty in being taken seriously in any other way, and continuing to have to struggle to develop their full potential as human beings. This emphasis on female sexuality is paralleled in the quite different responses that can be observed when the behaviour of males and females becomes a matter of public concern, for it has been found that, when boys and girls are arrested for similar public order offences, the investigations centre on strength and violence where boys are the offenders, and on sexual behaviour and promiscuity where the offenders are girls. The majority of anorexics are female. Those who make the ready assumption that anorexia nervosa is rooted in sexuality are thus treading a familiar path.

The idea that gender-role expectations lie behind the emphasis on sexuality in this theory are not lessened by references to the physical attractiveness of anorexia nervosa patients that occur in otherwise clinical texts on the subject;[8] nor by such comments as 'She's a pretty little thing', made by male members of medical teams during ward rounds.

This assumption was not shared by the two earliest female medical authorities on anorexia nervosa, who have a much wider focus on the nature of the problem.[9] Both developed theories where sexuality is one issue among many that are relevant in explaining the condition, and both found in practice that Freudian ideas are inappropriate in this instance. The current rise in incidence among males also seems to strip this view that emphasizes female sexuality of its conventional plausibility.

References

1 Neuman, P. and Halvorson, P. (1983). *Anorexia Nervosa and Bulimia – A Handbook for Counselors and Therapists*, New York, Van Nostrand Reinhold.

2 Gull, W. (1874). 'Anorexia Nervosa', *Transactions of the Clinical Society*, London, 7, 22–8.

3 Dally, P. and Gomez, J. (1969). *Anorexia Nervosa*, London, Heinemann Medical Books, 115.

4 Dally, P. and Gomez, J. (1969). ibid., 113.

5 Gostin, L. (1983). *A Practical Guide to Mental Health Law*, London, Mind, 10–12.

6 Society for the Advancement of Research into Anorexia (Sara), Billingsthorpe, Sussex, Newsletter no. 12, April 1986.

7 Crisp, A., Norton, K.R.S., Jurczak, S., Bowyer, C. and Duncan, S. (1985). 'A treatment approach to anorexia nervosa – 25 years on', *Journal of Psychiatric Research*, Oxford, 19, No. 2/3, 393–404.

8 Dally, P. and Gomez, J. (1969). ibid., 93.

9 Bruch, H. (1974). *Eating Disorders*, London, Routledge and Kegan Paul.
Palazzoli, M.S. (1974). *Self-starvation: From the Intrapsychic to the Transpersonal Approach to Anorexia Nervosa*, London, Human Context Books, Chaucer Publishing Co.

PART II

· FIVE ·

The picture at low weight and foundations for help

Theories of anorexia nervosa that recognize the way a person can be trapped by the effects of starvation share common ground in that they lead to the view that the condition has different stages and, more importantly, that each stage requires different responses from the helper. There is no single counselling or therapeutic approach that is appropriate or sufficient throughout. The helper must employ different skills at different times. These theories also share the view that something very important changes when a person's weight is reduced to approximately 80 per cent AEBW, though there is disagreement about what kind of change it is that is important.

Though many theorists who take starvation into account have been led by the assumptions they make to the view that anorexia nervosa is essentially concerned with sexuality, we suggest the change that takes place at around 80-per-cent AEBW is more widely relevant in the way it applies to living at a moment-to-moment level. For every moment is affected by altered thinking, and by influencing thinking starvation influences experience as a whole.

Around 80-per-cent AEBW: across the threshold into low weight

Intellectual shut-down and preoccupation with food proceed by such gradual steps that an uninformed observer may not at first appreciate that a person is crossing the threshold into low weight. However, the change in thinking in all people that takes place in the band of weights between 81–78-per-cent AEBW (i.e. around 80 per cent) is as noticeable to those alert to this altered psychological state as the cessation of menstruation in female sufferers is to those who focus on physical change.

Conversely, when weight is rising the opening up of intellectual functioning can seem quite dramatic, particularly to a helper who has been working for many months or years with a sufferer whose weight has been consistently below this level.

The sufferer who is at or who stays below this threshold is likely to appear distant and unreachable. Those meeting her who are unaware of the reasons for her distance can get drawn into seeking 'the truth' about this elusive and unfathomable person without realizing there is less to find than there might once have been.

> I was intrigued with Bel when I first met her. We were in a first-year tutor group (at university). She was very bright, and always looked pretty good. But she was kind of mysterious. So it was somehow never possible to get through. That wasn't just my experience. I remember Tim and Candy saying that too. It was a bit of a shock when she got so thin. None of us realized till then there was anything wrong.

Nor is it only potential friends who encounter this problem as one long-term sufferer revealed when she happened to say that the Jungian psychotherapist she had been seeing had told her he found her 'a difficult client'. She was so 'inscrutable and unforthcoming'. Her weight at the time was 73-per-cent AEBW. When she had begun psychoanalysis, she had been about 95 per cent of her AEBW, but already sliding downwards. The significance of her weight loss was missed by this psychotherapist.

The 'around 80 per cent' threshold is important for its relevance to the sufferer's understanding of herself and the world, and for the kind of communication that can take place with her. For this is the small band of weights from the top point of which, as her weight falls further, it becomes progressively more difficult to talk with her in an ordinary way. It is certainly not impossible to work effectively with a sufferer whose weight is at or below this threshold, but this possibility does depend on the helper's ability to make certain necessary efforts of imagination to cross this threshold and communicate with her in terms of her low-weight experience.

The task is analogous to talking to a person whose thinking is altered by the effects of alcohol or street drugs. How a person who has reached this level of weight restriction sounds is less familiar to most people than how a person sounds when drunk or stoned, but with practice the same level of swift recognition can be achieved. With some guidance and practice there is no reason why a helper cannot become skilled not only in recognizing the anorexic but also in communicating with her while she is existing at a low weight (see Chapter Ten). It is skill in communicating that provides the way out of the dilemma described in Chapter Three, where the choices facing the helper seemed to be between restoring the anorexic's weight in a way that is psychologically destructive and allowing her to persist with a lifestyle that has the potential to destroy her physically.

Different approaches and how weight gain is implicated

To acknowledge that the experience of starvation itself makes food control increasingly compulsive is, in practice, compatible with two approaches to the question of weight gain in those whose weight is below 80-per-cent AEBW. These two approaches produce radically different experiences for the sufferer undergoing therapy. They also lead to very different ideas about who is capable of providing help.

Weight gain as a prerequisite to psychotherapy

Theories that emphasize sexuality encourage, as we have said, an understanding of anorexia nervosa as having two stages marked by the presence or absence of sex hormone secretions, and the favouring of rapid weight gain to a normal or near normal level.

In practical terms rapid weight gain usually involves bed rest for the patient to reduce the amount of energy expended, and an increased diet which is built up rapidly, certainly to 3000 calories and often to as much as 4000–5000 calories a day, this latter being about twice the average calorie intake for an active adult female. The sufferer's unwillingness to consume this amount of food or contemplate so great a weight gain at one stretch means this treatment usually entails a considerable amount of coercion.

Because such rapid refeeding, with or without the use of drugs, can cause marked physiological reactions such as oedema, gastric dilatation and, if chlorpromazine is used, epileptic fits, this is an approach that necessitates in-patient treatment, often in specialist units. Nor would the necessary control of the patient be possible elsewhere. For these reasons rapid refeeding is an approach that is beyond the capabilities of the general practitioner and of helpers without medical training alike, and to concentrate on such an approach is to put severe limits on the amount of help available.

It cannot be denied, of course, that forcing the anorexic's weight to go up does provide the helper with a window of opportunity as the constraints of starvation ebb, but it is an opportunity that is, in practice, very difficult to use to good effect. Anorexics whose weight has been forced up by rapid refeeding have usually become very unwilling to take advantage of psychotherapy where it is subsequently offered. The process of refeeding violates so much of her person, and so many of her important principles, that she will not tolerate further contact with those who have done this to her. In the words of one sufferer: 'You manage to get yourself out of hospital and you feel disgusting and abused, destroyed and really in a mess, and you just think, "Sod the lot of them!"'

Gradual weight gain and psychotherapy in parallel

The alternative approach is to encourage the anorexic to gain weight gradually and to regulate this weight gain herself. Where this approach is used, in-patient refeeding is restricted to those anorexics whose emaciation is endangering their life and continued only until a medically safe weight is reached (see Chapter Eleven). This is usually 70 per cent or more of the patient's average expected body weight. This means that a girl whose AEBW is 8 st., whom anorexia nervosa has reduced to a skeletal 4 st. 7 lb. will be restored to somewhere between 5 st. 8 lb and 6 st. (i.e. between 70–75 per cent) before her treatment as an outpatient will be resumed. In other cases weight gain need only take place as fast as the sufferer herself will allow as she is given the necessary therapeutic support.

Enabling the anorexic to regulate her own weight gain means proceeding relatively slowly over a substantial period of time. It involves her first learning to hold her weight stable, and then gradually gaining weight. Individual anorexics can differ in the rates at which they will allow their weight to increase, but it is not often any faster than a pound a week, and is commonly much slower than this.

The aim in enabling an anorexic to initiate, sustain and regulate her own weight gain is to help her to maintain some sense at least of personal autonomy. At low weight, because non-eating has become central to her existence, this will necessarily involve her own careful control of food intake above all else. This approach, described in Part III, is in distinct contrast to those approaches that contrive to overcome the anorexic's food control.

Where a gradual approach is used, help can be given on an out-patient basis. There is no reason why either general practitioners or non-medical helpers should not play a major role in supporting the girl and assisting her through the process of change. Since it draws on human skills rather than on technical ones, it is also an approach that allows help potentially to be plentiful rather than rendered scarce by the need for expensive hospital units.

Different meanings of the same words

There is a difficulty in comparing these different approaches to helping an anorexic who is low weight and refusing food in that the same words are used by the adherents of each, but used to convey very different meanings. The result is a conceptual confusion that can leave proponents of each school of thought unaware that they are not actually discussing the same thing, however much it may look as though they are. This is a situation that can generate more heat than light.

The use of two ideas in particular needs to be clarified. It needs to be made clear what is meant by 'opposing the anorexic's food control'. It also needs to be made clear what is meant by 'weight gain'.

'Opposing food control'

Any therapy that recognizes starvation effects has, from the start, the eventual aim that the sufferer will achieve a weight that is at least at the lower end of the range of weights that are normal for her height and age. For as we have said, it is not possible to recover from anorexia nervosa while remaining substantially underweight. This aim is in opposition to the sufferer's desperate commitment to maintaining control. It is in opposition to the moment-by-moment struggle she is engaged in to shore up the dyke that holds back both her need for food and the pressures that are put on her to eat. But there is a great difference between approaches that use vast machinery to bulldoze the dyke and those that help the girl to dismantle the dyke herself, whilst acknowledging the push of the surge tide that is her hunger.

The helper who sets out to enable the anorexic to regulate her own weight gain, and in this way maintain some sense of personal autonomy, places herself or himself alongside the anorexic and works with the anorexic's own values and beliefs. By sharing the sufferer's perspectives the helper will find that the values and beliefs the anorexic has are more ambivalent, even when she is quite low weight, than would appear from her consistent refusal to eat.

There are, for example, some consequences of continued weight loss that the anorexic does not want, if and when these become real prospects to her mind. It is possible that she would prefer not to fail her exams, nor lose her job. She is usually very unhappy about the way she is upsetting the other members of her family, and the idea of being taken into hospital and being made to eat fills her with terror. Any anorexic would usually like to avoid some or all of these eventualities. But, constrained as her thinking has become as a consequence of her starved state, she can see only the alternatives of total control and maintained thinness on one hand, and total surrender to the impulse to eat and resultant 'instant obesity' on the other. Losing control is her greatest fear. Thus it comes about that, if the price of holding on to her food control happens to be losing her job, or upsetting her parents, then, if left to herself, this is the price that she sees herself as being compelled to pay. She sees herself as having no alternative but to stay totally in control over food and her body.

In working with the low-weight anorexic to achieve her gradual change, rather than totally against her, the helper will have to make adjustments, or efforts of imagination to see the situation as the anorexic sees it and let her know clearly that she/he understands her feeling of having no alternative but food control. Then the task is to begin to bring into focus some of the intermediate positions that the starving anorexic's style of thinking consistently eliminates. This is the strategy that makes the gradual dismantling of the dyke possible (see Chapter Twelve).

The helper who repeatedly brings into focus some of the unwanted consequences of starvation, but which follow from her extreme position, and who assists the anorexic in making such small changes as enable her to avoid them, is still opposing the sufferer. But in this instance the 'opposition' arises from clarifying conflicting ideas that already exist within the sufferer herself. Doubtless the anorexic may also feel opposed by the helper as a person approaching her in this way, for the helper will still be cueing into the anorexic's supreme fear of going out of control and will awaken a great deal of anxiety and panic in her merely by suggesting the very slightest move to an 'intermediate' position. But by focusing on the conflict that there is in the anorexic's own values and beliefs, and at the same time supporting her in making minute changes in the direction of resolving these conflicts (see Chapter Fourteen), the helper is offering the anorexic a way out that leaves her sense of control *intact enough* for her to cope gradually with further change, and avoiding the blatant and destructive clash of wills that is usually the outcome of the approaches described in Chapter Four.

The fact is that very modest increases in the amount of food the low-weight anorexic consumes can begin to alter the situation and make possible some of the other things she would also like. They may enable her family to feel less anxious and upset and, if family tension can be reduced, the relatives involved may find it easier to learn about the nature of anorexia nervosa as the problem that has beset them. Small but gradual changes may likewise enable the sufferer to keep her job or keep it till she feels she wants to leave rather than being given the sack because her progressive emaciation has reduced her competence.

'Weight' and 'weight gain'

Between the alternative approaches to therapy there are important differences as to what is meant by the term 'weight', and in the way this meaning relates to the idea of 'gaining weight'. Those who adhere to the principle of rapid weight gain appear to be using these words purely in terms of changes in measured body weight. If they are using them with any subtlety beyond this in the initial stages of therapy, then they fail to communicate this to the anorexic. It is this use of 'weight' that provokes such characteristic comments such as: 'They treated me just like a piece of meat. All they wanted to know was how much this piece of meat weighed, and how quickly they could fatten up this carcass.'

In using a gradual approach to weight gain on the other hand we are explicitly concerned with the fact that, as a result of the way in which her preoccupation with food is intensified by the effects of starvation, by the time she is low weight she has developed a 'food control self', a self for which weight inevitably is crucial as one of the clearest measures of her existence. It is not simply a physical measurement. It is her identity. 'You can't not weigh yourself. You've got to know. If you don't, you disintegrate. You just go to pieces. Terror and panic. Spinning off into terrified panic, like becoming nothing . . . nothing at all.'

It is the lack of a sense of self other than the self which is centred on the control of food, weight and eating that underlies the problem of anorexia nervosa. Because food control is her 'self', all interventions must acknowledge this, and indeed be calculated to maintain this control sufficiently for her to continue to function, and interventions when she is low weight are no exception to this. Her food-control self needs to be nurtured until she can gradually begin to let that self go and replace it with a self that is more certain, that is not so absolutely dependent on control. This in our view is the task of therapy. Weight gain that is purely physical, that is not accompanied by an experience that enhances her self in this wider sense, is no progress at all, except where it is necessary to keep her alive.

Important though it is to separate out weight as meaning 'who I am' and weight as measurement of pounds and ounces, it is essential that the helper does not discard either meaning. It is important to appreciating her position to be able to think in the way the anorexic does. But it is also vital not to lose sight of changes in her weight. This must be kept in perspective for the sake of her safety. So the helper must learn to process in parallel information about an anorexic's experience and information about her physical state.

Low weight and non-medical help

Generally it is not realized that anorexics can be helped, even when they are at low weight, by helpers who do not have medical qualifications; though they will need an irreducible minimum of ordinary biological information about the physical aspects of the condition.[1]

The bodily signs of anorexia nervosa, which include emaciation and loss of periods (amenorrhoea), low blood pressure (hypotension), slow pulse rate (bradycardia), mauve or blueness of hands, feet and other extremities (acrocyanosis) and an increased hair growth (lanugo) on the face and body, are all the normal adjustments of a healthy body reacting to increasingly inadequate nutrition. They are not strictly medical problems in their own right.

Monitoring physical safety

There is no need for the non-medical helper to withdraw as soon as, or just because, such physical effects develop. The process of gradual weight gain and personal change is one that is helped, as we have said, by human rather than technical skills. However, it is that point where emaciation becomes physically dangerous that sets the limit for helping the low-weight anorexic without medical advice or assistance. At and below this level, where her helper is not medically trained, the care of the anorexic must be shared.

The threshold where emaciation becomes physically dangerous is reached when a person's weight falls to between 65–60 per cent of her/his AEBW, or to 50 per cent of an obese original weight, whichever comes first. For example the person who originally weighed 16 st., but whose AEBW is 10 st. will already have reached a critical point when his or her weight falls to 8 st. (50 per cent). It is *this* that is the significant calculation, and *not* the 6 st. 7 lb. that would be 65 per cent of their 10-st. AEBW.

Whatever the sufferer's original weight, the grounds for medical concern will be much greater if this critical threshold has been reached by rapid weight loss than if weight has been low but relatively stable for some months. For, when weight is lost rapidly, there is less time for the body to adapt. A weight loss from 10 st. to 7 st. in eight months, for instance, is more worrying than the loss of the same 3 st. over two years followed by a stable 7-st. weight for a further year.

The kinds of control the sufferer has been and is currently using are also relevant to the question of physical safety. Where the helper has reason to believe that the sufferer's body chemistry might be disturbed as a result of persistent vomiting, or the use of excessive quantities of laxatives and/or diuretics, then a biochemical check on serum electrolytes is essential and can be requested from the patient's general practitioner.

While appreciating the sufferer's anxieties about food and weight gain, and supporting her in overcoming these, any helper, medically trained or otherwise, must be clear about his/her own anxieties concerning the anorexic's physical safety. Helpers must not only acknowledge their own fears but do something appropriate about them. This advice also applies to the wider circle of professionals who have marked anxieties about being able to cope with any severely anorexic client at all. It will still be useful to the sufferer if the professional, who for this reason is declining to take her on, makes it clear to her that it is his/her own worries about the anorexia nervosa and low weight that has led to him/her feeling unable to see her. The straightforward statement to be made is, 'You need more help than I can or know how to give'.

It is appropriate to pass her to another source of help if the other source is seen as more likely to be able to be effective. Though a series of rejections is best avoided, it is not damaging to let the anorexic know her condition has the power to cause grave anxiety. Rather this can be helpful in the long run. Solidarity in the expression of anxiety can help in getting the message get through to an anorexic, who is currently certain she is perfectly well, that perhaps all is not as well as she thinks it is (see Chapter Nine).

Counsellors or therapists who do decide to help an anorexic may find it essential, in order to keep a check on their own fears, to decide in advance upon the weight level beyond which they will not be prepared to continue their help without organizing medical support. This may be a level above the threshold where the girl's emaciation would actually be physically dangerous, but which would be important nevertheless to ensure that counsellor's peace of mind. Meanwhile the anorexic will need to be told about this arrangement well in advance of her reaching the stipulated level, and told repeatedly. She will need this, not as a threat or as a warning but simply as *constant*, *reliable* information that her position is not as sound and well organized as she believes it is.

It goes without saying that, if her weight does still drop to the stated low level, the arrangement to contact the nominated doctor must be carried out without any postponement, no matter what the anorexic says. The helper must be reliable, even if it is painful for both parties.

A stepladder for recovery

The gradual approach to weight gain follows from our view that any two-stage division into non-functioning low weight on the one side and viable weight on the other, where the sufferer can 'pass for normal', is too simple. It fails to acknowledge either the variety of changes in experience that starvation brings about, or the gradual way in which these changes actually take place.

Not only is there a whole variety of experiences related to restricting food intake, but they are placed like rungs on a stepladder throughout the entire process of starvation and weight change from the initial, rapidly induced sense of euphoria to the severe breakdown of rational functioning and ability to relate to the world that occurs at very low weight. Their effects are subtle, particularly in the way they mesh with the person's values and beliefs and blend into the person's understanding of who she/he is. However, unless the helper develops a facility for moving mentally across the communication threshold into 'low-weight thinking', the many subtle distinctions in the anorexic's behaviour and experience that there are when she is below 78-per-cent AEBW, and well into the whirlpool of starvation, will be lost to the helper's awareness. Certainly those who make a basically twofold distinction in the stages of the illness, and who assume little or nothing of any therapeutic significance can take place below the particular weight threshold where the 'all important' feelings concerning sexuality are switched off, miss a great deal that is important to the anorexic and in consequence lose precious therapeutic opportunities.

Seeing the process of recovery as moving on the rungs of a stepladder, and a stepladder that reaches down to other thresholds beyond the point where her thinking is clearly altered, is to provide a much closer fit with the subtleties of the sufferer's experience through every stage of the condition. Nor have we found that, where weight gain is gradual, the anorexic's progress in gaining weight will stop as she approaches an immediately pre-pubescent 'phobic' weight level. In our experience there is not one level only at which a sufferer will 'stick' or avoid reaching. There are many levels, and a wide variety of reasons too, for her 'sticking', few of which in practice have to do with sexuality.

For many sufferers the sticking point, or resistance, is related to the imminent need to change to a larger size of jeans. Others have their own personal 'magic number' weight levels, as expressed by such typical statements as, 'I can't be seven stone anything! I've *got* to stay under six stone, thirteen!' Thus it is often the case that the one pound that will move the sufferer from x st. 13 lb. to x + 1 st. is the one pound that is most difficult to gain. These sticking points are totally unrelated to possible menstrual thresholds. The above statement, for example, was made by a sufferer who at 6 st. 13 lb. was only 72-per-cent AEBW, and far from menstruating. The reluctance of another very tall, older and normally menstruating bulimic sufferer was just as great when it came to her moving from 10 st 13 lb. to 11 st. 'It feels like failure to be 11 stone.' But this weight would have been 94 per cent of this young woman's AEBW.

Those sufferers who were previously overweight are usually more frightened of weight gain and will stick as a result of this particular fear. Some stick because they are currently comparing themselves with slender friends or sisters, or with other anorexics who are currently at low weight levels and 'must do better'. Merely a glimpse across a hospital ward of another sufferer who looks thinner will be enough to stir this response. The low-weight sufferer who is allowing her weight to increase even very gradually is a person with many fears, many anxieties, and who feels many pressures. At any time, and whatever weight she has reached, these can become threatening, very overwhelming and sufficient to stall her progress in terms of further weight gain.

It is not that sexual issues never play a part where resistance to weight gain occurs, but clinical experience just does not seem to provide enough evidence to suggest that this is where it usually or inevitably occurs. From the point of view of the helper who chooses to work gradually, the notion that anorexics stop gaining weight only at a phobic pre-pubescent level can be destructive. It is often difficult to negotiate with her family to allow the time that is needed for the girl to change slowly, and this idea encourages them to lose patience – which is often hard to keep anyway – when she sticks at a lower level. So they feel they have to revert to coercive forms of treatment. At worst the joint decision between family and helper to discontinue ineffective treatment can lead to neglect and rejection of the sufferer who no longer has anyone to consult.

At any level there are plateaux in the process of therapy, just as there are plateaux in any other process of learning and change. As a reflection of this, an anorexic's weight can remain stable for a while, or it may fall slightly. These plateaux can be temporary. There is no need to assume that they signify 'The End of Progress', but the sufferer will need continuing and consistent help. Where she learns that she can live through adjustments and changes while she is still low weight, she is the more likely to manage each later adjustment with a little more confidence as her weight gradually increases, and that includes any adjustments at that later stage where she begins to feel sexual interest again, and where menstruation returns.

Following the analogy of the stepladder, we can see the therapy that allows slow weight gain, and provides emotional support and understanding at each stage when the anorexic's weight is low, as securing the ladder's foundations, making the lowest rungs safe first, before encouraging her to climb higher. Where an anorexic is helped to gain weight gradually, while at the same time learning to change her attitudes and beliefs about herself, the progress she makes will be her own. She will experience the changes as her own creation. Thus her sense of real autonomy will increase.

Where on the other hand she feels she has been coerced into gaining weight, she will see herself as having 'weakened', or as having been taken over by a superior force. Such an experience will either strengthen her resistance to change because she will hold more firmly on to her conviction that her food control is the right thing for her, or it will cause her deeper despair because of her total failure, and she will continue to swing between these two extremes.

Mapping low weight

The way in which a starving person's style of thinking becomes polarized and predictable after a measurable loss of body weight makes it possible to map the area the low-weight or emaciated anorexic inhabits. This not only helps others to begin to understand her world and appreciate the way she is constrained within it. It also provides a background for making the mental adjustments necessary for effective communication and care.

The single most significant piece of information a helper can have is the sufferer's current weight in relation to her height and age. For this gives an immediate 'map reference'. It provides the skilled helper with enough information to have a shrewd idea of how the sufferer is probably thinking and experiencing herself and the world. Finally therefore we will outline a number of identifiable low-weight stages, looking at each one first from the point of view of physical emaciation, then from the point of view of patterns of thinking and experiencing.

The communication threshold: 'around 80-per-cent' AEBW

The change in thinking that takes place when weight falls to approximately 81–78-per-cent AEBW marks the communication threshold in the case of the person whose weight was originally at or around an average expected body weight for her/his age, height and sex.

From a small sample it would appear that for obese people communication difficulties occur around 80 per cent of their original obese weight, if weight loss has been swift. This means that if person B (whose AEBW is 9 st. 7 lb.) has been an overweight 15 st. for the last eight years and then this weight falls to 12 st. in five months, B at this point will have the same altered thinking as A at the point where A's weight has fallen from A's 8-st. AEBW to 80 per cent of this (i.e. 6 st. 6 lb.). B's thinking will be altered even though, at 12 st., B is still 2 st. 7 lb. *above* her or his AEBW.

Meanwhile, in those who are underweight before weight loss, altered thinking occurs sooner, after the loss of fewer pounds. Thus, while to lose a stone or a stone and a half in weight may be a fashionably coveted aim, in terms of changes in attitude, behaviour and ability to communicate it can be seen that these 14–21 lb. are a crucial percentage of a person's body weight.

When the sufferer's weight is at or below the 'around 80-per-cent' threshold she/he is within the 'low-weight' stage of the illness. Problems in communicating are already likely to have arisen by the time weight has fallen to this level. Yet as long as weight remains at or around 78–81-per-cent AEBW the person's physical appearance will not cause adverse comment. This degree of low weight does not produce striking physical features, though menstruation in female sufferers will be slighter and/or intermittent, or may even have ceased if this amount of weight loss has been extended over some time.

Those who are close to the person who is newly anorexic may have a sense of uneasiness about her, particularly if they are aware that she has lost a significant amount of weight, or if they know that she has been cutting down on food and they notice no sign of her returning to a less restricted pattern of eating, despite having achieved a 'better figure', or 'feeling more fit'. They may have noticed changes in behaviour, such as her increasing preference for spending time alone, and they may be beginning to suspect that her weight is still falling. But generally the sufferer's bright, wide-eyed appearance, alertness, enormous energy and increased physical activity deflect anxiety at this stage. Certainly, when a sufferer is with people who have not known her when her weight was higher, the fashion for extreme thinness ensures that this symptom passes unnoticed, often for a long time.

It is as the anorexic's weight falls below the 81–78-per-cent AEBW threshold that she clearly moves into the world of extreme, rigid, black-and-white thinking, of preoccupation with food and not eating, of feeling clear, directed and in control (see also Chapter Two).

> At last I had life organized. Things were different. I was in my own world. Controlling what I ate was everything. I weighed every bit of food; knew the exact contents of every packet; how many calories there were in half a peanut. My clothes went on in the same order. Every moment of every day was absolutely routine. [80-per-cent AEBW]

Enveloped as she is in her altered state the anorexic does not know she is ill, or hooked on starvation. In the early stages, far from feeling there is anything amiss, she will feel better about herself than she has done for a long time.

> I was happy all that summer. I'd lost some weight. I didn't eat much, and worked long hours at the stables. No one interfered with what I did. I just got on with it on my own. It was always easier if I didn't eat. I was happier than I'd ever been.

During the summer in question this particular sufferer's weight moved from 83 to 79 per cent of her AEBW.

Moving towards the classic picture: 75–69-per-cent AEBW

By the time weight has fallen to 75-per-cent AEBW the helper will begin to see the classic physical picture of anorexia nervosa, and this will certainly be noticeable by the time it has dropped to 69 per cent. The sufferer will look clearly frail. Her limbs will have become more stick-like. Her shoulder blades, spine, cheek bones, collar bones and hip bones will be more clearly prominent, and the bone structure of her hands will be quite marked. She will no longer have a healthy or pinkish glow. She will appear pale and sometimes rather blue. Her hands, nose and other extremities will take on a bluish-mauve colour (indicating acrocyanosis) as her body attempts to conserve heat by closing down the supply of blood to its peripheries. Her skin will be dry, her nails brittle and cracked, and she will usually be cold to the touch. Her hair will be dry and brittle too, and she may by this time have a covering of downy hair, or lanugo, on other parts of her body which would not normally have hair growing on them, such as her cheeks and her back.

Because thinness has not only become unremarkable, but a fashionably desirable state, even at a weight that is as low as 75-per-cent AEBW an anorexic may be seen as 'rather thin' but still be described by others as having a 'model' figure. Parents and friends who see her day in and day out can become visually accustomed to her emaciation and dulled to its hazards.[2] Subjective judgements of those looking on are important in many respects and certainly create experiences for the anorexic that cast doubt on the idea that help should be sought. This is a recurring problem in relation to providing help, as the following contrasting cases show.

One eighteen-year-old, at a weight of 75-per-cent AEBW, was told by her friends, who knew she was anorexic, that she was 'a Cambodian look-alike', and that she reminded them of E.T. (the alien from outer space in Spielberg's film of that name). This upset her. She wanted to look attractive. The experience pointed up the conflict between this desire and her wanting to stay in control, and in the event it led to her making a small step in the direction of eating just a little more. This girl had already increased her own weight slowly over approximately eight months from a low point of 68 per cent. Another eighteen-year-old meanwhile, at the same 75-per-cent level, became confused and doubtful about whether there really was anything 'wrong' with her totally constrained anorexic lifestyle after a workmate, ignorant of the girl's difficulty with eating, assured her during a conversation at the dress shop where they both worked that she 'really had a nice figure and wasn't too fat'. The confusion this experience created was unhelpful for the girl who was at this time finding it hard to increase her food intake from 700 to 800 calories per day and was thus set to continue to lose more weight.

Should others see her body undisguised by clothes, a sufferer's thinness can arouse discomfort and disgust at this stage. But the real extent of her emaciation may still remain hidden by her wearing layers of clothing. This may be her way of contriving to hide her thinness, particularly where she feels her control will be threatened if others find out how thin she really is; or extra clothing may be to keep her warm. For by this time she will also be suffering the discomforts of low weight. She will feel continually cold and tired and the protruding bones in her buttocks will make it uncomfortable for her to sit on hard surfaces, especially in the bath. She will also become noticeably more accident prone and more irritable.

As the whirlpool of starvation draws her further in, the more intense will be her need to sustain her control, and the more intense her fear of losing it. Against this need, as we have said, every other aspect of her life loses significance. Her job, career, education fade into the background. Her ability to relate to others diminishes.

> I wanted to keep my job, or I thought I did until my boss said he couldn't keep me on any longer, then I realized I didn't care. The only thing that matters is that you don't eat. That comes before everything else. I was six stone five [67-per-cent AEBW]. I had to get down to six stone. It's the most important thing in your life.

On any matter concerning food, weight or eating she is absolutely rigid, stubborn, apparently self-willed and inflexible. Where she maintains her control she will remain satisfied, calm, happy. When her control slips, she will become very panicky, irritated, frightened, angry, and filled with self-recrimination. Those around her tend to suffer the backlash from these mood swings but, however hard they try, they are less and less able to get through to her. When her control slips the anorexic's 'negative' emotions take over. Her feelings of frustration, violent anger and despair can result in more widespread destruction.

> Her behaviour is absolutely appalling and completely irrational. I don't know any other father whose twenty-two-year-old daughter gouges the kitchen table with the bread knife, just because she has to eat. Or sits in her room banging her head against the wall.

Few people appreciate the extent to which anorexia nervosa and bulimia can wreck family life, either by the way it erupts into physical violence to people or property, or by the suffocating tension it creates. It can make any sharing difficult.

> We shared a flat with Del in the second year. We knew about her anorexia, but it was really difficult. We'd come home and find things like she'd squirted washing-up liquid over the pizza to stop herself eating it. Or else she'd eaten every single thing so you'd get back from lectures and there'd be nothing to make a meal with.

The lower the anorexic's weight, the more clear it becomes that she is not engaging with what is happening around her. Her forgetfulness will become increasingly obvious. The anorexic night sister, for example, who was able to remember the telephone messages she had to pass on to the day staff when her weight was 70-per-cent AEBW, found that, when her weight dropped to 66-per-cent AEBW, she could remember that there had been a call, but could not remember what it was about. Another sufferer described herself as 'having holes in my memory'. She will become increasingly clumsy. One girl at 71-per-cent AEBW remarked that she kept bumping into doors. Another noticed herself constantly 'tripping up and making mistakes like pouring the boiling water over my hand instead of into the cup.'

Emaciation and danger: 68–50-per-cent AEBW

From this point on, as she continues to lose weight, her appearance will become increasingly skeletal. She will be physically weak and obviously accident prone. Between 68 and 63-per-cent AEBW, road using becomes clearly hazardous. At this stage a red traffic light may be seen by the anorexic driver, but it will not carry meaning.

Increasingly she will be in danger of physical collapse. The point where her condition becomes life-threatening will depend on the rate at which she is losing weight. Changes in her attitude and pattern of control are important indicators of the whirlpool's gathering momentum and should not be ignored (see also Chapters Eleven and Twelve). A weight level of 50 per cent constitutes a medical emergency. Without food at this weight the sufferer will die very soon.

By the time an anorexic's weight has fallen to 65-per-cent AEBW the extent of her emaciation will no longer be easily hidden by clothing, which will look more as though it is covering a wire coat hanger than a body. Nevertheless, because she is likely to be well covered up, it is important for the helper to be aware of the physical changes that can be seen in those parts of her body that are visible, such as her hands and face, and to note the significance that increasingly prominent bone structures and the extension of bluish-mauve colouring beyond her hands to her wrists and forearms have for continuing weight loss. Those who do catch sight of her uncovered are usually shocked and repulsed. But for accurate information about her position there is no substitute for weighing an anorexic in minimum indoor clothing and without shoes, particularly at this stage of low weight.

Her polarized thinking and its lack of connection with the real world will be quite apparent. At this stage it will sound like 'madness'.

ANOREXIC: I can't stay here. I've got to go home now.

NURSE: You're dangerously thin (i.e. 59-per-cent AEBW). You have to put some weight on before you can go home.

ANOREXIC: You're going to keep me here for ever.

NURSE: No, we don't want to keep you here for ever.

ANOREXIC: So I can go home now.

NURSE: No, you've got to put some weight on. You're not safe as you are. When you've put on enough to be safe, then doctor says you can go.

ANOREXIC: So you are keeping me here for ever.

NURSE: No, just until you've put on the weight doctor said.

ANOREXIC: But I'm fine, and you're keeping me in here for *nothing*!

NURSE: You look much too thin to me.

ANOREXIC: I'm not too thin. There's nothing wrong with me. I don't see why you should keep me here for ever. [Pause] Can I have some more of that stuff for these bedsores? [These have developed in spite of the rubber cushion she is using to protect her buttocks where her bones are sharply protruding.]

Interest in anything other than maintaining non-eating will have entirely diminished by this time.

> He's terribly strong-willed about refusing to eat. But otherwise he's not interested in anything at all. He has two dogs, very beautiful red setters. He loved those dogs, even until a short while ago. I think he loved them more than anything in the world. But now there's nothing he cares about. Not even the dogs. I find that terribly alarming.

Alarm of course is entirely appropriate. This man's weight had fallen to 55-per-cent AEBW at the point when the above account was given.

Sometimes, when a person is extremely low weight, the psychological changes this produces are so bizarre that it is difficult to know what psychiatric condition that person is suffering from. Appearances may suggest the onset of an acute psychosis (a sudden break with reality). Nor is it possible to make an accurate diagnosis of such states until a certain amount of weight has been regained. This very extreme or bizarre behaviour tends to occur when the less complex brain functions begin to disappear. These are the functions, as we have said, that are concerned with memory, with controlling the movements of the body, and with being able to know where one is, or locating oneself in relation to the rest of the world. The anorexic may experience herself at this stage as being controlled by her surroundings. For example, she may hear physical objects demanding that she behaves in a particular way, or voices continually criticizing her.

> There's no respite from these voices. It's the books on the bookshelf. They're nagging and nagging. They want to be arranged in the right order. I've got to do it. They say so. They keep on at me, criticizing all the time. Then when I've done it, they start again. Telling me I ought to have lined them up exactly with the edge of the shelf, it's not good enough otherwise.

This person is not a schizophrenic hearing voices, but an example of the effect of *acute* starvation on top of chronic low weight. This girl had, for two days, stopped eating the small amount of stewed apple and yogurt she had previously been taking each day.

Once a diagnosis of anorexia nervosa has been made, even though such bizarre, extreme behaviour has occurred, it is still no longer necessary to consider other psychiatric diagnoses such as schizophrenia. Nor does such a psychotic episode indicate a more depressing prognosis for the anorexia nervosa itself. A sufferer who has experienced psychological change of this kind is no less likely to achieve recovery than one who has been only mildly disturbed throughout her illness.

Such experiences can be very frightening for the anorexics themselves who feel on the verge of going mad. Sometimes long-term sufferers become aware of their own individual weight threshold below which they are likely to get this disturbed; when further weight loss of as little as a pound or two, or an event such as the weather turning cold, can bring about effects which terrify them because they feel distinctly unreal. So a long-term anorexic may choose to eat slightly more at this point in order to avoid experiences of this kind.

The sufferer's response to the experience of starvation

Anorexics, as we have said, are not always recognizable by their extreme thinness. No square but the last (i.e. death) on the games board described in Chapter Three is stable and, as sufferers move among the other squares, their weight can fluctuate dramatically. Some begin their anorexic career imperceptibly, maintaining themselves on the threshold of low weight for many months before a further drop in weight or other change in behaviour alerts others to the fact that all is not well.

A long-term or experienced anorexia nervosa sufferer who has endured many fluctuations in her weight – from quite low levels to levels clearly above the threshold where her weight is viable, and even to an obese weight and back again – may become aware of the way her thinking changes as she makes these transitions; but this is unusual. Generally she will have no awareness of the way she becomes intellectually constrained. Nor, when she is low weight, is she readily able to imagine what it would be like to exist in anything other than the low-weight state she is in at the moment. But the one thing she will certainly be aware of, when she has lived through any significant weight fluctuations, is how very much better and safer she feels when she is low weight, and how her emotionally more comfortable state compensates for the physical discomforts of being very thin. Like the emptiness and feeling physically lighter, the anorexic's perpetual feeling of coldness and tiredness are positive experiences. They tell her she is in control.

> Yesterday I felt quite good. Well, not good . . . because I was feeling really cold, and sort of weak. But that was all right because that meant I hadn't given in and eaten anything. So yes, I did feel good. You know when you feel like that you can manage to get through the morning. [72-per-cent AEBW]

An experienced anorexic carefully manages her food intake to maintain this kind of optimum 'good' feeling, but the panic and desperation she experiences at the prospect of her control being threatened is overwhelming. It is analogous to the panic of the drug addict who is faced with going without a fix.

> As long as you can keep the emptiness, the feeling you can float along on that 'high', then you're all right. But if you get forced to eat you're terrified. So you don't get into that situation. You avoid being anywhere you might have to eat. Then you can cope. It's your fix – you're a starvation junkie.

There may be some, including many anorexics, who would reject the idea that their thinking and experiencing at low weight can be mapped because it seems depersonalizing. It strips them of their individuality. But the sad truth is, though it may take an anorexic some time to realize this, that by restricting her eating and reducing her weight she has done this very effectively for herself. Consistent food restriction does not produce uniformity solely in terms of physical emaciation or 'slimness'. It produces psychological uniformity too. The more constrained the anorexic or indeed any other starving person is, the less variation there is in that person's actions and in his or her responding. At low weight anorexics are all much the same in the way they think, feel, relate to others and experience day-to-day events. The lower their weight, the more 'standard' they become.

Simply to thrust this information upon any individual anorexic is not helpful, however. It may destroy too quickly the lifestyle that she still needs to cling to. If she can be helped slowly to learn the truth of this for herself, then the benefit in the long term will be greater and more lasting.

It is only when an anorexic reaches the stage above 80–83 per cent, where her thinking changes and her awareness opens up once more, that a greater variety of ideas can begin to emerge. Difficulties still remain, and how these come about and why they persist will be discussed in the following chapters. But the quality of communication between the girl and her helper will be different, and the possibilities for learning in the context of therapy and elsewhere will be greater.

References

1 See Slade, R. (1984). *The Anorexia Nervosa Reference Book*, London, Harper and Row, 32–67.
2 Slade, R. (1984), ibid., 45.

· SIX ·

Viable weight and the picture that is hidden

As her increasing weight approaches 78–81-per-cent AEBW, the sufferer will change physically and psychologically. There will be a change too in the way others respond to her.

Physically, where she previously appeared pallid and drawn, she will now have a glow in her cheeks and her lips, earlobes and fingertips will have a healthier pink colour. Although she may still be on the skinny side of normal weight, she will no longer look like a famine victim. Where she is seen to eat more food, those close to her will be reassured. Psychological changes will be noticeable mainly in the way it seems more possible to communicate with her. For this is the level where there is a transition from the separate, self-contained state she maintained at low weight and begins to be more fully aware of and responsive to people and situations. She may resume her school or college work or her career, so it will seem she is getting on with her life.

It is around this point therefore that those close to her begin to relax and turn their attention to other matters, believing she must now be all right. As far as the world is concerned, when a sufferer who has been low weight reaches 78–81-per-cent AEBW, anorexia nervosa disappears. But from the sufferer's point of view she is not better. She is worse.

. . . but evermore came out by the same door as in I went

Compared with the sense of well-being she achieved when she was low weight and restricting food intake, her experience when she regains weight to this level is disturbing. As the effects of starvation lift, feelings become stronger, intellectually she comes alive to all the subtleties and complexities of the situations she finds herself in. She feels thrown into an overwhelming turmoil, inadequate and utterly confused.

> When you put weight on everyone thinks you're better. My family didn't think there was any need for me to keep on seeing the therapist, so I stopped.

> I was still scared of putting on an ounce. I started dieting again, without letting on. It was useless, I couldn't even keep to that. It got really desperate. I was just going round in circles . . . felt suicidal. Like there's no other way out. But everyone thought I was OK . . . You can't explain the hell. You just can't explain what hell it is.

It is during this process of weight gain that the sufferer relives the experiences that created her anorexia nervosa in the first place; so bringing to mind the quotation from the Rubayat of Omar Khayam: 'Myself when young did eagerly frequent doctor and saint, and heard great argument, about it and about: but evermore came out by the same door as in I went.'

The sad consequence of there being two different sets of criteria at work over the question of 'being better' is that well-meant comments turn out to be destructive. A remark about the way she looks that seems ordinary and pleasant to the onlooker saying it will be received by the sufferer in a negative way. Hearing someone say, 'You're looking better,' she will instantly think, 'That means I'm looking fat.' To be told she is looking healthy induces immediate panic. Any comment of this kind confirms her worst fear. 'Someone's only got to say you look well, and that's it. You know you're fat. You don't eat for the rest of the week.'

This can still be a sufferer's reaction after one or two years of 'improved' near-normal eating. Just a single remark to this effect, however innocent, may be all the prompting needed for an anorexic who is emerging from the low-weight stage to tighten her control, reduce her food intake and set her spiralling down again.

Being told she is looking well underlines for her the difference between other people's assumptions and her own experience. It emphasizes her separateness and deepens her sense of isolation. Feeling more separate can reinforce her conviction that in her food control she possesses something unique and special, which in turn can vindicate her withdrawing from other people's company. The greater isolation thus created makes it easier for her to re-establish or continue her pattern of food restriction without others interfering with her regimes, or criticizing her. Equally experiences of this kind, which illustrate to the sufferer how wrong people's assumptions are about her, increase her despair of ever being understood.

The helper who has been suggesting that the way forward requires some weight gain may find the anorexic confronting her at this stage with statements such as, 'You said it would be better, but nothing's changed. I've just got fat and bloated and lost my control.' It takes a great deal of skill on the helper's part to encourage an anorexic to maintain a viable weight long enough for some of the confusions to be resolved (see Chapters Thirteen and Fourteen). A therapist who has a track record of having helped the anorexic create small increments in her feelings of autonomy, while her weight was lower, will have more credibility in the anorexic's eyes at this stage, and will need this credibility.

Though clearly there is more to helping her than merely avoiding the issue of the feelings others' well-meant comments arouse in her, it can nevertheless reduce her sense of being pressured when others refrain from remarking on her increased weight, her healthier appearance and so on. Meanwhile the helper who knows that, as her weight rises, the sufferer will predictably have to cope with people expressing their pleasure at her more healthy appearance can usefully warn her that she is likely to react with fright and panic. The helper cannot protect her from her panic, but there will usually be some comfort for her in knowing the helper understands what she is going through, and this may help her to avoid her standard reaction of immediately restricting her eating.

Being invisible

Just how great the psychological discomfort is for the sufferer in maintaining herself at a weight around or above 80-per-cent AEBW is not generally appreciated. It is well known that anorexics do not like being 'fat' or 'heavy'. But what this means to them tends to be dismissed as 'distorted' and as 'out of touch with reality'. Few people know how sufferers actually feel.

Certainly many of the helpers they meet are professionally committed to giving much less significance to feelings than to symptoms that are observable and quantifiable. But neither professional bias nor the lack of encouragement that is given to expression of feeling in hospitals or other institutions is sufficient to explain the general lack of awareness that there is about the way the anorexic/bulimic feels as a whole when her weight reaches a viable level. For, in so far as she is able to do so, the sufferer deliberately and systematically tidies her feelings away. By carefully preventing them from reaching the public domain she herself contributes to the ignorance there is about the way she feels, and so to the mystery that surrounds the condition.

Yet she is not to blame for this for, as she endures the day-to-day experience, she cannot easily stand outside it and explain it – a difficulty that will be elaborated in Chapter Eight. However, the result is that, when she is low weight and her feelings suppressed by the effects of starvation, theoreticians of all kinds rush in to fill the gap that is created by her inability to provide a coherent explanation for her determined food restriction. But as her weight reaches a more viable level and she puts on what one anorexic referred to as her 'false front', it seems there is no gap to fill. As long as her weight and behaviour appear normal, no explanation is considered necessary. Indeed, there seems to be nothing to explain.

So well in fact does she hide her feelings that the way her later bulimia or compulsive eating is related to her former anorexia nervosa is also hidden. Because the episodes appear to be discontinuous, few theoreticians perceive that there is a clear relationship between the two problems. The medical profession in particular is still prone to discuss anorexia nervosa and bulimia as two separate illnesses.

It is unfortunate that the sufferer hides the way she feels because, invisible though they may be behind her competent, efficient, hard-working and acceptable exterior, these feelings, when her weight is viable, are sufficient in themselves to explain her condition. It is in these feelings that the information lies that makes her supreme need for food and body control intelligible.

The key to the self-starvation whirlpool

There are three underlying characteristics that are particularly marked in the sufferer. These are her intense morality, her extreme sensitivity, particularly to the needs and feelings of others, and her profound sense of her own worthlessness. Though descriptions may be cast in different theoretical terms, there is a large measure of agreement amongst authorities on anorexia nervosa that these are key characteristics. However, while they can be separately identified, they do not create discrete experiences but weave together seamlessly to produce an anorexic style of thinking that protects and defends against ineffectiveness, failure and overwhelming confusion, so creating the person who becomes drawn into the whirlpool of self-starvation.

It is as she emerges from low weight that her morality, sensitivity and extreme sense of worthlessness can be seen more clearly.

Morality

The sufferer's intense moral awareness means that she has strong convictions about what she ought or ought not to do, how she ought or ought not to behave and even how she ought or ought not to feel. As one sufferer said of herself, 'I'm just full of shoulds and oughts.' She is characteristically very rule bound.

At a normal or near normal weight, when her thinking is no longer directed by the polarizing effects of starvation, the 'shoulds' and 'oughts' emerge as thoroughly conflicting. Hence her ineffectiveness and confusion about what she ought to do and how she ought to be.

She applies her moral rules to food, eating and exercise as to everything else in her life. Significantly, however, it is only where she applies them to food and body regulation that she finds herself able to be decisive. It is in her clear single-mindedness and *lack* of conflict regarding food and body control that the potential lies for the degree of control she achieves in these areas. Her rules have an alien quality, as expressed by the sufferer who referred to the moral prescriptions she applied to herself as 'The System', and talked about what 'The System' required of her.

The extent of the self-restraint and denial in terms of food restriction and exercise that are the classic symptoms of anorexia nervosa is a standard that the anorexic is actively striving to maintain. This is why her behaviour does not have the passive connotation usually associated with the word 'symptom' (see Chapter One). Although those who concentrate on physical symptoms can miss the moral quality there is in her food control, to the sufferer this is an undisputed virtuous action. This is the phenomenon that confronts the helper working with her.

Public rules and personal rules

In moral rules there is a duality. At one and the same time they exist as important features of an individual's psychology, and as public rules in the culture to which she/he belongs. In the one form they have an important function in integrating the many divergent processes in a human being and in producing coherent actions. In the other form they are one of the ways in which the group exercises control over its members.

Broadly speaking therefore, when people subject themselves to a particular kind of rule, common sense provides two sorts of explanation. It may be sufficient to point out that many people in a certain group behave in a particular way because in the culture of that group this way of behaving is important. Sometimes, on the other hand, something about the fervour and extremity of a person's commitment to a rule suggests that it is doing some personal psychological work for them.

In the case of the anorexic's food control it is probably true to say that most theorists have chosen to delve into the individual's psychology in search of an explanation. For at first sight it is implausible that life-threatening emaciation could be compatible with the moral rules of the sufferer's social group. Some fairly complicated theories have gained a certain credibility in this way, usually leaning on some particular view of psychological development. One suggestion noted earlier was that an ascetic lifestyle created by moral rules defends people particularly in adolescence from their sexual feelings. Another was that the anorexic's control is typical of the kind of morality found in an early stage of cognitive development, and that her development has been arrested at this developmental stage. Yet, as we have shown, the extremity of the sufferer's behaviour is in large part the result of starvation itself and, as the whirlpool sucks the individual in, it hides the extent to which public rules organize the individual's behaviour.

Initially food and body control is only a part of a potential sufferer's system of rules but, as weight falls, her moral code becomes increasingly, and ultimately totally, centred on controlling food. Conversely what emerges, when starvation is reversed, is the standard pattern of beliefs and moral attitudes of that section of society that is her background. The condition has its roots in and draws support from the everyday ideas of those around her. It is starvation that pushes these familiar values to almost unrecognizable extremes.

This is not to suggest that those who are a part of the sufferer's usually middle-class and rather conforming social group believe she ought to deny herself food to the extent that her actions endanger her life. Rather it is to bring into focus the fact that, for reasons that will be considered in the following chapter, sufferers typically adhere very strongly to a cluster of values that centre on hard work, self-control, personal responsibility, high standards of achievement, deferred gratification and not receiving rewards that have not been *earned*. It is to point out too that these values can be applied to food and body regulation as effectively as they can be applied to work, educational achievement, career success, personal relationships and to sport. In this last sphere there is explicit encouragement for them to be extended to body regulation.

It is important to appreciate the continuity there is between the sufferer's personal rules and those of her/his social group, for many problems that arise in attempting to help stem from this (see Chapter Nine). The anorexia nervosa/bulimia sufferer is a person who places very high value on control. So as long as she is behaving in a controlling and controlled manner she has moral right on her side. It is the continuity between her moral attitude and that of her social group that explains why the condition can be lethal.

Public rules from two sources

There are in fact two sets of rules to which the sufferer adheres. One bears the clear imprint of the female role, often in quite an extreme form. The other, following the sterner theme outlined above, comprises the values of the Protestant or 'work' ethic. These are the two sets of rules that combine and conflict to produce the sufferer's value confusion (see Chapter Eight). But the imperative that feelings and emotions should be hidden belongs to both.

Worthlessness

Improbable though it might seem from the way she appears to the outside world and from all her apparent successes, the sufferer has a deep sense of personal worthlessness. She does not value her achievements, her skills, her experiences, her feelings. She does not value herself. Where others see her as intelligent, she sees herself merely as someone who works hard, or who has fooled the examiners. 'They marked it wrong,' she will say, 'because I know I did a rotten essay, and they gave it A minus.' Where others see her as bright, cheerful and capable, she sees herself as a fraud. 'I hate it when they say how good I am. *I* know I spend all the time working in the library because if I didn't I would eat. So of course I got high grades, but it's just a lie. It's all phoney.'

Where others see her as helpful and considerate, she sees herself as someone who lets other people down. Where others see her as a success, she sees herself as a total failure.

> Jay was bright, very outgoing, seemed confident. She put a tremendous amount into everything she did. She was captain of the first hockey team at school, and it was a good team. She walked into university. I think she'd have got a first if it hadn't been for this anorexia. And you say she feels a failure. I can't see that.

On standardized psychological tests designed to quantify low self-esteem anorexia nervosa/bulimia sufferers generally score as low as it is possible for these tests to measure. Statements that may be part of such tests, such as: 'All in all, I am inclined to think that I am a failure' and 'I feel I do not have much to be proud of',[1] receive their strong agreement. Furthermore they will typically endorse their agreement with comments such as 'I'm not just *inclined* to think I'm a failure, I'm a total failure,' and 'It's not that I don't have much to be proud of. There's *nothing* about myself I can find to be proud of.'

A helper will not only need to be aware of, and accept the anorexic's belief in her own worthlessness, but also must understand that in the ordinary course of events her belief in her own worthlessness is unassailable. She does not just think she is bad. She knows it with every fibre of her being. It is an assumption she brings to all her transactions with others, to all her relationships. Furthermore it is self-sustaining, for she rejects any view that is not consonant with her experience of herself as someone who is bad, useless, undeserving. She finds some way of nullifying any response or opinion that does not confirm this fundamental belief.

Thus she filters out all praise, compliments, appreciations, love, and so keeps her low self-esteem intact. In the words of one anorexic's boyfriend:

> I can honestly tell her I think she's intelligent and attractive. I can tell her I like the way she paints, she's a good cook, loads of things I like about her. But it gets to be a kind of meaningless game. Anything I say like that just bounces off her like a brick off a dustbin. Say anything critical though, and that goes *straight* in.

While the sufferer will accept criticism as a fundamental truth about herself, she sees praise and compliments either as evidence that the person giving them lacks any understanding of how awful a person she really is, or as a transparent attempt to manipulate her. The person who is saying pleasant things about her is either plainly stupid, or they are devious and out to get something from her.

Thus, while a helper will need to acknowledge how badly the sufferer feels about herself, certainly if she is to appear to have any degree of competence in the sufferer's eyes, the helper who is tempted to employ easy reassurances will be dismissed as either a knave or a fool.

This sense of extreme worthlessness is a feeling she has had for a long time, well before she became explicitly anorexic/bulimic. Sometimes the condition develops after a particularly nasty event in a person's life, but often this is not so. Research generally has failed to find a pattern of obviously traumatic events that have preceded the sufferer's initial weight loss. The fact that there seems to be no clear preceding event has tended to add to the mystery that has surrounded the illness. What does appear to happen, however, is that feelings of profound worthlessness and low self-esteem coalesce around an event that to anyone else can appear to be relatively trivial, but which to the potential sufferer is the straw that breaks the camel's back.

It is because she feels so ineffectual in every other respect that the sufferer's success at food and body control become so important to her at this point. Where it seems that everything else is going wrong, this is the one thing she *can* get right, the one area in which she feels effective and relatively confident. Hence the enormous relief that it is to her. It becomes her way of clawing back some sense of self-worth, of attaining some self-respect. To this extent food and body control resolves her feelings of low self-esteem.

Throwing her self away

Worthless as she feels, she gives no value to her own feelings. If she does allow her feelings, then her rules dictate that they have to be the 'right' feelings. But since she cannot guarantee she will have the 'right' feelings, she treats feelings and emotions generally as irritating intrusions, and better obliterated. 'I oughtn't to be so unhappy. I shouldn't feel like that, and I don't want to. If I can't feel positive, it's better if I don't feel anything.'

This is, of course, exactly what an anorexic achieves when she is low weight. If she admits to any feeling, she will tend to push this to one side, often with a dismissive gesture, as if disowning the experience. If her feelings are too clearly evident to be denied, she will deride and devalue them. Her frustration is unnecessary, her anger unjustified and wrong, her jealousy unpleasant. She has no right to feel upset. Her happiness is unwarranted, her need for comfort too demanding. Her caring for others is inadequate; she ought to do more. Her sense of confusion is illegitimate, and so on and on. Whatever her emotion, whatever sense of her self she experiences, she invariably judges it in harsh and negative terms. Because her feelings and emotions are so unacceptable to her, she consistently and determinedly attempts to suppress or deny them. So she ends up with a sense of being separate from them and consequently separate from her self.

Distanced though she may be from her feelings, there is little evidence to suggest that she is actively prevented from gaining access to them by unconscious defences. Often she is too well aware of them. Her rules and her sense of worthlessness combine to create a moral resistance to acknowledging the feelings she has.

It is generally easier to live effectively, in a self-directed and autonomous way, if feelings are treated as facts that provide the individual with basic information about her/himself. But the sufferer morally prohibits herself from accepting the very information that would indicate to her what she wants, or needs, or indeed who she is. In this respect her position is analogous to that of a student who does not like a particular subject, who is convinced it is completely worthless, and who therefore makes determined and concerted effort to pay as little attention as possible to it. As any teacher will know, such a student is unlikely to have the kind of knowledge which will enable him or her to have the confidence to work with that subject in an effective and creative way.

Humiliation in the guise of help

The helper's task lies not so much in enabling the sufferer to become aware of her feelings as in enabling her to begin to change the way she values those feelings. The timing of such change has to be well judged by the helper. Simply pressing her to look at or express the way she is feeling is not necessarily a particularly helpful or liberating experience for her. Because she believes that she does not have the 'right' kind of feelings, this can merely bring her face to face with so much of herself that she cannot bear. She will experience the forced exposure of her feelings as humiliating, degrading, as reaffirming her sense of badness and inadequacy, as undermining her confidence further, and so *confirming* her low self-esteem.

Consciousness raising and other techniques for increasing self-awareness need to be used carefully, therefore, particularly in the early stages of a helping relationship. Pushing her to confront more of her bad self than she feels she can cope with can easily create just another failure; another experience of feeling that she is out of control. It will generally result in her clinging all the more desperately to food and body regulation. In effect these techniques can produce a similar experience to the reawakening of feeling that is brought about by rapid refeeding and can equally reinforce her belief in the virtue of keeping herself tightly regulated. Food control is the anorexic's haven, and she will return to this haven whenever she feels frightened, threatened, angry, desperate or otherwise unable to cope. Likewise under stress the bulimic's swings from control to chaos will become the more violent and chaotic. These events can be prompted by very minute events, as biographies of sufferers bear out.

Sensitivity

The person who becomes anorexic/bulimic is highly sensitive to the feelings of others. This may seem implausible to those who are living with the anorexic and who daily come up against her intransigence over food and endure the continual tensions and disturbance that this brings. Anyone who feels their family life is being or has been wrecked by a member who is locked into food/body control might be forgiven for finding the idea that she is sensitive to other people hard to believe. Altered thinking, preoccupation with food and non-eating and a desperate fear of losing control have much to do with this, of course, when she is low weight. Below the threshold that is around 80-per-cent AEBW she is not so much selfish as immersed in a 'non-food' self that she sees as having to be maintained at all costs.

As she emerges from her low-weight and starved state her awareness and sensitivity increase, and this, as we have said, has unbearable consequences for her feeling of being able to cope. For she picks up the slightest atmosphere. She is alert to every resonance in the web of relationships that there is in any group of people. She perceives individual needs, feelings and preferences with remarkable acuity. Equally she is highly aware of and responsive to the obligations, prohibitions, expectations and demands that these can and do generate.

Responding and responsibility

There are two aspects to sensitivity. One lies in being perceptive and aware. The other lies in responsibility. But the sufferer does not distinguish between them. This is not because, at a level of ideas, she is unable to differentiate the two aspects. Her difficulty is that her own personal moral rules will not allow her to make a distinction between being responsive and being responsible. Her belief is that she ought to be sensitively aware of others' needs and preferences and, in being aware, that she ought to respond. Her low self-esteem supports and sustains this obligation: others are more important than she is, their needs more pressing, their preferences more significant, so she ought to be sensitive to them. Hence: 'My parents [friends/spouse/children] have a right to be happy. I shouldn't upset them. I should make them happy. I want to please them. I ought not to let them down.'

She is so convinced of this belief that she will typically see the helper who is 'insensitive' enough to suggest otherwise as lacking standards, as being morally deficient for not appreciating this as the right attitude to have. So she will deem the helper useless and despise her/him for it. This is a style of thinking that, as we will show in Chapter Nine, serves to enable her to keep her rules and beliefs intact and resist change. However, because she cannot allow herself to be aware of another person's need, to acknowledge it, and then not at least to try to make an effort to respond in a caring way, the sufferer is defenceless against others' wishes and obligations, whether clearly stated, or covert but sensed by her. She does not feel she has the right to refuse. If she does refuse or withdraw to avoid the situation, she feels unutterably guilty. So she is vulnerable not only in relation to her family and friends, but potentially in relation to anyone she meets, including the would-be helper. Responding is the sufferer's responsibility. Characteristically she feels responsible for the whole world.

How sensitivity becomes a burden

Even if she could allow herself the choice point that there is between being aware and actively responding, even if she were to allow herself the possibility of not taking on a perceived need or obligation without feeling guilty and wrong, she would still have the problem of knowing whether responding was something she herself wanted or not. For constantly dismissing her wants, needs and feelings as worthless leaves her with no clear idea of her own personal preferences.

The sense of obligation is not entirely of the sufferer's own creation. There is some evidence that the structure of her family is such that she is the recipient of whatever obligations and expectations there may be. One authority suggests the reason for this might lie in the tendency she found for anorexics to come from families where there were no sons to fulfil the family's aspirations.[2] We have not found this so much as that the sons in anorexics' families have tended to be 'failures' in some way by their family's standards, and that this has created the greater obligation for the potential anorexic to succeed.[3]

So acute is the sufferer's sensitivity that she responds to emotional needs in other people that they do not recognize in themselves; or should they be dimly aware, they are unwilling to own these needs.[4]

> I ought to try for Oxford. My father would be really pleased if I went to his old university. He says he'd be happy if I got a place anywhere, but I know he'd be disappointed really about Oxford, and I don't want to disappoint him. The trouble is that Oxford doesn't combine modern languages with business studies, which is what my French teacher says would be more useful.

It is quite commonplace for people to be unaware of their real feelings and/or deny feelings they do not wish to own. But the problem with responding to emotional needs in others that those others are not aware of in themselves is that, by the nature of this situation, it is not possible to check or clarify that one's response is appropriate. So it is easy for the person who is thus responding to become uncertain of him/herself. It is also impossible to fulfil everybody's needs, meet everyone's preferences and take up every obligation, whether these are heard, stated or sensed. Either way the sufferer's sensitivity becomes a burden to her, and a burden she cannot easily alleviate by exercising her own personal preferences because she is not in the habit of allowing these.

> It's a good job. I ought to feel pleased. But I don't. I only applied for it because they thought it'd be good for me. My mother's pleased. It would be

selfish to spoil that for her. But I somehow resent it. But if I gave it up I'd feel guilty. The careers teacher went to a lot of trouble getting me the interview. And there were loads of other applicants who'd have been glad to have got it. Anyway, I ought to have a job. And I don't know what I'd do if I left.

External control

Though intelligent and capable of highly complex thought processes, the sufferer's harsh and unrelenting moral judgements of herself, her low self-esteem and her extreme sensitivity leave her entirely vulnerable to external control. Her experience is of being pressured or regulated by everyone with whom she comes into contact. So diminished is her sense of self that others' needs and feelings and expectations automatically become intrusions and obligations upon her. Devoid of any way of resolving the inevitable conflict that these needs and expectations create, she feels trapped and confused, and the more so the nearer normal weight she is, because she is the more opened up and aware.

From the point of view of psychological theories of anorexia nervosa, the sufferer's sense of being externally controlled can be misleading, for it is far more usual for external control to be associated with limited intellectual potential. There has been some debate therefore as to whether the sufferer's sensitivity to the emotional needs of others is a skill or a handicap. Since external regulation occurs quite normally in the early stages of a child's development, it has been proposed that its continued presence in people who are chronologically older is evidence that they are suffering from a conceptual handicap enduring since childhood; that their conceptual development has been arrested at this earlier stage.[5]

There is no doubt that the sufferer has great difficulty in making certain distinctions which other people make more or less successfully as a matter of course in their everyday lives, as when she does not distinguish between perceiving another's need and the obligation to meet that need. But the question is whether her failure to make such distinctions indicates that the anorexic/bulimic is deficient in ideas, or whether her moral beliefs, her low self-esteem and her extreme sensitivity combine and conflict in such a way as to deny her the possibility in practice of using distinctions that in a purely intellectual sense she is perfectly capable of grasping.

In our view it would seem to be unnecessary to postulate conceptual deficiency in anorexia nervosa/bulimia when these three clear characteristics, that are evident when she emerges from her low-weight state, constantly combine to produce the same effect. The problem would seem to be not so much that the sufferer is a person who, prior to experiencing the psychological changes wrought by starvation, had a limited conceptual capacity, but rather that she is a person in whom high intelligence and extreme sensitivity create an abundance of ideas that open up innumerable possibilities for action, but action that she cannot realize because her rules lead to her being unable to choose or order her priorities in terms of her own personal preferences. Thus her potential for highly complex and flexible responding is paralysed.

Hidden feelings

When the anorexic's weight reaches a more viable level (i.e. above 78–81-per-cent AEBW), her feelings are no longer so attenuated and predictably 'good' as a result of the psychological effects of starvation, and her awareness is no longer so shut down; not only does she have more feelings to hide, she also has to create the cover herself. The effects of starvation no longer obliterate them for her. While she was low weight, she was able to say truthfully that she felt fine, certainly if she had not eaten more than her intended minute amounts of food.

When her weight is viable, though she may feel a great deal, she will do her best to hide her real feelings and express only what she senses or assumes will keep everyone else happy. Yet in this, as we have said, she sets herself a task at which, conscientious as she may be, she can only fail, because by its nature such a task is impossible.

She feels inadequate at her persistent failure, and utterly lacking in confidence, and hides both her feelings and herself. For the more hidden and private a person she is, the less possibility there is of anyone discovering her total inadequacy and failure. The less chance there is too of disappointing and hurting others by her failure and her ineffectiveness. Whichever way she does or does not express herself, however, she is caught. If she says what she really thinks and really feels, she might upset others and this will make her feel guilty and hateful for making their lives a misery. If she hides her real feelings and does her best to please others she feels a liar and a fraud. Experiencing herself as false in this way does nothing to help her feel better about herself. Nor does it give her a sense of being real and authentic. So there is no way she can win; no way she can feel all right about herself, and hiding becomes all the more imperative.

Where there is such an imperative to hide what is really felt, then performance is all. A great deal has been made of anorexics' educational achievements, but their ability to perform is not limited to the academic sphere. It is no accident that they are characteristically excellent actresses, actors, dancers, and so on; that there are so many who stage their successful performance as media figures and continue to do so for as long as they are physically able. Theatre can supply a more than adequate mask for hiding real feelings. It is also a way of working hard at keeping everybody happy. The commitment that the anorexic or bulimic who is a professional performer has to pleasing his or her audience is no less great than that of the sufferer whose father asked the ward sister in the hospital where the girl was being re-fed:

> Has Dee given you one of her performances yet? She's a wonderful mimic. She's had us in stitches for hours with her impersonations. They're spot on. She can be really amusing – although she hasn't been recently. . . .

As we said earlier, people generally are unaware of the effort a sufferer can put into covering up her feelings, and they do not know the extent to which it is in the nature of the condition for her to make every effort to present a convincingly happy and pleasing exterior to the world. They have little idea of the extent to which she is protecting them from anxiety and pain, or how much hate, guilt and self-loathing she feels when she fails to do this.

So with her helper too, the sufferer will hide herself and take care of the helper's needs in a way so subtle the helper is never likely to know.

> They made me see a psychiatrist. He was very patient and kind. I went several times. But it didn't really get me anywhere. I pretended I felt better so's not to disappoint him. He was very nice. He didn't deserve such an awful patient as me.

While hiding feelings when her weight is viable is certainly symptomatic of the problem she is still suffering from, her struggle to do so is entirely consistent with social and cultural values. The sufferer is doing only what she has learned because she has been brought up in a part of society where hiding feelings – and especially such unacceptable feelings as sadness, anger, grief, pain, jealousy, resentment and hatred – is very much the required and proper thing to do.

References

1 Rosenberg, M. (1965). *Society and Adolescent Self-image*, New Jersey, Princeton University Press.
2 Bruch, H. (1978). *The Golden Cage*, London, Open Books, 24–5.
3 Slade, R. (1984). *The Anorexia Nervosa Reference Book*, London, Harper and Row, 177–8.
4 Slade, R. (1984). ibid., 182.
5 Bruch, H. (1974). *Eating Disorders*, London, Routledge and Kegan Paul, 51.
Slade, R. (1984). ibid., 105–9.

· SEVEN ·

The culture of control

The feelings of personal worthlessness, moral obligation and sensitivity to others' needs discussed in the previous chapter will be familiar to most women, at least to some extent. Many would also be quick to point out that it is not just the anorexic's feelings that are hidden. In a world where the work women do is taken for granted many feel they are as good as invisible.

In part anorexia nervosa is indeed a rather extreme example of such experiences. Many of the things sufferers say have an almost Victorian ring about them. The following, which is an excerpt from a magazine article written nearly a century ago, expresses sentiments that are typically those expressed by today's anorexics/bulimics.

> The term 'lady' describes one with a gentle heart, who considers others before herself, and is, in plain words, the servant of all.
>
> The housewife who comes down to breakfast with a scowl on her brow and finds fault with everything, contriving to make husband, children, and servants thoroughly uncomfortable, and setting their teeth on edge for the day before the meal is over, is not behaving as a lady, and half the time she is aware of it. She may have received a disagreeable letter; she may have found her skirt unbrushed; she may have a headache. Why should others be made miserable on these accounts? What use have her education and comforts been to her if they have not taught her to put small annoyances on one side and make things pleasant for all round her?[1]

The form of personal psychology that makes this one-way caring possible is also very familiar. For as we have seen, the systematic devaluation of the individual's own needs, combined with a high degree of sensitivity and awareness of others, virtually guarantees that life will be lived for other people rather than for the individual herself or himself. It is a personal psychology that is pivotal upon low self-esteem.

The female role: only part of the explanation

The similarity between some aspects of anorexia nervosa and the female role, together with the fact that at present the majority of those who are recognized as anorexia nervosa/bulimia sufferers are women, has been sufficient to convince many people that the female role alone explains the condition. Women in particular are constantly subjected to the quite explicit demand to conform to changing fashions in body shape, and it has been argued that the anorexic's extreme slimming is both an overconforming to the female role, and a rejection of it; for an emaciated body ceases to be a sex object.[2]

However, anorexia nervosa is not so simple. Characteristically those who become anorexic and/or bulimic have not been restricted to the nurturant activities of the traditional female role. On the contrary, they have been given every encouragement to make the best of their education and to pursue a successful career. In terms of the resources made available for the development of the necessary skills and talents, they are a markedly privileged group of women.

With such encouragement, however, comes another and in many ways conflicting set of values and beliefs which play just as significant a part in creating 'anorexic symptoms' as those described in the previous chapter. These are the values of the Protestant or 'work' ethic. But the connection between these values and 'anorexic symptoms' is often missed because the sufferer shares them with many professional people, including those who try to help her. Yet these are precisely the values that provide an effective training ground for the anorexic's extreme self-control, whilst at the same time making easy conformity to the female role impossible.

The Protestant or 'work' ethic

The rules or values of the Protestant ethic – so called because it has its roots in Calvinist theology – stress the moral worth of sustained effort and productivity, individual strength and personal responsibility. The belief is that rewards must be deserved and pleasures deferred in favour of more worthwhile pursuits, and certainly deferred until they have been earned.

Judged in terms of 'work ethic' values, the worthwhile person is the one who takes full responsibility for what he is, who accepts the obligation to make something of himself and believes his success and failure is largely of his own creation. Evidence of a person's goodness and worthwhileness is to be seen in what he or she does. Because it is an ethic of 'doing' rather than of 'being', time and resources have to be used well, not frivolously wasted. Nor can goodness be a once-and-for-all achievement. There is no virtue in the person who rests on his laurels. There is no level of achievement that justifies no longer trying to do still more. Those who follow these precepts are precluded from saying to themselves, 'I don't have to keep on proving myself. I don't have to strive any more. I am all right just as I am.' They must always aspire further, strive for greater success. Goodness must be continually reaffirmed. The sense is: 'I know I've been busy, but I can't just give up. That makes me feel guilty. I ought to be doing something more.' So the horizon is forever retreating. There is always something else to be attained. This is the cultural theme that gives sense to the late Duchess of Windsor's remark, 'You can never be too rich or too thin.'

These ideas gain much of their importance from the way they are used to justify and maintain the distribution of resources in our present social order. They have become the dominant ideology of industrial capitalism, an ideology which has been vigorously reasserted in the last decade, over which time the number of cases of anorexia nervosa/bulimia has also notably increased. For people who adhere strongly to these beliefs life is a serious business. They must be certain of being good and deserving, and this is something that has to be continually organized. So spontaneity is distrusted. There is little, if any, place for fun.

Inherent in the Protestant ethic is a profound mistrust of feelings and emotions, a mistrust that goes back to its Calvinist roots. It was of the utmost importance to the early Calvinists that they 'felt God's will working within them', because this provided the only evidence that they were among the saved. To this end they believed it was essential to regulate every detail of behaviour. For it was through the minutiae of personal conduct that 'the enemy of mankind finds his way to the soul'.[3] Awareness of feelings was far from being a source of information essential to the development of selfhood. It was dangerous. To give in to emotion signified weakness, a loosening of resolve that could constitute evidence of eternal damnation. The unguarded moment was not just a lapse but evidence of a lost soul. Amusement and frivolity were out of the question. The devil would find work for idle hands.

Though stripped of its original religious significance, the belief still persists quite strongly that giving way to feelings and emotions is a sign of personal weakness and that such 'weakness' hinders productivity, progress and success. In a word they are an impediment to everything that is deemed essential to prove personal worth. The anorexic's unwillingness to pay attention to herself receives strong support therefore from beliefs that are deeply ingrained in this culture. They receive support from the legacy of Puritanism bequeathed from generation to generation. It is the sufferer's own Puritan attitude too that underpins the expectation that, as a woman, she should cover up her own feelings while deferring to the needs of others.

> You shouldn't go burdening people with the way you feel. It's so self-centred. In any case they've got more important things to do than listen to me. I used to talk to my brother till he went to college, and my parents used to get at me for that. They didn't want me upsetting him with my problems. He had exams to pass. I was stuffing all this food and vomiting and crying all over the place. It was disgusting and I hated myself. But, if I was making a mess of my life, they didn't want me wasting his time and spoiling his success. And I agree with them. It was *utterly* self-centred.

Thus where she is accused, the sufferer will agree with her accusers.

> You ought to be useful and efficient, and be positive about things. What's the use of sitting here (with the helper) talking about me in this stupid, self-

> indulgent way? I ought to be able to do something about myself, manage on my own. It's not doing any good, feeling negative and irritable. Better to feel nothing than feel like this.

The sufferer's belief that, if she cannot have the right feelings, then it is better to have none at all is strikingly reminiscent of the beliefs of the early Calvinists. Although she does not know this at the outset when food restriction is first bringing about a sense of euphoria, being free of all but 'good' feelings is the state that physical and psychological emaciation create. In this light her unwillingness to 'recover' thus becomes the more understandable. For what she recovers when she puts on weight are the undesirable and untrustworthy feelings that she ought not to have, that she ought to be able to subdue or banish.

It is the work ethic that is largely the source of the deliberate, active striving quality that is fundamental to the 'anorexic attitude' discussed in Chapter One, the attitude that is a defining characteristic of the condition and crucial to its diagnosis.

The 'therapy culture' in conflict with the sufferer's culture

The idea that feelings and emotions are the core information an individual needs to be effective and that they are integral to the individual having a sense of 'knowing who I am' is an idea that is fundamental to many therapeutic approaches (see Chapter Fourteen) but is one that will seem implausible to the anorexia nervosa or bulimia sufferer who is convinced that feelings are untrustworthy, unnecessary and dangerous. Thus helpers who approach her with the simple belief that focusing upon and expressing feelings and emotions are positive activities, and a source of existential strength, will find there is a crucial difference of understanding between the sufferer and themselves.

The helper who attempts to encourage a sufferer to focus on herself, and accept her emotional experience as valuable, will not be preaching to the converted in the sense of working with an individual who already believes in this aspect of the therapeutic process. She/he will be attempting rather to communicate a way of being to a person who, particularly if she is a successful self-starver, will believe she ought not to be converted, who will construe this not as a way forward, but as subversive or sinful. Again the helper who remains unaware of this particular pitfall runs the risk of being swiftly dismissed as someone who is misguided, who does not have the 'right' beliefs.

Since the helper and the controlling anorexic are making opposing metaphysical statements, conversations between them reach unreconcilable end-game moves very rapidly. This is particularly important at the stage of the initial meeting between the sufferer and a potential helper. The very nature of an anorexic's moral attitude is likely to create a clash of cultures, rather than a co-operative venture. It is sufficient to prevent therapy getting started. Rather than becoming moral advocate, rather than becoming the person whose suggestions the sufferer should try to obey and whose needs and demands she should try to fulfil, the helper in this instance becomes devil's disciple, the person the sufferer should not allow to break her will.

The sufferer's own characteristic solution to her problem, if she allows that she has a problem, is to work harder, produce more, be more organized, more independent, more in control and stop wasting time; and often that means 'stop wasting time over help'. She will believe there is nothing wrong with her that 'a good slapping' or 'a really good telling off' would not put right. Alternatively, all that is wrong with her is that she has not exercised enough will-power and self-discipline to achieve the necessary 'goodness'. Thus she will maintain: 'I doubt there really is an illness called anorexia nervosa. I don't believe it exists. There's nothing wrong with me that enough hard work wouldn't put right.'

If on the other hand she has reached the stage where she can acknowledge that she does have a problem, this often translates into the belief that she has not tried hard enough to be 'normal', which by this time is the goal she feels she *ought* to achieve, but does not know how.

Social standing

Though they permeate the culture, Protestant ethic values are particularly congenial to those who are relatively privileged, particularly if they feel their higher incomes and social standing are the just reward of their effort and industry. One of the most consistent sociological findings is that it is predominantly in this relatively privileged section of the community that anorexia nervosa/bulimia occurs. Usually the sufferer's family's status is upper or middle class and, if this status is not explicitly conferred by wealth or 'father's occupation', her family is either aspiring to achieve higher social standing or struggling to regain status that has been lost.[4]

It might, of course, be argued that these values are so widespread in this social group that they could not possibly play such a significant a role in creating and maintaining anorexia nervosa. For compared with the very many adherents of the values, cases of anorexia nervosa, at least in its classic form where emaciation is fully developed, are relatively few. But while the ethos is important, it is not so much from its existence that anorexia nervosa develops as from the intense commitment to these specific values that is found in sufferers' families. Moreover the pattern of circumstances that creates this commitment is present so often in the backgrounds of anorexia nervosa and bulimia sufferers that it is possible to make certain generalizations about them with a degree of confidence.

Circumstances that intensify commitment to the work ethic

Sufferers characteristically come from families that are strongly committed to the work ethic, and where there is often the feeling that everything must be done from the highest possible motives. Their adherence to these beliefs is apparent in the way that many of their members have lived their lives, not only in the present generation but in previous generations too. The sufferer's family is typically one in which major change in social position has been experienced. Her background is one in which social mobility – upwards or downwards – has played or is playing a significant part.

Social mobility

Amongst the biographies of their parents, grandparents and great-grandparents there are lives that read like classic tales of rags to riches. But the riches, in terms of enhanced social and economic status, will have been achieved as a result of thrift, diligence, frugality, sobriety and individual striving. These are the stories of the miner's sons who became university professors, and the labourer's sons who became doctors and preachers. Equally there are stories where forebears went from riches to rags: biographies that indicate that the struggle is, or has been, to regain lost status and lost respectability. These are the stories of the shame of fortunes lost through gambling, through drink, or through family upheaval of an otherwise 'unacceptable' kind, as, for instance, through bankruptcy or the 'unwise' marriage of the middle- or upper-class girl to the lower-class boy, or of the middle- or upper-class boy to the lower-class girl.

Movement from one social class to another is known to be a source of stress. It is a change that involves making adjustments for differences in conventions of behaviour, for altered expectations and new patterns of consumption. Those who are upwardly mobile tend to find themselves estranged from the people they grew up with, but they will tend to feel anxious and ill at ease in the social class they have attained. Downward mobility, meanwhile, brings disappointed expectations and the need for adjustments that are often painful. Those who find themselves unable to keep up their social status attempt to do so by clinging to the 'old rules', but without the resources to do so easily.

> We never had any money. That's what we were always told. And it was a real struggle. But we were all sent to expensive private schools. All four of us. We had to be properly educated. That was essential, no matter what we went without. Of course, it showed at school. We were never like the others.

Those whose improved social status is recently attained have the task of properly fitting to new and unfamiliar rules and expectations of what is proper, or the done thing.

Moving from one social class to another thus increases sensitivity to outside opinion. Sufferers' families will often have led very private lives. Children's friends are likely to have been vetted. There will have been the preference for outsiders to arrange to call beforehand. Social occasions have to be controlled and manageable, rather than allow spontaneous 'dropping in'.

The status that has been achieved, or clung on to, in these families is usually reflected in the present generation in the careers and occupations of the sufferer's own parents. Either one, or other, or both parents are likely to occupy professional positions, or be employed at a high scientific or managerial level, or run their own small businesses. Significantly they will be working as lecturers, ministers of religion, doctors, consultants, teachers, judges, social workers, policemen and so on, and thus are engaged in occupations which explicitly require the application of Protestant- or work-ethic values as a workaday task.

'Missing' people

A close look at a sufferer's family history usually reveals that in previous generations there has also been a striking number of people 'missing', either because they had died, or were divorced, or because for some reason or other they had disappeared and deserted the family. In other words, there is a high probability that one or both of the sufferer's parents – and if not her parents, then her grandparents – were thus deprived of a parent, or in some cases both parents, usually before the age of fourteen.[5] This loss will characteristically have been endured, like every other adversity, in an ethos of emotional control, where the rule is that feelings ought not to exist and so grief must not show.

Apart from people who are missing, sufferers' family trees also characteristically reveal a high incidence of people who were handicapped, either physically, or as a result of their being alcoholic, and it is twice as likely that these handicapped members will have been male. The corollary to this is the 'strong' grandmother, or great-grandmother who recurs in the family folklore, the woman, that is, who might otherwise be understood as emotionally undernourished and seeing herself as having no choice but to take control, be independent and successful, and by sheer hard work and determination improve her lot for herself and for her children. Thus success or survival has very often been achieved against great odds. It is also clear that whatever the adversity, and in whatever generation, the response has been for this family to have drawn itself in more tightly and demanded that its members exercise even greater virtue, greater loyalty and greater self control.

The transmission of values

While the anorexic grows up in an ethos of strong Protestant ethic values, the way these are transmitted by each parent is complicated by gender roles and her parents' own experience of them. Her mother is likely to have been ambivalent about encouraging her daughter to adopt the straightforward, traditionally nurturant female role, since her own experience, and the experience of her mother and grandmother before her, is likely to have shown her that, to survive, a woman needs to be more independent than this. Within the context of 'death, desertion and disablement' in the family's history[6] there tends to be a feeling amongst mothers of anorexics that other people, and men in particular, are not to be trusted. Self-reliance is essential. Their daughters should be able to 'stand on their own two feet'. These mothers are likely to have alternated between encouraging independence in their daughters, and so expecting high standards of performance at school and work, and encouraging them to be nurturant to other family members, and so expecting extreme loyalty, caring and sensitivity within the family, while being cautious of their contacts with the outside world.

The vulnerability of their children will generally have evoked painful memories of their own unmet emotional needs. Their sense of being unable to cope with their own feelings will not only have led to their rejecting emotional neediness in their child, but also will have vindicated their belief in the desirability of self-control.

The stiff upper lip, carefully maintained by the emotionally controlled parent, will scarcely give permission for the child's expression of feeling, for this threatens to disrupt rational order and arouse fears of yielding to primitive chaos.

It has been argued that this alternation between encouragement of nurturance and rejection of feelings is the crucial experience of all female children in a society in which it is women's role to nurture others without themselves being nurtured.[7] While this may or may not be true for women in general, there is certainly every reason to believe from what is known about the backgrounds of anorexia nervosa/bulimia sufferers that this is their particular experience.

The sufferer's father meanwhile is equally likely to have been ambivalent about expecting his daughter to adopt the conventional female role. The fathers of anorexics are often absent from the day-to-day life of the family: both physically absent as a result of working abroad, or a hundred miles away and emotionally distant. Typically they are austere, demanding, engrossed in their work and stern in their criticism. 'I came home from school and said I'd got 95 per cent in a physics exam, and all I got was, "Hm, and what happened to the other 5 per cent?"'

They want competence, achievement and success from their children. They will usually have given their daughters no encouragement to be frivolous or feminine. Intellectual prowess is acceptable; stupidity is not. It is notable that physical exercise and sport are also important avenues for achievement and prowess in sufferers' families. Often a sufferer may have felt that it is only through her academic achievements or her skill at sport that she can relate to her father.

> Try as I might I couldn't get through to my father. He was so distant and unemotional, and the only thing he was interested in was sport. I wanted him to approve of me. I was brilliant at sport. I thought if I was good at that he might like me, or at least take some notice of me – you know? Give me some recognition and approval.

Sufferers' families are also likely to be facing stress in the present time. In an economy which is in relative decline, and where the nature of production is changing, there are generally greater odds against achievement and success than there are in an economy which is expanding. A parent may have been made redundant or may have had to cope with the change created by early retirement. A family business may be verging on bankruptcy. Given the family's marginal status that follows from its recent social mobility, experiences such as these will tend to re-echo the insecurity of earlier generations. Yet committed as they are to their belief in the value of hard work, consistent striving and personal responsibility, its members have the greatest difficulty in adjusting their expectations to an economic situation in which the chances of 'appropriate' and 'just' rewards are ebbing away. They still respond to adversity by striving harder. Thus there is the feeling about the sufferer's family that in some way its members are hanging on to their present middle-class status by their fingernails. Hence the importance of education and career success.

Creating the symptoms

It is in the ethos that the work ethic creates that the anorexic learns many of the forms of self-control that one day will be called symptoms of anorexia nervosa. This ethos is one that influences not only body regulation, but also the extremity to which this is carried.

The moralization of body regulation

The imperatives of the Protestant ethic are quite routinely applied to the areas of food and body regulation. An anthropologist looking at our society from the outside might well conclude from clear evidence that we believe that by controlling our bodies we can make ourselves morally good. This is explicit in public policy on deviant behaviour, where the penal innovation of the 'short, sharp, shock' clearly rests on the belief that harsh and persistent routines of physical exercise will bring about moral improvement. But there are probably few individuals who do not respond, at least sometimes, to a moral lapse or degrading experience by reasserting or establishing some kind of body regulation to make themselves 'better'.

It is important for the helper to appreciate the extent to which body regulation is offered either as preparation for a career or as a career in itself, at all levels of education. Many schools, colleges and other high-status institutions place great emphasis on the value of sport, where the connection between self-regulation and moral goodness is quite explicit. With the stress that is placed on playing hard, and developing ultimate physical control, sport appears to have become a secular vehicle for beliefs that originally had religious significance within the Protestant ethic. Performance in sport is held up as the epitome of excellence, with enthusiasm and commitment culminating in festivals like the Olympic Games where its values are ritually celebrated, and without reservation. It is the more influential too because of the unthinking support it obtains from those who hold powerful positions in education, industry and government.

The great majority of those who become anorexic have not only been very good at some form of sport before their emaciation became noticeable, but also very committed. In the initial stages of the illness there is often little to differentiate the person who is on the way to becoming anorexic from the person who will one day run or swim for England. Because of this many sufferers pass through the early stages of anorexia nervosa with the full co-operation of their parents and their schools. It is no accident that the highest incidence of the illness occurs not only in dance schools and schools of drama and modelling but in sports colleges, and in university and college departments that offer sport as part of their higher-education curriculum.

How moral imperatives fit extreme actions

We saw in Chapter Two how continued starvation and weight loss result in thinking in polarized extremes. But, while starvation pushes a person's values to absolute positions, it becomes clear that, rather than protecting against extremes, the moral imperatives of the work ethic can be entirely compatible with them as ever more diligence is required, and ever greater striving to reach new and higher goals. This goes a long way towards hiding the nature of the anorexic's actions, particularly when the problem is in its very initial stage.

There are individuals whose moral codes are moderate, flexible, and tentative; but when values are employed to create, or to restore social order – as work-ethic values are currently being employed – they seldom have these qualities. Hence it is quite usual for moral views to be expressed in extreme black-and-white, 'all or nothing' terms. It is not considered enough for children to be encouraged to be 'moderately good', or 'good enough'. The demand is generally that they should be 'good' or 'very good'. The message all too often is: 'Your best isn't good enough. Try harder!' – a message epitomized by the official motto of one private school: 'Beyond the best there is a better'.

If there is any adversity it must be the sufferer's own fault, and so to avoid blame it must be met by a redoubling of effort. It is wrong to give in. No achievements, however great, are as valuable or worthwhile as those which we have had to strive for. There is no gain without pain. These are the ideas, reiterated in countless pep-talks, that find their echo in what is sometimes referred to as the psychopathology of anorexia nervosa.

The competitiveness that is engendered in this ethos meshes with the sufferer's polarized thinking. Her imperative is that she must be an outright winner, otherwise she has absolutely failed. Characteristically she is highly competitive and will compete against herself.

> I got down to six and a half stone last time, and I've got this thing in my head now: I've been six and a half stone before, so I've got to get it lower this time. Otherwise I might as well be second man on the moon, and that's not good enough. If I'm not first, I'm nowhere.

Hence the anorexic is the person who has the determination and the will-power to go on long after others have fallen by the wayside. But as she strives to win, it is her sense of self that is at stake. Even as she was being helped to her hospital bed, one skeletal young woman said desperately: 'They're not going to make me eat. They can't. I won't let them. I haven't given in so far. They're not going to make me give in now. I'm not giving in for anyone. I've got to beat my personal best.'

The assumption that moral principles work in opposition to basic and unrestrained impulses leads to their being expressed in extreme terms. Otherwise the fear is that these principles will not be strong enough to hold such impulses in check. But people who are vulnerable to anorexia nervosa, who do not have a firm sense of self, are in danger of taking these precepts literally. They can come to construe moral principles not as a restraint on what they are, but as a prescription for what they might become.

> The feeling of guilt and intense self-loathing just grew and grew. I had this private vision of being wrong in every way – physically, emotionally and intellectually – as a whole person I was wrong in every situation. I never got

> over the sense that, although I'd got an A for the work I'd done today, I might not get an A tomorrow. So I had to do the same tomorrow – and there was no security that I could do the same. Then there came this enlightenment. It gradually became apparent that control was the answer: control that self to make it appear as it *ought* to be, by working hard, being useful, being kind and helpful. The only way forward seemed to be to *do* things to change what I was. But I only got temporary relief by succeeding. There were some rewards, but never enough to make it more than temporary. And controlling what I ate was just the last manifestation of what I had been doing all along.

Rather like the requirements for becoming a lawyer or a doctor, an accountant or an international sprinter, being anorexic demands a great investment of time and effort and considerable self-discipline. Driven though her choice is by her deep sense of being unable to achieve in any other way, it is not unusual to hear an anorexic speak of her preoccupation with food and body control as her 'chosen career'. 'When I left school, I only had two ambitions. One was to write, and the other was to be thin. I became thin – but I never managed to write.'

Striving towards extremes does not necessarily guarantee the good behaviour that has been suggested as marking out the anorexia nervosa sufferer. She is by no means always identifiable as 'the best little girl in the world'.

> I got into a load of trouble at school. If I was with one lot it wasn't too bad. They never went too far, so I'd go that much further, and I could do that without getting clobbered. But when I was with the others, they always had to go over the top. I still had to go one further. Yes, that was it. I had to be best at being worst.

Moving the spotlight away from women

It is commonplace in discussions of anorexia nervosa to point out the pressures exerted by the fashion industry upon women, and there is no doubt that the female image as projected by the media does have influence. But, with the connotations it carries of cheap commercial exploitation, the fashion industry is an easy target for blame. As such it tends to draw attention away from the part played by the pressures exerted by the work ethic. Indeed it seems to say something significant about the underlying assumptions that exist in our society about femininity, about the female role and about other factors pertaining to the basic irrelevance of women, that it has been easier to advance an explanation of anorexia nervosa entirely in terms of the frivolities of fashion and cosmetics than to indicate the relevance of the stress created for serious-minded young women by the ebbing away of opportunities for success in middle-class occupations during a period of economic change.

This viewpoint also results in overlooking the way these same moral pressures, and equal and opposite conflicts, exert their influence on boys and men as well.[8] Nor is this irrelevant at a time when social and economic change, together with mass unemployment, are stripping away the structure that has for so long supported the male role. As straightforward achievement and anticipation of success in the workplace have become more uncertain, it is notable that the obligation to strive, for people to make something of themselves and create their own individual success, has over the last decade increasingly been transferred to sport. The growing numbers of runners, joggers, swimmers and lone cyclists include men in particular. There is generally a lack of awareness about the changes in brain chemistry that take place with excessive exercise to produce a sense of well-being and success. This lack of awareness, together with the positive moral values that surround their persistent activity, means little or no attention is given to the evidence that there are males who become addicted to their sport.

Nor is there a physiological process as clear as loss of periods to bring men or boys to medical attention or alert those close to male sufferers to the significance of their greater mental rigidity and control. So the incidence of anorexia nervosa and bulimia in the other half of the population goes unnoticed, and diagnosis is also delayed.

> I took my son to the doctor several times. I thought it was anorexia, but the doctor said he'd never heard of a boy with anorexia. He wouldn't listen to me. He just dismissed my worries. To him I was just an over-anxious mother. But Giles was getting thinner and thinner. Assuring me he was eating when I knew he wasn't, and I didn't know what to do, or where to go.

Recognizing the problem and providing help at an early stage can, as we have said, be a way of reducing the amount of time a person spends as anorexic or bulimic. Delayed diagnosis is a disadvantage that particularly affects male sufferers.

References

1 *The Lady*, 1 October 1896, in London, quoted in *The Lady*, 12 September 1985.
2 Orbach, S. (1978). *Fat is a Feminist Issue*, London, Hamlyn, 165.
3 Tawney, R.H. (1926). *Religion and the Rise of Capitalism*, Harmondsworth, Pelican, 124.
4 Slade, R. (1984). *The Anorexia Nervosa Reference Book*, London, Harper and Row, 119–21.
5 Slade, R. (1984). ibid., 121–2.
6 Slade, R. (1984). ibid., 125.
7 Eichenbaum, L. and Orbach, S. (1982). *Outside In Inside Out*, Harmondsworth, Pelican, 27–47.
8 Slade, R. (1984). ibid., 197–9.

· EIGHT ·

On becoming a person: through food control

For the many reasons described in the preceding chapters the anorexia nervosa/bulimia sufferer constantly devalues herself and pays little, if any, attention to her own emotional needs. Consequently she has little idea of what she wants, and little idea of who she *is*. She is very uncertain of her self. But she has discovered, usually inadvertently, what a superb solution food and body regulation provides to the problem of feeling otherwise so unsure, and how well it fits the moral standards that are important to her, and the aspirations she holds dear.

Being . . .

In this process of discovery her ability to restrict her food intake has become not just the difference between being good and being bad, or being a success or being a failure, but the difference between her being and her not-being. It has become her solution to being at all.

This is how it is that she feels that she exists as long as she is in control of her food and her body, and that, if her control goes, her sense of who she is disappears as well. It is this experience of the certainty of her 'self' residing in food and body control that is the source of statements like 'If I don't control my food, I'm nothing. That's the only way I can get anything done,' and 'I'm all right when I'm not eating. I have to have that organized. If I don't, I just go to pieces. Everything disintegrates (i.e. I disintegrate).' Thus it is her food control that is her core, that holds her together and gives her a sense of direction. In all her statements the use of 'I' and 'I am' and the value that she gives to these words are entirely bound up with success or failure at food control, which then, as we have said, reflects on every other aspect of her life. This is the centrality that is evident in her characteristic attitude (see Chapter One). 'An anorexic is not simply a girl or young woman who doesn't eat and can be considered cured when she resumes eating. She is someone who doesn't know how to live except by non-eating.'[1]

Where she becomes bulimic, the sufferer is on a more obvious switchback between disintegration and chaotic eating and the certainty of control. While her eating may look disordered, and she may describe it this way, her certainty is the certainty of knowing she can do something: she can act to regain the control that is essential to her being. Cyclic episodes of stuffing–starving, or binge–vomiting temporarily provide a sense of order that stands in contrast to the confusion in the rest of her life, the confusion that she is the more aware of at her higher weight. To this extent these episodes provide her with the relief of directedness and achievement. Control is still the locus of her 'self'.

> At least when I'm going to have a binge it's something definite. I can start it, I can even enjoy it in a strange sort of way while I'm eating all this food, and I can finish it. There's an end to it. So I know where I am.

When they have been bulimic for several years, sufferers can lose the sense of control achieved this way and so lose this temporary haven of selfhood. Then they find themselves in a state of total despair.

. . . and nothingness

Behind the conscientious, hard-working exterior that supports the sufferer's food-control self there lies a hollow emptiness, a 'nothingness' so profound it is terrifying for the sufferer to experience. It becomes essential for her to maintain her protective exterior, and she resists any suggestion that she might look further than this.

ANOREXIC [whose weight is currently 73-per-cent AEBW, after eleven months in therapy]: But I still don't think there's anything wrong. I can go out of here and look perfectly all right. I'm efficient at work. I can get on with what I have to do.

HELPER: Yes, you can do that. Concentrating on how you feel now, though . . . what feeling do you have, right now?

ANOREXIC [in a dead tone]: Nothing.

HELPER: Nothing. [Affirming her] If you were to have a feeling now, what feeling would that be?

ANOREXIC [dull and hopelessly]: I don't know.

HELPER: If there were something you'd like, now . . . What might it be?

ANOREXIC [pausing for some time, then wistfully]: I suppose I'd like to be loved . . . But (in a more definite but hopeless tone) there's nothing in here to love. Nothing. I am nothing. I'm just empty. I feel as though I've got a hollow glass ball here, in the middle of me.

It can also be frightening for a helper who is unaware of the nature of the problem, who accompanies the sufferer to this void, not knowing that it is there.

The sufferer is aware of this sense of nothingness, even though others are not. This for her is her real deep-down sense of who she is. This is the source of her angry, dismissive statements about herself, as when she says: 'I'm not worth bothering about. I'm nothing. Nothing at all. A cardboard façade around a hole.' Equally it is the source of her despair: 'If you (the helper) were to take anorexia away from me, you know, draw it away with your hands [bursting into tears] there'd be nothing left.'

In so far as food control provides certainty, it creates a sense of self for anyone who is failing to gain an experience selfhood in any other way. This is the experience of becoming a person through food control, the experience that makes anorexia nervosa/bulimia a solution to an existential problem.

How is an existential problem to be recognized?

There are many who might find it difficult to work with such ideas as 'existence' and 'an existential problem'. To those who see themselves as essentially practical people, words like 'existence' almost invite dismissal. Or they might ask 'What does it actually mean?' Or 'How can you know that's what the problem is?' So there is a need to be specific about the nature of a fragile sense of self, and to consider more closely what counts as evidence of an underlying existential malaise, and the circumstances in which it is likely to be evident.

This is also relevant in relation to the problem of identifying or diagnosing the condition where the sufferer appears so very plausible and shows a face to the world that is highly acceptable and 'right'.

Dither and indecisiveness

The clearest indication of the sufferer's existential unease is her inability to choose and make her own independent decisions. This may not show so much in relation to decisions concerning a career or leaving home, for these are often taken care of at the level of cultural and family values, though inability to choose is still present.

> Everyone used to be going off to do exciting things in the summer, and I'd think about doing this, or doing that, write off here, get brochures there, and the end of term would be getting nearer, but I'd be no nearer knowing what to do. And in the end my father would step in and arrange it so I'd come back after the holiday and could say where I'd been and what exciting things I'd done too.

Her indecisiveness is evident in her inability to order her priorities over completely mundane matters. If she has a series of tasks to do, she cannot decide for herself which one of them to do first. She ends up in a state of total, agonized dithering.

> It's over the smallest things, like having to decide what clothes to wear. Or I think I want to paint a wall in my room, but then I feel I ought to clear up the kitchen first, because my flatmate is on nightshifts and she doesn't get time. But there's the jumper I started knitting. I can't sit down to that but I ought to because winter's coming and I need it, but that feels selfish, so I go and feed the cat and start to clean the kitchen. But I ought to be writing all the letters I haven't replied to, but I haven't got any stationery and that means going out, and if I go out I'm not clearing up the kitchen, or painting my room, and I waste all this time going round and round in circles. A whole

> two hours starting things and not finishing them. Ending up making a cup of coffee and then not being able to decide whether I ought to drink it. [Sounding angry and frustrated] I'm supposed to be intelligent. But how can I be if I can't organize my life? When I can't decide to do the silliest little thing! I'm stupid, and that just proves it.

The nearer a normal weight she is and the more aware of the numbers of options available, the more she has to dither about, so her indecisiveness becomes the more paralysing. This can become noticeable in her being completely physically immobilized, unable to decide whether to stand up or sit down, to stay in the room or go out.

> She said she was going out, and she seemed to make all sorts of preparations, but she ended up just standing there, door open, on the doorstep. She was there ten minutes or more, sort of hovering in a vacant, undecided way.

This is where her conviction of her own worthlessness and her pattern of responding to others' needs and obligations leave her. Denying her own needs and feelings, she denies herself the information on which preferences are based, and on which choice and decision-making depend.

With no immediate knowledge of her own personal preferences, she strives to apply logic, rationality and externally derived rules to every choice and every decision. But the demands, needs, interests of everyone around her inevitably conflict. So she ends up like an anxious accountant, continually trying to make absolutely sure the books are balanced.

> My parents are pleased I got into medical school. But it's difficult for my brother. He didn't get into such a good university. He scraped in. He's doing biochemistry, but it's a struggle. They've arranged for him to have private tuition. They make him feel he ought to match up to me and that's what I hate. We've always got on really well together. He's great, I really like him. But I'm a thorn in his side. I don't like hurting him. But if I give up, I'll upset my parent, and I don't want to upset them.

As she strives to weigh up every implication of every action, all she achieves is level upon level of intellectualization and level upon level of analysis which do nothing to move her forward. For logic and rationality are but handmaidens to personal preference. They do not by themselves resolve conflict. It is the sufferer's attempts to use them to do so that result in her coming to exist permanently in a state of confused indecision. It is this that creates the 'intellectual wheelspin', the feeling of gaining no traction, of being unable to make any contact with, or impression upon the world. 'When I push, nothing moves. It's like being a car with the engine really going, revving like mad all ready to go, but with the brake full on. You feel frustrated. So frustrated. And utterly hopeless.'

Lack of spontaneity

It is paradoxical that the more visible face of this dithering indecisiveness is efficiency, organization and routine. The onlooker needs to be aware of the rigid tenacity with which the sufferer clings to her routines and to observe that they are but a limited part of her life. They are carefully related to maintaining food and body control.

Any situation that threatens her routines of food and body regulation will result in her clinging more rigidly to them. In this is the evidence of her control-dependence. Changes of any kind will not be tolerated. Even the suggestion of change will arouse panic. This may reveal itself in small ways in the early stages. It will be noticeable in her reducing her food intake. If she has lapsed and eaten or had food forced upon her, she will starve more strictly and/or exercise more relentlessly. She will be most calm where she has everything planned and predicted days in advance: food and meal times, work, bed-time, every detail of how to meet a day's worth of obligations.

> It's terrible if you get asked to go for coffee after a lecture. It's anti-social not to go, and I don't want them to feel I'm rejecting them, but if you go you never know how long it's going to be, and when you've planned to go to the library, you know you've organized to be there at a quarter past eleven exactly, then something like that just throws you out. But I don't want them to think I don't appreciate that they've asked me to come for a coffee.

Tentative and fragile as she is, unless she has twenty-four hours to plan a change into her routine, she feels in danger of being completely anihilated by people and events.

> If there's any chance I have to eat when I'm with anyone, I make sure I don't eat the day before. That's what I did last week-end. The conference was on the Monday and I knew I'd have to eat with all the other delegates at midday. I ate a bit on Saturday; just an apple and some cheese. Sunday I didn't have anything at all.

It is as well to be aware that the lower her weight is, the more the anorexic's lack of ability to make real choices will be masked by her 'decidedness', her 'greater clarity'. She will be the more directed by her food-control self. Meanwhile, where she is bulimic, her panic at threats to her control can become desperately clear.

> In an attempt to make her break the habit, my father tried to stop her (the speaker's sister) going into the bathroom to be sick, and she went absolutely wild. It was quite violent, and my father was white with rage. It didn't make anything any better. She just ended up in floods of tears, and totally refused to eat anything.

Controlling others . . .

Her own imperative to control her food and body leads to her controlling others' lives. Though this may have the appearance of 'the strong personality', attention to the source of the impetus for control will reveal its anorexic roots.

> We all decided to go for a drink. No one specially minded where. Someone suggested the pub on the corner, but what we actually found ourselves doing

> was trekking half way across town to a bistro where Susie knew she could get a particular red wine. That was the only thing she would agree to. She was really stuck on that. We didn't want to break up the crowd. So it turned out we went there, just because that was what she wanted.

Likewise as pointed out earlier, relatives can feel as though they are being taken over by her.

> I asked her to wait till we'd finished the meal before she began clearing up. But she was determined to get everything put away. She had the knives and forks out of our hands before we'd finished the last mouthful. And my kitchen's not my own any more. She gets so tense if I go in when she's cooking. I feel completely overruled by her. My husband says I shouldn't let her, but his answer is to disappear into his study, or go out to play golf.

. . . or follow-my-leader

Unable to choose and decide on the basis of her own preferences, and so form her own opinions and initiate her own actions, the sufferer attempts to resolve her own non-existence by following the examples of others. This will be more clear at higher weights when she is more aware of people and situations around her, though it can happen at quite low weight too that in subtle, and sometimes not so subtle, ways she is taken over by others' ideas and opinions. As one nurse observed of an anorexic patient: 'She's going round talking to everybody and just taking on the thing that every last person says and repeating it to the next.' This compliance, the flip side of her rigid control in relation to food, is evidence of her being externally controlled: following the rules, sensitively pleasing, doing the 'proper thing' whoever she is with, whatever context she is in. Another sufferer said despairingly:

> I have to see how other people do things. They're all right. They've got themselves together. They get on with their lives. I'm really nosey, I've got to find out what they do. They've got the answers, and I haven't. So I have to copy them. But then I despise myself, because I ought to have my own answers.

Overtly or covertly sufferers allow others to resolve their indecision and organize their life for them. Their conviction that everyone knows better than they do, that there is one 'right' or absolute way of doing things, and that others have the key to this, permeates every relationship. It can also render the unwary helper ineffective in quite subtle ways. The client who says: 'But that's what Cara said, and Cara's my therapist, so she *must* know. She *must* be right about me,' is handing the helper the task and the responsibility of defining that client. The helper who is unaware that the sufferer is following the helper's lead can unwittingly take on the task of leading and so become drawn into perpetuating the sufferer's inability to initiate her own actions or define herself in her own way.

Even if she is aware of what she wants or needs, her ability to decide is still paralysed by conflicting pressures. She still struggles to be fair and reasonable and logically to balance the accounts, but ends up with her fragile autonomy undermined, with no sense of achievement, nothing to lessen her confusion.

> I wanted to do domestic science for O Level, and they wanted me to do maths. They thought that was more important, but it wasn't important to me. I didn't want to do maths, but I ended up doing it for them. What I really wanted to do was do maths and fail, and that would have served them right. But I didn't want to fail for myself, so I had to succeed for me, and do the maths for them, and I ended up feeling like I'd achieved nothing.

Food/body control: a solution to confusion

In the context of the experience of having no sense of self, anyone, male or female, is in danger of discovering that they feel more real, more in command of their life, by controlling food intake. Where every other action is fraught with the possibility of failure, where the rule is that failure and personal inadequacy are not allowed, where the demand is that the individual must be independent and strong, then a food-control self comes into its own. These acts of control are straightforward and uncomplicated. They give a sense of supreme autonomy for they are independent of anyone else. Success is measurable and immediate and belongs unequivocally to the person who has achieved it. Where personhood is food control, then personal fulfilment can be obtained from moment to controlling moment. Certainty of self can be gained in the here and now. Here is evidence of doing something 'absolutely right', of achieving socially approved ideals. So this food-control self is morally superior, a tangible way of realizing perfectionist aims.

> It gradually sort of happened. I found life was organized. In control of every detail. Whatever I ate I weighed. I didn't eat a single calorie more than I'd worked out. I was fine. I was still teaching. My lessons were going haywire. I couldn't understand why, but I was sure it wasn't my fault. I'd never done so much preparation for lessons than I was doing then. They said I'd lose the job. I was too thin. But I didn't care what anyone said. I'd got this thing. And nobody, but *nobody*, was going to take it away from me.

Whatever form it happens to take, food/body control is insidious in the way it gains hold.

> I'd never really lost much weight, though I'd tried dieting, on and off. I don't think I ever lost more than half a stone like that. Then I discovered I could make myself sick, and that became something special for me. I didn't binge then. Not like I have been recently. I just used to get rid of the food after each meal, and that felt better. I had this secret thing. No one but me knew about it. But I felt I could cope when I'd got that. It sounds silly . . . but it was the feeling that I'd got something nobody else had, and I was going to keep it. I never got really thin. But I was more confident. Confident I wouldn't get fat.

Having once become control dependent the person's self-concept is anchored in this and is so anchored whatever their current weight happens to be. Thus:

> I'm in a most extraordinary situation at the moment: severely overweight (even by medical standards), bulimic in my eating habits, yet totally and completely anorexic in my mind. It's odd really, because despite the vast change in me physically, I'm just the same mentally as I was at my lowest weight. My mind is a complex, intricate tangle of problems, fears and difficulties. I am still struggling with the bulimia, although I feel I am getting somewhere now. In the last three weeks I have managed five days of fasting which is major achievement for me, as normally I binge every single day. My weight is still dreadfully high but I have lost half a stone recently. I just live for the day when I will be five stone or less again; it means everything to me, it really does. I will still have most of the problems I've got now, but at least I'll be a weight I feel safe with and that will help me bear the other things.[2]

The difficulty there is in expressing nothingness

There are cultural patterns, strengthened by events in her family's history, that encourage the sufferer to hide her feelings (see Chapter Seven). It has also been pointed out that the overwhelming confusion and paralysis of action she experiences on gaining weight are in themselves sufficient to explain her food control, were they not so hidden (Chapter 6). There is a particular difficulty however that obscures this crucial information. This is that feelings of confusion and nothingness are by their nature almost inexpressible. 'It's just such a mess. You can't describe a mess. It's just confusing. There's nothing else to say. . . . Nothing. You're utterly confused and a mess. It's hopeless.'

Sufferers can have a sense well beforehand that something is not right, and find it impossible to explain. 'For a long time I had a feeling there was something wrong with me. I didn't know what it was. It was something. But I couldn't pin it down. Like trying to get hold of something I couldn't grasp.' Likewise it is impossible for a sufferer who feels non-existent to assert or insist upon the significance this has in her life. Even though she may try to express her sense of nothingness, because she appears so efficient and successful, she is rarely believed.

> I did once try to explain to my father that I didn't feel there was anything that was really me. You know, I didn't have any idea of who I was. No sense of identity. But he dismissed the idea. I was just being silly.

As the following account illustrates, being unable to express the nature of the problem has important implications in relation to asking for help at all, let alone obtaining help that is appropriate.

> I have been anorexic since puberty and had 'treatment' for 'something' when I was nineteen. I am now 39 and have spent the last twenty years in total isolation from my fellow human beings, not knowing why I couldn't make contact with people and feeling guilty about asking for help as I did not know what to ask for help for.[3]

Being unable to express the self that she is, the sufferer's depression and sense of hopelessness grow deeper and deeper. She is frustrated and despairing, and the more so when others fail to understand how it is to feel as she does.

> You get to the point where you can't do anything. You sit on the floor, leaned up against the wall, not knowing which way to move. So you just sit there, paralysed. And there's this stupid counsellor saying, 'You've got to be true to yourself.' But [wailing suddenly with frustration] how *can* I be true to myself when I haven't *got* a self to be true to? There isn't a feeling of being me!

Compared with the profound existential unease there is in the sense of 'never knowing what to do, never knowing whether what I'm doing is right; constantly feeling if it's all right over here, it's not all right over there, and I can't get it right in both places, so I'm wrong whatever I do,' a food control self is comforting and safe.

The sufferer's strong commitment to work-ethic values plays a significant part in her structuring of her understanding of her confused, paralysed, empty self. While all human beings can feel these ways at some times and in some circumstances, the sufferer's moral code denies her a way of accepting such feelings in herself and denies her any language in which to express them 'positively'. So her paralysed action becomes 'laziness' or 'time wasting'. Her dithering confusion becomes 'sloppiness' or 'not having a grip'. Her ineffectiveness becomes 'a failure to achieve' or 'a lack of standards'. The actuality of her experience of nothingness, and the potential for this really to become a problem where it persists and perpetuates itself, is then dangerously obscured by being overlaid by her enormous feelings of guilt and self-blame at 'being wrong'.

It is her moral stance, together with the very intangibility of her experience, that contributes to the sufferer's dismissing the suggestion that she has a problem at all, no matter how great her distress. If she senses something is wrong, she believes it is entirely her fault, and her values dictate that it is her responsibility to put it right. Yet this too is an impossibility where it is so difficult for her to know what it is she has to put right.

Meanwhile, as she turns to food and body control as the only way she feels she has left of getting anything right, cherished values cast a gloss of virtue on the gathering effects of starvation. So, by the time those around her have begun to be alarmed by the severity of her food control, they are meeting an individual whose sense of identity has already formed around her ability to restrict food intake.

The significance of indecisiveness

It is difficult to exaggerate the importance of the sufferer's indecisiveness and the lack of a sense of self that lies behind this; for they provide the impetus and the rationale for food and body control. Both practically and theoretically they are at the core of anorexia nervosa/bulimia.

The failure to appreciate the direct link that exists between the need for effective action of *any* kind as a confirmation of self and the use of food and body control to provide this confirmation has led to a proliferation of theories that miss this central point. There is the danger in this too that such theories tend to draw the helper's attention away from the quality of experience that the anorexic's food control and the bulimic's continual attempts to re-establish food control are warding off in the here and now.

The helper who begins, on the other hand, to work with the sufferer's indecisiveness and sense of confusion will tend to obtain immediate confirmation, in the way she responds, that this is the core problem. Meanwhile, provided she is not very severely constrained by the effects of starvation – which she generally will be when her weight is below approximately 70-per-cent AEBW – the sufferer will usually begin to feel a glimmering of being understood, and the helper will begin to have a sense of having a grasp of the problem, and some leverage to assist change.

A feature of most theories of anorexia nervosa is that they incorporate reasons why the sufferer should not be expected to accept the proponent's view of her condition; the reasons for her behaviour are held to be buried in her unconscious, or shielded from her by a phobia, or distanced from her understanding by her arrested intellectual development. So the assumption is that only much later will she come to realize the correctness of others' theoretical views of her. But as we have said, theoretical ideas that do not depend for their validity on the sufferer's own experience can be oppressive to her. Because of the difficulty she has in trusting and believing in her own feelings and in expressing anything of herself, she very easily feels put upon, interpreted, analysed, taken over, invaded by others' views, fenced in by others' predictions. This is how anorexics/bulimics who are typically highly intelligent, well educated and articulate, come to be so defenceless in the face of academic theorizing.

Sources of confusion

The sufferer's dithering indecision would melt away had she any feeling of what she wanted for herself. But, because her own wants are precisely what she will not allow herself, she has no basis inside herself, no ground on which she can come to her own decisions (see Chapter Fourteen).

It is not that a weak or fragile sense of self on its own creates a problem as destructive as anorexia nervosa/bulimia. People who have a poorly developed sense of self are certainly vulnerable to external control. But as long as the received values and priorities are consistent with each other, it is entirely possible for those who hold them to act effectively, to engage with the world in terms of these values and priorities and maintain a sense of self-worth. Such people may well endure the cost of never reaching their full human potential, but they are spared the profound sense of paralysis experienced by the anorexia nervosa/bulimia sufferer.

Rather it is that the standards and expectations which the sufferer tries to fulfil are contradictory. There is conflict between the requirement to strive that springs from the work ethic and the expectation to be sensitive and caring that springs from the requirements of the female role. Some degree of value conflict is a far more common experience for women than it is for men. So too is the feeling that value conflict brings of 'being wrong whatever I do'.[4] In the sufferer's case, however, these experiences are particularly severe. The experiences of her parents, grandparents and great-grandparents certainly have resulted in the passing on of highly ambivalent messages to their children. But gender roles themselves provide an illuminating example of the conflicting expectations that beset her.

Gender roles

Gender roles are important because they provide one of the ways in which people order their priorities. The requirements and expectations of the male and female roles guide a person's choices and shape their decisions, particularly in situations where conflicting responses are possible.

For instance, faced with a situation in which one could be either sensitive or assertive, males responding in their gender role would resolve the conflict by being assertive, a resolution typified in such attitudes as 'We'd like to be nice guys, but we've got the world to run.' Conversely, females responding to the requirements of their gender role would resolve the conflict by being sensitive, a resolution typified in such attitudes as 'I'd like to tell you what I think, but I don't want to hurt your feelings.' This latter is an example of what has been referred to as 'the compassion trap'.[5] These are expectations that press on men and on women. It is not that men by their nature cannot be sensitive, nor that women by their nature cannot be assertive. But the influence of gender roles on personal development is so strong that this frequently seems to be the result.

When psychological tests were used by one of the authors (RS) to examine gender role in anorexia nervosa, it emerged that none of the sufferers felt they ought to conform to the conventional female role. Some described themselves in terms of male role characteristics, and others in androgynous terms – androgyny being a way of referring to people who ascribe characteristics to themselves which are drawn from both the male role and the female role. [6] This result was perhaps hardly surprising in view of the extreme commitment to the work ethic and other circumstances of their family history, as we have described.

Again it is not the fact that girls and women who become anorexia nervosa/bulimia sufferers have adopted male or androgynous roles that seems to be the problem, for both are compatible with a woman living her life in a way that is highly effective. Rather, as the same psychological research has shown, sufferers seem to have taken on contradictory halves of each gender role.[7]

Trying to make bricks without straw

Each gender role usually describes certain desirable ends together with certain characteristics which make it possible to attain these. Thus men are expected to be competent, independent and successful in the world, and they are allowed, and expected, to be assertive and single-minded in order to achieve this. Women meanwhile are expected to be sensitive and caring; likewise to do this they are allowed a certain freedom of emotional expression.

The anorexic/bulimic meanwhile takes on some of the obligations from each role, yet either way denies herself the means to fulfil them. She is convinced that she ought to be strong, independent, emotionally controlled, which are male role characteristics; but according to her rules she must not be assertive because assertiveness is selfish and hurtful to others. So she is conflicted here. She both wants and believes she ought to be sensitive, caring and responsive to others' needs but, while emotional responsiveness both requires and is enhanced by the expression of feelings, she does not permit herself this. True to the particular half of the male role requirements she adheres to, she believes allowing herself feelings is self-indulgent and weak. So she denies herself essential ingredients for effective action within the female role too. Either way she tries to make bricks without straw. Forbidding herself the tools that are needed to achieve either goal, she ends up feeling ineffective and inadequate whichever way she tries to act.

This pattern of taking on some of the expectations from each gender role, whilst ignoring those other aspects of each role that would enable the expectations to be fulfilled, applies equally to male sufferers. But in their case the parts of each role that are assumed and parts that are denied are generally reversed, so, for instance, they believe they ought to be assertive, but actually feel sensitive and caring, and likewise they end up feeling ineffective and inadequate whatever they do or do not do.[8]

The danger in resolving the sufferer's conflict for her

In theory, if the sufferer's problem has its roots in conflicting expectations, a solution could be to remove one side of the conflict. Progress might be made, for instance, if the sufferer were to scale down her career aspirations and take on a more straightforward and conventionally female role. Alternatively she might develop her more male-role interests and capabilities, pursue a career and do this at the cost of being sensitive, caring and nurturant.

Sufferers do in fact quite often find that people who try to help them overtly or covertly advise them to relinquish one or other set of values or role expectations, the recommended one depending on the helper's own particular inclinations and prejudices.

> The consultant seemed to think it was my duty to put on weight and get my periods back so I could get married and have babies. When I was talking to one of the nurses afterwards, she let it out that he'd like a family himself, but his wife can't have children.

But neither approach is likely to be satisfactory because both sides of the sufferer's conflicting values are strongly supported by the culture and experience of their families. If it were possible for sufferers simply to drop one set of expectations in favour of the other, they would have done this for themselves long ago, as many girls do in their teens when they give up trying to be competent and qualified in favour of being decorative and nurturant. This is a well-documented explanation of academic under-achievement and failure in adolescent girls.[8]

This is not to deny that there are sufferers who make some recovery by dropping one set of expectations. The illness is so protracted that, while the sufferer is bound up in it, the family's values and expectations may themselves alter or modify over the duration in such a way as to make this a possible solution. So it is always worth helping the sufferer to check whether this might be so.

Others achieve some change by taking on a set of rules, or external controls, that they can use to guide them in their decision making and that provides a focus for their existence that is not food and body control. For some this involves religious conversion. For others caring for animals becomes a central preoccupation. Others find a way of living that provides food rules for them. 'I do keep to a strict vegan diet. But it does the trick. It does the controlling for me. I'm aware of what I'm doing. I'm not stupid. But I can't manage any other way.'

For helpers to exercise their own prejudices and encourage the sufferer either way is to fail to address the problem. It is to leave her in the position of saying, as one girl said: 'That's all right for them, but I still don't know what *I* want.' It is to perpetuate her sense that 'Whatever I have, I always seem to want more,' and 'I'm never satisfied. I always want too much. I *ought* not to want so much.' So she will remain deeply dissatisfied with herself still, and with no understanding of how she comes to feel this way. The root task of therapy is to foster in the sufferer a sense of her *own* selfhood.

Since her pattern of food restriction is potentially life-threatening, the specific problems created by her anorexic or bulimic behaviour must be addressed at the same time. Meanwhile, the lower her weight, the greater the difficulty there will be in reaching her through the barriers that starvation itself creates. These are topics we will return to in Chapter Ten and subsequent chapters, however. The prior task is to consider the way helpers may feel towards the sufferer and her problem. For there is always the possibility of their being drawn to her style of thinking themselves, and anyone who is will be the less able to help.

References

1 McLeod, S. (1981). *The Art of Starvation*, London, Virago, 182.
2 Anorexic Aid Newsletter: *Contact*, High Wycombe, Bucks, September 1986.
3 Anorexic Aid Newsletter: *Contact*, High Wycombe, Bucks, December 1986.
4 Baker Miller, J. (1978). *Towards a New Psychology of Women*, London, Pelican, 52–63.
5 Dixon, A. (1982). *A Woman in Your Own Right*, London, Quartet Books, 54–9.
6 Slade, R. (1984). *The Anorexia Nervosa Reference Book*, London, Harper and Row, 192. Bem, S.L. (1974). 'The measurement of psychological androgyny', *Journal of Consulting and Clinical Psychology*, Washington, 42 (2), 155–62.
7 Slade, R. (1984). ibid., 194–6.
8 Horner, M. (1972). 'Towards an understanding of achievement-related conflicts in women', *Journal of Social Issues*, New York, 28, 2.

PART III

· NINE ·

Perspectives that maintain the ability to help

By its nature anorexia nervosa and its counterpart bulimia have great potential to disturb those who attempt to help. They are remarkable for the extent to which they challenge the helper's own personal beliefs and lifestyle. This is because the ordinary standards and values that many people cherish play an essential role in creating a potentially lethal illness.

Comparing starvation effects with the effects of alcohol, and the attitudes that are held in relation to each, is probably the clearest way of illustrating how the helper's beliefs are challenged. For lack of awareness of the role that values, attitudes and beliefs play can render attempts to help totally ineffective.

Food control and the use of alcohol compared . . .

Chapter Two showed how self-starvation and excessive exercise are like alcohol in that they induce certain psychotropic effects, or altered states of consciousness that can be experienced as a sense of well-being. In much the same way as a few drinks can give a person 'courage' to face a difficult or uncomfortable situation, so the starvation 'high' can create a sense of well-being and prevent awareness of those aspects of the person's life that are difficult to countenance by inducing a feeling of being confidently active. It was also pointed out that the psychotropic effects of starvation occur more rapidly than is generally realized. A relatively few hours without food can create a sense of euphoria. Like the excessive use of alcohol, continued starvation also gradually disrupts the biochemical basis for normal intellectual functioning. (In the case of starvation in people who are already physically mature this effect is entirely reversible, but with sustained alcohol abuse the damage may be permanent.) Thus starvation and alcohol are both potent means of changing the way people think. Decisions to continue are in both instances made from a different physical and psychological position from the decision to begin. Thus both have the capacity to entrap their users into a spiral of personality deterioration.

Because, when a person's weight is below approximately 70-per-cent AEBW, further weight loss of even quite small amounts can bring about major shifts in mood, and further changes in thinking, self-starvation like the need for alcohol is likely to become a permanent life-style.

. . . and contrasted

The difference between food/body control and the use of alcohol lies in the way their use is valued. Except in limited subcultures, such as certain groups of young single men, excessive drinking is regarded as undesirable. But people who exercise extreme self-control in relation to food generally attract considerable admiration. It is true that the moderate use of alcohol is tolerated, particularly as a way of easing social situations along. But this is tempered with an awareness of the possible dangers. Campaigns are launched against drinking and driving. People are aware that drinking leads to going out of control, so parents warn children about the hazards of alcohol. But no effort is made to warn of the hazards of sustained food restriction and the biochemical changes wrought by excessive exercise. For food restriction and strict exercise are seen as being achieved through self-control; self-control is virtuous, and being virtuous can hardly be wrong. Indeed the visible consequences of self-regulation are used to proclaim to the world the moral qualities of the individual.

The different values we place on the use of alcohol and on food/body control would appear to derive not so much from what may happen to the individual as a result of these activities as from the implications they have for social order. The individual who drinks to excess may suffer personal harm. But as a disinhibiting drug alcohol can lead people to neglect their social responsibilities, so its abuse is a potential threat to significant institutions such as the family. Similarly, since caring for the home and for children is a designated female responsibility, drunkenness in women tends to attract far greater disapproval than drunkenness in men. The need to combat such threats is constantly reasserted by politicians and moral leaders in the community. Thus the burdens and privileges that go with such social arrangements are maintained.

Meanwhile food and body regulation not only fit dominant social values. Whatever harm they may in fact do to the individual, they normally pose no threat to the established order (except possibly in the case of hunger striking). So they are extolled as pre-conditions of national well-being.

Symptoms of excessive virtue

The person whose body is thin and lithe is not easily construed as greedy, slack, self-indulgent and given to wayward appetite. Even the marked symptoms of undernutrition that occur with anorexia nervosa are interpreted positively. Hyperactivity suggests a busy, committed, achieving person. It is the antithesis of indolence and slothfulness. So, even where the person is quite emaciated, it becomes difficult to see hyperactivity for what it is. Sleeplessness likewise readily lends itself to positive interpretations. Getting up early is good for the soul. The person who goes running at 5 a.m. elicits admiration and feelings of guilt: 'I'd feel better if I could get up at that time. I should be organized like that.' Thus the fact that the anorexic's early rising is the result of hunger-induced restlessness, and her running part of a compulsive exercise routine that she dare not break, is lost in a blur of moral approval. The sufferer's withdrawal from social situations, though a symptom found in all starving people, loses its symptom status because isolating oneself is often taken as the mark of a person going places. 'Going it alone' signifies individuality and ultimate success. Thus the sufferer intent on starvation and other controlling routines easily obtains not just permission to be alone, but approval for her 'independence'.

Although the harder she works the more she may succeed in driving away thoughts of food, although her perfectionism is the expression of her polarized thinking, although organization and ritual are essential to her maintaining her food restriction, the anorexic is nevertheless seen only as 'very thorough' and 'very reliable'. Indeed the success of many a business or organizational enterprise may well have been achieved on the back of an anorexia nervosa sufferer.

> I must admit that a lot of our success in the early days was due to the girl who worked here when we were getting the business off the ground. She was amazing. She used to be in here at seven in the morning – regular as clockwork. You've never seen such organization. We were always up to date on everything. She was the most efficient secretary I've ever had, and she didn't leave this office till seven or eight at night either. Then I believe she used to go and do a shift for the Samaritans. A real worker. It's a pity she's not here still, now the company's bigger. I'm looking for a personal secretary. I'd have given her the job. Of course, we didn't know then she had this anorexia thing . . .

Hoarding is also symptomatic of her totally controlling lifestyle. At low weight an anorexic is likely to save everything from money to the sticky edges on postage stamps. She is the rare creature who accumulates savings while living on a student grant. But hoarding usually gives little cause for concern, particularly amongst members of her own family. It is quite consistent with the belief that resources should be used 'sensibly'. However, while she will squirrel away sometimes very considerable sums of money while her weight is low and she is successfully starving, she will characteristically run through it all with equal and opposite recklessness, should she move into a bulimic phase of the illness. For example, a legacy of £1000 from her grandmother lasted one sufferer six months as a result of her binges and, as she said, 'I couldn't tell mummy and daddy why I had nothing to show for it. They expected me to have bought an electric sewing machine, at least.'

The preference for physical explanation

Because it can be disturbing to realize and acknowledge the extent to which the anorexic's extreme actions grow out of ordinary values and everyday notions of moral goodness, many parents find more comfort in believing that their child is suffering from an as yet unspecified brain disorder or endocrine disturbance. This is easier than countenancing the idea that the standards they live by are implicated in the development of the condition that is causing them so much distress.

The most recent instance of the wish to believe in the existence of a simple physical cure is in the enthusiasm there has been for the suggestion that a specific mineral deficiency might be involved in the aetiology of anorexia nervosa. 'This led to hundreds of anorexics asking their family doctors for zinc salts and to some practitioners actually prescribing them, in the absence of any scientific evidence to demonstrate their efficacy.'[1]

Nor are parents alone in the preference for physical explanation. The predominance of physiological research in anorexia nervosa has gained much of its plausibility from the general unwillingness to accept the idea that moral goodness can have undesirable or bad consequences. Thus the history of research into anorexia nervosa is an intriguing example of the subtle way in which society's cherished beliefs shape scientific hypotheses. There is a cruel irony in the frequent assertion that anorexia nervosa is a mysterious illness. It is not so much a mystery as a case of organized blindness, for generally there is no point at which the preconceptions with which people approach anorexia nervosa enable or encourage them to see what is really happening to the sufferer.

Seeing what is there

Though ready social approval attracts attention away from falling weight and other signs that a person is entrapped in food control, it is nevertheless essential from the point of view of help that onlookers recognize and acknowledge these signs for what they are. There are otherwise very few safety nets in which sufferers can be caught before they plummet into low weight and land on Square 1, or another square on the board (see Chapter Three).

It is especially important for workers who are professionally concerned with the pastoral care of young people – hostel wardens, teachers, ballet teachers, games coaches, university and college lecturers and counsellors, school nurses and so on – not only to recognize warning signs, but to be aware of how their own values and attitudes may be received by those under their guidance, or in their care, whose sense of self may be more fragile than it would appear.

> Cathy's coach passed a comment after a disappointing race about her being a little too heavy. As a well-ordered, introspective perfectionist, she began a rigid diet next day. Her weight dropped from $8\frac{1}{2}$ stone to $7\frac{1}{2}$ stone. She parted from the coach, and to this day he does not realize the misery his chance observation caused. Cathy's promising career as a runner ground to a halt. As later she wrote in her diary 'It's gone on four and a half years now, and I'm so frightened. I stopped going to athletic club because I hate the idea of racing. But I feel lost without running and scared I'll lose my identity if I don't run.'[2]

Just as people make allowances for the effects of alcohol when listening to a person who is drunk, so they must also learn to listen and allow for the effects of starvation in anorexia nervosa. In much the same way as expressions of bravado are understood as 'the beer talking', so commitment to being positive, having will-power, being rational and controlled needs to be understood as 'the starvation talking'.

There are great disadvantages in waiting for a sufferer to become obviously emaciated or to begin to incur accidents and injuries at low weight just to 'be sure this really is anorexia nervosa', because of the way the possibility of communicating diminishes as weight drops. This is so whether weight loss is a consequence of anorexia nervosa or has arisen as a result of any other circumstance. To wait until emaciation alone is severe enough to appear to justify action is to wait until the best chances for initiating therapy have been lost. The changes in personality that accrue with persistent starvation are not easy to alter either, once they become well established.

From praising control to imputing madness

Conventional values and standards create certain difficulties for the sufferer too in the way that she experiences changes in attitudes towards her. Eventually, instead of receiving approval, albeit unjustified, for being very slim, she finds her slimness abruptly redefined as emaciation and as a symptom of mental or sometimes physical illness. 'People can be so cruel when they realize you're anorexic. They'll have been all nice, and kind, and helpful and then suddenly – well, they treat you as if you're mad!'

It is when this category change occurs that it is often no longer felt to be necessary to talk to the sufferer about her actions. Treatment too may be imposed without her consent (see Chapter Four). She experiences this redefinition as a devastating betrayal. It does nothing either to help her feelings of confusion or worthlessness.

> I was getting thinner, but no one said anything. The staff at school used to come into the library at lunch time and find me there, working. But they never said anything. There was a sort of conspiracy of silence. Then one day, after O Levels, they announced I was going to hospital for tests, to find out what was wrong. I felt a thorough hypocrite occupying this hospital bed, especially while I had this great sense of well-being.
>
> Then I was *told* I was going to have insulin treatment. That was one of the few times I broke down. I actually cried in front of my father. The doctor said, 'Yes, they do get hysterical. That's one of the symptoms.' The thing was – it never occurred to me I was doing anything wrong. Or that I was in any way crazy. Eventually I found out what was wrong with me from a textbook belonging to another patient – actually with a certain sense of relief. Because at last I had found out what I was being accused of.

It is far more constructive for those around her to tell the sufferer about their suspicions as soon as they arise, and to tell her about them repeatedly.

> It felt like being down a long dark tunnel. Mum used to shake me and cry at me, saying I would die. But she was so far away. And I could hear my

therapist saying the same. But it was safe down here in the dark. Life looked easy, I was so far down this tunnel (73-per-cent AEBW).

It will seem, of course, that whatever anybody says, she will not listen, though, in fact, she is so biologically and psychologically altered, she cannot hear with any understanding. Because of the way self-starvation works, she will not be able to reverse the whirlpool process merely because those around her are repeatedly giving her their observations. But where concern is expressed, and expressed early and repeatedly, this tends to avoid the more destructive later experience of being suddenly betrayed. There is also just the chance it might be directly constructive.

> What was important was the letter from my friend. She said she knew I wasn't eating, and she was very worried because she cared about me. She said she'd already seen her cousin go through anorexia and it was a terrible experience, and please would I be careful what I was doing. I was already right in it by that time, and I didn't know what I was doing. I just knew I didn't want to stop – and didn't know how. But Vicki's letter meant a lot to me. My therapist helped me see that much.

Admiring the anorexic

Helpers working with anorexics are likely to find they share many of her values and aspirations regarding food regulation and self-control. Commonly they come from the same social background, share cultural ideas concerning body regulation and likewise take this as a valid area in which to achieve success. The sharing of values will be most evident where the sufferer is straightforwardly anorexic and not yet bulimic and raises crucial issues in terms of providing effective help.

The bulimic meanwhile is someone who is evidently out of control and like the alcoholic or drug addict tends to elicit negative judgements. People tend to be fascinated by the bulimic's behaviour and can be voyeuristic about her excesses. But they have no wish to be like her. Those attempting to help any bulimic are more easily able to see themselves as different from her/him. They more easily feel they can identify 'the problem' as something apart from themselves.

Where helper and anorexic do share the same strong values, the anorexic will often appear to the helper as having gone further along the same path and to have achieved more. Thus the extremity she has reached may easily be perceived by the helper as the anorexic's greater success. This means that, even at quite low weight, the anorexic generally maintains the ability to call out approval for her actions from helpers, who then find themselves in the confusing position of approving of the means whilst being professionally obliged to disapprove of the ends.

This is a situation that frequently arises in hospital where young nurses are required to feed anorexic patients. Whilst they may be aware that 'somehow she has taken things a bit too far', they find themselves otherwise sympathizing with the patient, admiring her and wishing they were thinner themselves. Often young nurses feel the amount the anorexic is being asked to eat is 'far too much' because their own dietary intake is inadequate and patchy. Their doubts are clear to the perceptive anorexic and contribute to the difficulty she already has in believing she ought to eat as much as is being asked.

Many attempts to help sufferers are undermined by the sense of hypocrisy there is in the helper's feeling obliged to work in opposition to her/his own values, wishes and aspirations. For example, during a ward round an anorexic patient was met by a team of hospital staff and her problem discussed sincerely and professionally. But walking away from her bedside the social worker turned to the ward sister and confessed: 'I wouldn't mind a bit of anorexia myself. About a stone and a half's worth. That would do me nicely.' With this comment the social worker illustrated her own lack of self-acceptance and made it clear that she valued precisely the same actions as the anorexic. Likewise a helper who is slim and elegant will (unless she is evidently at home with her body and not fighting to keep it that way) commonly make little headway with the anorexic because she too signals that her values are consistent with the anorexic's own. Whatever a helper may say, the sufferer will perceive from the way the helper presents her/himself that this helper has the same beliefs and aspirations in relation to thinness, success, self-control and so on, and, where such contradictions exist, the helper's response to the sufferer can hardly be unambiguous.

Contradictory attitudes also make it difficult to obtain a consistent approach to an anorexic patient where professional helpers are working as a team. An instance is provided by a debate that arose over whether a new patient (a smart young woman who had carefully been restricting her food intake and whose weight had fallen to 76 per cent of her AEBW) was primarily depressed or whether she was anorexic. The reaction of both the newly arrived male senior registrar and the skinny female student social worker on placement to the team member experienced in working with sufferers was: 'But why do you think she's anorexic? She's not thin!'[3]

Many people who have an enduring sense of their own personal failure are drawn to the feelings of success and power that come with restricting food intake and pursuing rigorous exercise. Nor is anyone necessarily free from such a sense of failure, nor exempt from the possibility of being drawn to these ways of making themselves feel 'better', just because they have taken on a helping role, professional or otherwise and of whatever status.

Attitudes in helpers that are consistent with the anorexic's own attitudes invariably reinforce her commitment to food/body control. For the helper's feeling of needing to control her/his own food intake and weight, whether spoken or not, will feed the sufferer's need to feel better about herself. Her sense of her own worthlessness is so profound that any helper must, by definition, be better, so where the helper admires the anorexic's food/body control this works as 'proof' for her that this helper is inferior. This is 'proof' of her own superiority, and she clings to this to boost her pride in herself and to maintain her self-respect. It is this same pattern that leads to her dismissing anyone she considers to fall short of her standards of excellence which are so high as to ensure that everyone must fall short. So she traps herself into finding no therapist, doctor, counsellor or friend who is *really* good enough for her.

Meanwhile she will also swiftly dismiss helpers who demonstrate that they have the same standards and attitudes as she has, yet ignore this fact about themselves, whilst at the same time trying to persuade her to lower her own standards and break her precious control. She will judge them not just as extremely lacking in perception but also as two-faced, and she will take only minutes to rumble their inconsistency. Painfully aware of her own false pride, the anorexic is characteristically ruthless at debunking hypocrisy in others. Her moral victory here is essential. The only alternative she has, if she does not 'win' this way, is to fall into her pit of total worthlessness.

Helpers may be envious of the anorexic or stand in awe of her, not only because she is able to be so controlled over food and is thin, but also because of her academic qualifications, career, social status, wealth, practical skills and so on, and this can trigger the sufferer's feelings of worthlessness too. She will equally see the helper's awe of her as misplaced and undeserved, and her/his envy as isolating and exacerbating her sense of not being understood. Her thinking will be:

> I manage to look clever, but I'm not really. I'm just despicable and low. It's all false. I'm just a liar and a hypocrite. You wouldn't feel inferior to me, not if you *really* knew what I'm like underneath.

Becoming drawn in and ineffective as help

Anyone who takes the anorexic at face value will be little use to her as a helper. The more any helper is seduced by the ideas and beliefs the anorexic expresses concerning the importance of being rational, of exercising will-power, being determined, hard working, self-controlled and independent, the more she/he is impressed by who the sufferer appears to be, the less likelihood there is of that helper being able actually to help.

Extreme examples occur quite frequently of would-be helpers getting sucked in by the sufferer's persuasive beliefs and attitudes and her alluring values. Delia's mother, for example, became so drawn into the arguments her daughter used to justify her adamant refusal to eat that, even when the girl was admitted to hospital as a medical emergency, weighing only 4 st. 12 lb. (58-per-cent AEBW), she was quite unable to help. She hovered at the bedside, clearly anxious and caring, but could not bring herself to pick up the glass containing the prescribed fortified milk drink and feed it to her obviously dangerously emaciated daughter. The drink stayed on the bedside cabinet while mother stroked her daughter's forehead and, by her presence, kept the nurses away. As she commented to one of the nurses, who had to ask her to go outside so that the patient could be fed: 'Delia is so strong-willed, I can't help admiring her. When she's so determined I can't really bring myself to break her will.'

Respecting what she saw as evidence of admirable attributes, this mother was effectively blind to her daughter's physically dangerous state.

Intervention: problems and strategies

The above problems stem from a fundamental misinterpretation of the self-starver's actions. But it is understanding that such a misinterpretation exists that provides the rationale for the informed helper to intervene.

Being unwelcome to the anorexic herself, and often in opposition to what many other people consider to be praiseworthy behaviour, intervention is generally fraught with conflict and emotional upheaval. Having found in food control a solution to her previous dissatisfaction and uneasiness with herself, the anorexic will rarely experience what is being offered in the name of help *as* helpful. Resistance can be particularly strong in the initial stages of the illness when the feeling of being in control has been newly achieved and weight is drifting down for the first time. At this stage, as we have said, self-starvation is a heady new experience. So she resents anyone preventing from persisting with her newly discovered lifestyle, and she is distinctly impervious to criticism.

Knowing that self-control and thinness are by definition good, she typically assumes that anyone who is critical of her is merely jealous of her success. Schoolfriends' comments that she has lost enough weight and ought to stop dieting are discounted as expressions of envy. Many girls who have started dieting with their friends, or mothers, and who have subsequently become anorexic report that they ignored all warnings and entreaties to eat for the same reason.

> There were times when I was at school and I hadn't eaten much. Sometimes I'd eat nothing at all for a few days; though I never did that for more than six days running. Then my mother and I went on a diet together. She couldn't stick to it. I could. It was easy. I knew how. She kept saying I ought to stop, I'd lost enough weight; but I just thought: she's saying that because she's jealous. I thought she didn't want me to succeed because she'd failed.

Where she is convinced she has no need of help, or deeply fears attack on her control, the anorexic will naturally not seek help herself. Concerned others do this. But this leaves the difficulty of persuading her to agree to meet the helper, and characteristically she will make use of any chink in the situation to avoid change. One headmistress, for example, was aware that one of her sixth-form pupils had become anorexic, and she was alert to the implications of this. She saw the girl's examination prospects as likely to be affected by her obvious weight loss. But all attempts to help were frustrated by the parents' conviction that their daughter's isolation and preoccupation were simply because she was working hard for her approaching A Levels so that she could take up the place she had already been offered at medical school. This was a view that the girl herself endorsed wholeheartedly, and the school staff were helpless in the face of the family's conviction that no problem existed.

Another sufferer leaned on her boyfriend's appreciation of her thinness to reject her parent's worries about her picking at food and avoiding all set meals.

> They kept on about me seeing the doctor, but I got Pete to say I'd had a meal with him. He didn't think there was anything wrong with me, and I knew if

> Pete said I'd eaten they wouldn't get at me too much. My brother and his girlfriend had just split up, and that caused them enough trouble.

Yet another avoided help because her mother had no faith in the general practitioner's ability to help and favoured seeing a counsellor, while her father thought the general practitioner should 'do his job and get the girl to eat', so no appointment was made with either possible helper. Where opinion is divided, the sufferer's routines persist.

The only approach to the problem of the sufferer's resistance that is likely to succeed is one where sufficient time and discussion are allowed for prior agreement to be reached between all those concerned with her that she does indeed need help. Only after this has been done is it productive for their concern to be expressed clearly and directly to the sufferer, until she gives in to pressure created by this unambiguous statement of joint concern and reluctantly agrees that help should be sought. The sufferer may see no need for concern, but where those around her are unified in expressing their anxiety, and unified in their strategy for dealing with this, there is more chance that she will actually reach help, and sooner rather than later.

Those who are teachers and employers and who are suspicious of a pupil or employee's preoccupation with food/body control will be helpful if they ensure they carry out the personnel-management aspects of their own job effectively by carefully, but persistently, requesting, for instance, that the suspected sufferer meets the demands inherent in the particular work or school situation rather than being allowed to avoid them. It will in the long run be more beneficial to the sufferer if her employer does not tolerate the inefficiency that follows her growing inability to remember tasks that her job involves, and if teachers of perfectionist anorexic students require essays to be handed in after an appropriate number of hours' work, rather than let them take extra days over them, or if the suspected bulimic is confronted with her patchy attendance at work. Thus the problem may begin to be brought out into the open and eventually helped. Onlookers who perceive something is wrong can also help by voicing their discomfort to their superiors, as one university lecturer did when he bluntly told his professor he could no longer teach his second-year seminar group 'with this appalling skeleton sitting in the same room'. The sight of her made it impossible for him to concentrate on teaching. It was only at this point that notice was taken of the girl's plight and the resources of the university health service called upon to help her with her 3-st. weight loss.

Different professional views about the causes of anorexia nervosa, and different opinions as to the appropriate treatment make it difficult to negotiate a unified approach at this level too, and again she will take advantage of any lack of cohesion. Anorexics can, and do, slip adroitly between different professional groups in their search for 'help' that does not make them confront weight and food issues and so does not threaten their control. A useful strategy therefore is for everyone concerned to reach an agreement for her to see one named helper.

Justifying intervention

Working with resistant clients can raise moral and legal issues that do not occur when people seek help willingly. In anorexia nervosa this problem is particularly acute. This is not only because of the positive moral connotation that is placed on the effects of starvation but also because, unless the helper takes careful steps to avoid it, any intervention can seem to be in opposition to that very conscious, directed, and systematically organized behaviour which is the hallmark of ordinary, responsible human action, and which is also the key to recognizing the illness. It is in this ambiguity over the 'illness' status of anorexia nervosa that the potential lies for attempts to help to degenerate rapidly into destructive confrontations.

There does need to be some justification for a therapist, doctor or any helper to work in opposition to the clearly expressed wishes of the client. But in this helpers are not simply pitting their view of correct conduct against that of the sufferer. Rather they are using their knowledge of how confusion, and subsequently starvation can create behaviour that looks as if it arises from personal or moral strength. With experience a helper gets a sense of when these processes are taking place. As we have shown, there are clear indications of a person's polarizing between rigid control in relation to their eating and body and dithering indecisiveness in every other area of their life, and there are clear indications of the early effects of starvation.

There are times when helpers will find they need to explain these indications, perhaps to counter the charge that they are perversely attacking either the sufferer herself and her deeply held personal beliefs, or flying in the face of cherished social values. Where such a situation arises, helpers will find that the comparison between self-starvation and alcoholism can usefully be drawn upon.

Self-interpretation and virtuousness

Anorexia nervosa would not exist if it were not possible for a person to welcome and value the gathering effects of starvation. When changes wrought by starvation are taken morally and physically to be an improvement, it is very difficult for any onlooker to get their concern through to the sufferer.

The problem the onlooker faces is that, in the anorexic's understanding of herself, physiological information and moral standards are completely conflated. So she meets expressions of concern with frank disbelief, or the conviction that the facts of physiology do not apply to her. Characteristically the anorexic's view is that she/he is physiologically unique. Thus, even after stating correctly that 1400 calories is the daily minimum requirement for an unconscious head-injury patient, an anorexic nurse will firmly insist: 'I'm different. Three hundred calories a day is plenty for me.' Her evidence is not based on physiological facts but on her experience of elation and euphoria, the 'good' feeling that results from her altered brain chemistry.

Different languages and their implicit values

While physiological terminology may have its own clarity and precision, relying on this terminology alone can make it more rather than less difficult for the helper to understand the subtle blend of physical changes, and personal interpretations of these changes, that the sufferer creates, either in low weight or by vomiting and purging.

There is a clash where the language of symptoms that a helper may use meets the language of personal virtues that is used by the person who is dependent on food/body control. It is very easy for an anorexic to feel that her precious sense of control is being dismissed when her feelings are referred to as 'merely the result of her low blood sugar'. Even if a dismissive attitude is avoided, the words themselves are inherently evaluative. Symptom language has strong negative connotations, whilst personal virtues are positive by definition. To refer to someone as being 'anorexic' is to pathologize the person who, in the language of personal virtues, is 'striving to hold on to her moral integrity'. Thus the more attuned helpers are to the subtle implications of value involved in the words they use, the more effective they are likely to be.

The well-fed helper does not share the anorexic's experiences, and this together with the different ways they are valued is sufficient to prevent helper and sufferer ever agreeing about what the problem is, or indeed whether there is a problem at all. Thus the condition gains a reputation for being intractable.

Certainly many therapeutic skills are needed, even to establish a working agreement about the task in hand. But the first step is for the would-be helper to appreciate the sufferer's position fully, *to begin where the sufferer is*. Helpers must also appreciate what the consequences are for the anorexic in terms of her feelings, sensations and her understanding of herself, should the helper get her to eat even a little more food or should her control slip so she eats more by accident. Helpers must appreciate and allow for the fact that, when the starving anorexic eats, this switches off some of the pleasant feelings she has grown accustomed to and at the same time switches her rapidly into other feelings that she does not like in herself; from being on a starvation 'high', she experiences herself as plunging into deep depression as the effects of starvation-induced alterations in brain chemistry are reversed. Even a little food is sufficient to produce this 'mood crash' or 'food hangover'.

Anyone who has just eaten a meal will for a while feel less energetic and perhaps rather sleepy as their body diverts blood away from their muscles towards their stomach in the process of digestion. But the anorexic experiences this fatigue as extreme. The thinner and weaker she is, the more unacceptably tired and heavy she will feel after eating. The 'solid lump of food' in her stomach meanwhile is a physical discomfort that reinforces her emotional discomfort. The sufferer is not easy-going or forgiving about these feelings and sensations, even though they are normal and will quite predictably happen when a starving person takes in anything but the most insubstantial amount of food. They are an unwelcome and frightening experience for a person who is totally dependent on the 'right' feelings that she has when she does not eat. A drop in energy, a full feeling in her stomach and the sense of having a hangover are all the 'proof' she needs that eating is wrong for her.

The helper's recognition of the sufferer's experience of having a 'mood crash' or 'food hangover' enables its terrors to be shared. She usually accepts these descriptions as exactly fitting her understanding of what happens when she eats. Eventually, as the sufferer begins to take in the idea that a 'mood crash' is an ordinary if worrying event, she may feel able to be a little more self-accepting over its occurrence.

There are also other changes that take place on eating that are likewise unwelcome and frightening for the sufferer, such as an increase in heart rate and temperature that result in her feeling hot, flushed, sweaty, uncomfortable and possibly rather dizzy. These changes are often particularly marked in the sufferer who is nearer normal weight, who has been starving and then massively overeats. The extreme fullness of her stomach can also be excessively painful. The person who regularly vomits to relieve herself of the food she has eaten and/or purges will also experience subsequent feelings of weakness and lethargy. Again these are feelings and sensations that follow normally where the sufferer controls ingestion of food in these ways. They are brought about by the loss of chemicals from the body with the elimination of body fluids. But the sufferer does not know this. From her experience of herself after vomiting episodes, and persistent and increasing use of purgatives, she is convinced she is utterly lazy and good for nothing, that everything would be better if she could avoid food altogether.

Sufferers typically monitor their body states very closely and are often aware of the most minute changes. But they are effectively prevented from comprehending basic information about the way their body works because their physiological experiences and moral values have become so fused, and because the effects of starvation have become so intimately bound up with self esteem. So they do not have appropriate interpretations of their body states, nor of the changes that take place in relation to eating and not eating. An important task therefore is to assist her gradually in separating out facts from values, and to provide her with such basic practical information as will help her do this. It involves both helper and sufferer attending to the fine detail of the sufferer's experience in specific episodes of taking in or not taking in food. The helper will also need to accept that it will take considerable time before the sufferer will modify the assumptions about her own body that she is working on, particularly where she is a successful self-starver.

References

1 Cockett, A.D. (1968). 'Zinc deficiency and anorexia – cause or consequence'. The Institute of Family Psychiatry, Ipswich, paper no. 85.

2 *The Sunday Times*, London, 22 February 1987.

3 J. Welbourne, personal communication.

· TEN ·
Getting through

A number of points have emerged so far that are of paramount importance, particularly as we turn now to consider the kind of interventions that are of direct practical help.

These points are that:

(a) Because physical starvation is involved *the helper must respond differently at different stages of the illness*. There is no single counselling or therapeutic approach that is appropriate or sufficient throughout the whole spectrum of the various manifestations of an eating disorder.

(b) *All interventions must be calculated to foster a sense of self:* to increase, not decrease the sufferer's self-respect. This applies even when some weight gain is urgently required for the sake of physical safety.

(c) Since non-eating and body regulation are central to a sufferer's idea of self, and weight gain constitutes changing this 'self', such *weight gain needs to take place only as fast as the sufferer is able to cope with it*. This can be expected to take months, if not years, as she is helped to create a self that is not a 'food-control self'.

To these a further point can now be added, which is that:

(d) If the above are to be achieved, the helper will need to get through to the sufferer in a direct and effective way. *All alternatives to coercion depend on communicating.*

Whatever their connection with the sufferer, few people want or like the destructive confrontations that arise, usually when stores of patience and goodwill have been exhausted. Nor is anyone against communicating. Indeed its value is an article of faith, particularly to those in the helping professions. But the injunction to communicate with the anorexic or bulimic will ring hollow to those who have tried and failed.

The problem in this instance is that feelings of goodwill and a commitment to communicating are not enough. To be effective, a would-be helper needs information about the nature of anorexia nervosa/bulimia.

Acknowledging the sufferer's style of thinking

In addition to being informed, helpers must also be prepared to make certain mental adjustments, or efforts of imagination, as we suggested in Chapter Five, if they are to place themselves in the sufferer's position, particularly when she is at low weight. To meet her in the physiological and psychological place she is, the helper will need to change the basic assumptions on which conversations usually proceed. Only then will helper and anorexic or low-weight bulimic find they are talking about the same thing.

In the practical task of getting through to the sufferer, these necessary changes of assumption merge together. The helper, with some practice, will be able to make the adjustments automatically, rather like simultaneously translating into a different language. But to be clear about the changes involved it is useful to set out the ordinary assumptions that are usually made and compare them with the sufferer's understanding of her own experience.

	Ordinary assumptions	*Anorexic/bulimic experience*
(i)	Regulating food and body is one important thing amongst many in her life.	Regulating her food and body is the only important or significant issue in her life; it is her sole measure of personal worth. (Centrality of food and body control: Chapters One and Eight.)
(ii)	She is intellectually and emotionally the same person as she was before she lost weight.	She has changed herself by controlling her food/body and feels she is a better person as long as she remains in control. (Altered thinking and feelings: Chapter Two.)
(iii)	She has the same kind and range of physical experiences as the helper.	Some of her physical experiences are outside the experience of the adequately fed helper. (Different physical experiences: Chapters Two and Five.)
(iv)	Her personal skills and achievements must be as valuable to her as they are judged to be by the helper.	She believes she is utterly worthless in every respect. (Low self-esteem: Chapter Six.)
(v)	Helpers tend to assume that the values implicit in the words they use are shared by the sufferer; that she must believe emaciation, intellectual 'shut down' and emotional distance are undesirable.	While the helper may use negative words about her, she uses words with positive connotations. Emotional distance and intellectual 'shut down' are, for her, a sense of calm and the ability to be decided. (Different implicit values: Chapters Five and Nine.)

It is this mismatch that exists between the assumptions others make about her and the sufferer's different but undeclared understanding of her own position that creates the breakdown in communication. The sufferer, particularly when she is low weight, is so used to this that, having been previously sullen and distant, she will often sit wide-eyed with surprise when a helper demonstrates her/his awareness of how she thinks and feels. A working relationship between helper and sufferer can often grow from this point.

Feeling isolated and separate is a core experience for her. It is 'as if she has passed through a glass beyond which people can see her and they can hear what she is saying, but they seem incapable of understanding her'.[1] Many images of separateness occur in autobiographical accounts of the illness. The image of glass separating them from others is a particular image that one of the authors (MD) has found sufferers frequently use, and not necessarily only at low weight.

Because the personality changes wrought by starvation are cumulative, and because they are usually well established by the time her food/body control has come to be seen as a problem, it is the helper who has to adjust for the sufferer's different perceptions and different understanding. It is the helper who must make the effort of imagination to pass through the glass and make contact with her; for, imprisoned as she is in what one girl referred to as 'her glass fortress', she cannot make the adjustments herself to reach back. Once the helper has 'passed through the glass' however, she/he will begin to comprehend the remarkable simplicity, completeness and organized predictability of the world the anorexic inhabits, how it becomes essential to her to protect this world from being destroyed, and how this task of protection can seem so much simpler and easier for her, the thinner and more constrained she becomes.

It is by adjusting for this characteristic style of thinking, and for the way its changes are weight-related, that the helper will be able to appreciate the truth for the sufferer of the statements she makes, to see how it is she is neither lying, nor mad, nor incomprehensible to herself. But, while making these adjustments, it is imperative that the helper at the same time stands firmly on this side of the glass, securely in a non-anorexic world. This tends to require a high degree of self-awareness on the helper's part and the ability to separate her/himself from the sufferer's style of thinking and evaluation of personal experiences and so avoid becoming drawn into it (see Chapter Nine). It is essential for a helper to appreciate the sufferer's position and style of thinking, but equally essential to do this in such a way as to retain the freedom to promote change.

It would be wrong to give the impression that, once the helper has learned the skill of translating for an anorexic perception of the world, easy co-operation and harmony will prevail. On the contrary, many of the helping strategies we will describe necessarily involve some conflict. But the helper's skill here will lie in drawing out and working with the conflicts that already exist within the sufferer and paralyse her effective action, whilst not becoming part of them. The difference is in the nature of the conflict, and between an approach that seeks to impose change on the sufferer, whatever she thinks, and an approach that suggests changes because of the conflict in her own thinking (see Chapter Nine).

Returning to the stepladder

Though it can at some stages and in some situations be quite difficult to detect, whatever the sufferer's weight, the centrality of food control is always present. Though it may centre on different activities and present very different appearances at different times, her defining attitude is always the same.

A sufferer whose weight is around her average expected body weight and whose current pattern is stuffing/starving or binge/vomiting will at this stage be totally focused on the problem of how to avoid food and eating, and how to regain the control she loses as a result of the continual, humiliating, cyclic failure to do so. But she has the capacity to think in complex and varied ways. At low weight on the other hand it is the starving person's total preoccupation with food and the contraction of intellectual capacity that together create her inability to think about anything else. Centrality of food control at this stage is the consequence of an actual inability to conceptualize much beyond food and of the polarized thinking that renders her incapable of grasping the possibility of there being intermediate positions.

A sufferer who is not at a very low weight can respond to appropriate therapy far more rapidly than one who is emaciated and very constrained intellectually. The way in which it is possible to hold conversations with a sufferer who is 75-per-cent AEBW and still in full employment, for instance, is different both in content and in process from the more concrete, limited colloquies that can be had with a sufferer at 60-per-cent AEBW who is exhausted and in crisis. Where intellectual potential is not so closed down by starvation, a person can more readily hold in focus for herself the new experiences created in the context of therapy and has some capacity to process these experiences.

Therefore the adjustments listed at the beginning of this chapter require different emphases at different stages of the illness. Since there is not one, but a number of tasks involved in getting through, depending on where she is, the helper will need to tailor these adjustments to the requirements of each individual sufferer. Just as there are clear levels that can be differentiated physically, in terms of bands of weight and related appearance, and psychologically, in terms of intellectual capacity and emotional experience, so there are levels that can be differentiated in relation to getting through to the sufferer. In other words there is a stepladder for communicating too.

Working with this idea, the last four chapters are organized around four different stages of the condition. For those reading this book with a particular sufferer in mind these steps should provide at least one picture they can recognize. The task of this present chapter meanwhile is to point out and illustrate some aspects of communicating that apply in general.

Adjusting for the centrality of food control

As we have said, the centrality of food and body control is the key to diagnosing the illness, and necessarily so in its anorexic stage. It is the presence of this core attitude that will confirm for the helper that it is anorexia nervosa she is meeting in any particular case.

With practice a helper can quickly learn to 'tune in' to the authentic ring of the anorexic conviction that life is possible only as long as food and body are in control. Statements about food/body regulation will tend to be delivered with a confident assurance, and the sufferer's social poise will also deflect questioning and suspicion.

> I must plan what I eat in advance, otherwise I can't organize anything else. Once I've done that I'm all right. Then I know where I am. I don't often eat out, or anything like that. I usually prefer my own company anyway. [At 85-per-cent AEBW]

Illustrations were given in Chapter Eight to enable the helper to begin to clarify the existential quality of the content of 'anorexic' statements. It is useful to be attuned to hear, as well as see, evidence of the sufferer's characteristic attitude; for, as we have said, anorexics/bulimics are not always identifiable by their extreme thinness. For instance: 'I never miss my jogging. That's too important. Whatever the weather's like, it doesn't matter to me. I have to go out for my jog. I wouldn't feel right if I didn't'. [At 90-per-cent AEBW]. It is also useful for the helper, and concerned others, to be aware that there can be a hidden agenda in statements such as 'I always get so involved in my work, I find that when I'm working I really don't need to eat . . .' [At 89-per-cent AEBW]. Further questioning is likely to reveal that the speaker regularly goes all day without food, and then considers:

> It's not worth the trouble preparing myself anything when I get home late in the evening. I might just have a slice of bread and a piece of fruit. I can't be bothered at that time of night. Besides, I don't like to have too much food in my stomach when I go to bed. I hate going to sleep feeling bloated.

A person's thinness will, of course, make it easier to hear the central importance of food and body control in the things she/he says.

Because the anorexic's commitment to food/body control is in the nature of a lens or prism through which every comment, question, observation, encouragement or suggestion passes, all the 'being' or life statements she makes about herself need to be translated by the helper into food statements. Conversely, where the helper uses life statements, she/he must be aware that the anorexic will receive and understand them as food statements. Thus, when the helper asks the anorexic how she is feeling and the anorexic says, 'I'm feeling fine,' the helper must understand that for the anorexic this means, 'I'm in control.' In other words, she has not eaten anything she did not mean to eat, she has probably eaten less than the amount she planned to allow herself and she is feeling good and safe. Her underlying account to herself runs something like: 'I haven't eaten all day, so I can allow myself salad this evening, and a slice of cold chicken (8 cm square) and still be in control.' She probably has familiar and reassuring aches because she has had time to jog the two miles to the appointment with the helper instead of taking a bus and so has burnt off more calories than she would have done otherwise.

Conversely statements such as 'I don't feel very good today' or 'I feel terrible' translate as 'My eating is out of control.' Her experience and her underlying account to herself in this case runs something like:

> It's 12.30 and I've eaten four whole ounces of cottage cheese. I only ever eat two ounces at 12.30. It's made me go completely to pieces. I'm terrified. I might eat and eat and never stop. I hate myself when I can't stick to what I know I ought to.

It must be remembered too that statements about 'feeling terrible' will be made with most urgency and greatest conviction by the hospitalized $4\frac{1}{2}$-st. anorexic (59-per-cent AEBW) who has just gained the first pound of weight.

The helper who, by translating thus, can move into the self-starver's world will more easily understand the situation from her perspective and so, genuinely, be able to accept the positive statements she makes about herself as being true for her – however unlikely that may seem from the way she looks! Genuine acceptance, which will be felt by the sufferer, is fundamental to helping her change.

The helper's position described here contrasts with that of the onlooker who sees the anorexic as fashionably skinny, agrees with her when she says, 'I feel fine,' and is drawn in because there is no mismatch at all between the anorexic's views and the onlooker's own views. It also equally and oppositely contrasts with the position of the onlooker who sees the girl's stick-like appearance, notices the bluish-mauve colour of her hands, hears her say, 'I'm feeling fine', does not believe her and dismisses what she says. In these instances there is a complete mismatch between the anorexic's and the onlooker's views. Sufferers always notice the hearer's disbelief and dismissive attitude. They can become angry and hostile at not being believed, and they can feel totally unjustly treated.

The anorexic will take this response as one more judgement against her, yet another failure, yet another experience of not being understood. Thus where there is no adjustment to her anorexic style of thinking attempts to reach the sufferer rapidly reach their uncomfortable impasse.

HELPER: I wonder if there's anything worrying you?

ANOREXIC [blandly]: No.

HELPER: Nothing at all?

ANOREXIC: No. Nothing's worrying me. [Translated: I've really got my eating under control, and I'm not worried about anything when I've got that sorted out.]

HELPER: You look rather worried.

ANOREXIC: No, I'm all right. [Translated: The only thing that's worrying me now is you. I'm scared you're going to start pressuring me. I've got it organized and I don't want to be undermined by you or anyone else.]

HELPER: But other people are worried about you. Your parents, for instance. That's why you're here.

ANOREXIC: Yes, I came because I know they're worried, but I don't see there's any need for them to feel like that. I'm OK.

HELPER: I'm rather concerned about how thin you are.

ANOREXIC: But I'm not. I'm fine. There's no need for you to worry about me. You can see I'm all right.

Here the helper thinks, 'But she's skeletal. What does she mean?' and conversation grinds to a halt. The helper on the other hand who continually adjusts for the sufferer's perspective has the possibility (for instance where 'translation' is indicated) of moving into her world and communicating with her in her own terms. This not only avoids an impasse. It demonstrates to the sufferer that the helper understands her position. It is a way of really meeting her. Thus the above conversation might instead take the following course.

HELPER: Is there anything worrying you?

ANOREXIC [blandly]: No.

HELPER: Nothing at all?

ANOREXIC: No. Nothing's worrying me. [Translated: I've got my eating in control, and I'm not worried about anything when that's all right.]

HELPER: You look a bit worried to me . . . [Deciding to try a 'move' towards her] I imagine the people who think you're thin pressure you a lot to eat more. And I'm wondering whether, right now, you're worried I might start pressuring you like everybody else?

ANOREXIC [appearing startled, and then finding herself agreeing]: They're always trying to make me eat all this food. But I don't want it.

HELPER [indicating acceptance of her last statement by mirroring her determined tone]: No, you don't want it. But it's probably very hard to make them understand that you feel much better when you don't eat. You can get more done, perhaps?

ANOREXIC [still rather surprised that this therapist appears to understand]: Yes. I do, but they won't believe me.

HELPER: And I guess you do eat something?

ANOREXIC [opening up]: Oh yes, I eat the things I like. [Translated: I like eating a small range of low-calorie foods such as . . .]

HELPER: What kind of things do you like?

ANOREXIC [enthusiastically]: Vegetables. I love vegetables. And cottage cheese. I eat a lot of cottage cheese. [Translated: That is, a small amount which is always exactly the same so I still feel safe.]

In meeting the anorexic by adjusting for this centrality it becomes possible to help her bring the detail of her need for control into the open. This is one essential step towards her eventually allowing herself to experiment with risking some change (see Chapter Twelve).

HELPER: How are you feeling?

ANOREXIC: Fine.

HELPER: You're feeling fine. So I guess you've got your eating organized.

ANOREXIC [brightly]: Oh yes.

HELPER: Would you like to tell me about that? What have you eaten today, for instance?

ANOREXIC: Well, I don't eat anything till the evening.

HELPER: So you haven't eaten anything so far today.

ANOREXIC: No, I never do. I don't need to.

HELPER [noting last comment, but letting it pass in favour of bringing in a suggestion of change]: Suppose you'd eaten a slice of toast for breakfast before coming here . . .

ANOREXIC [looking alarmed]: I couldn't do that.

HELPER: No, but suppose you had. How d'you think you'd feel?

ANOREXIC: Terrible.

HELPER: Yes, I agree. You'd feel terrible. Like you'd let yourself down?

ANOREXIC [pausing before risking admitting this]: I'd be a total failure . . .

HELPER: And my guess is you wouldn't eat for the rest of the day.

ANOREXIC: No. [Looking panicky] Not if I'd eaten that for breakfast.

HELPER: You look as though the very thought of it makes you panic.

ANOREXIC [relieved the helper has noticed her panic, but doesn't seem to blame her, or think she's silly]: Yes, it does. [Pause] It seems silly to get into a panic over a slice of toast . . . but . . .

HELPER: At the moment that's what you do.

ANOREXIC [firmly]: I would if I ate it – but I don't. Not if I can help it.

Adjusting for altered thinking

As starvation progresses, the anorexic thinks about a smaller range of things, thinks about them in an increasingly polarized way, and everything that is thought about is thought about in non-food terms. These are the main intellectual changes that starvation creates (see Chapter Two).

These changes intensify as weight falls and become less severe as weight rises. This means that, of the adjustments the helper needs to make, the exact adjustment that needs to be made for altered thinking will depend utterly on *this* person's weight level on *this* day, and how it has recently altered; whether it has gone up or down, and how fast.

Intellectual changes can be masked for a considerable length of time by habitual performance. For instance, while her weight drops, a sufferer is likely to continue to obtain high marks in her academic work at first because she will make up with many hours of dedicated, repetitive learning what she cannot do by abstraction or by the creative synthesis of new ideas. How well she performs will also depend somewhat on her particular history as an anorexic, the significant factor usually being the length of time she/he has been maintaining a low-weight state and at the same time fulfilling day-to-day obligations. If she is studying medicine, geography or any subject where the task is to assimilate material in a predictable, pre-organized form, she will be able to continue to do this even at quite low weight. But if she is studying A-Level or university mathematics, or another course where problem solving via new decisions is required, or the flexible and creative reorganization of ideas, then she will begin to fail much sooner. She will not be able to perform even after a relatively small drop in weight below 85 per cent. Her ability to understand and assimilate new information will be restricted and this will become increasingly apparent as she becomes more emaciated. As one ex-sufferer said:

> It showed a lot when it came to doing essays. You sit in the library and make notes and more notes till you're drowning in notes. But you can't handle them. The last thing you can do is turn them into a coherent well-argued essay. You can't decide where to begin, or what to put in, and it seems impossible to leave anything out.

It is for this reason that it is pointless for a helper to present the low-weight sufferer with the 'grand analysis' in the hope that, by telling her her starvation is progressively impairing her intellectual capacity, she might be encouraged to eat. Attempting to get through by rational argument is as unproductive as attempting to discuss complex issues with a person who is continually under the influence of alcohol. She only has the capacity to respond in the most simple polarized way and, in any case, will not want to believe anything that is out of line with her own rigid views, or contrary to her 'improved' experience of herself. She does not take kindly to anyone who attempts to deprive her in any way of her greatest achievement, i.e. her recent or sustained weight loss.

It is far more effective a strategy for the helper to adjust to her, and so talk about specific deficits that can be judged as most likely to be happening at the weight she is in the hope that the sufferer herself will be able to recognize that what the helper is mentioning has begun to occur in her own life.

HELPER: You've lost another pound. I know that's not worrying you . . .

ANOREXIC: No.

HELPER [aware that the girl is now around 72-per-cent AEBW]: I'm aware it's easier for you not to eat. Your weight's gone down again. But I wonder . . . Have you noticed yourself changing any other way?

ANOREXIC [silent, and looks blank]: —

HELPER: I wonder if you're feeling the cold much more? And taking longer about doing things. . . . Because perhaps your concentration might be a bit patchy? Or as though you've got gaps in your memory?

ANOREXIC [in a changed tone]: Funny you should say that. I don't concentrate as well as I did. It's hard to keep my mind on things. When I'm at work . . . even writing letters, it takes ages.

HELPER: You're noticing that yourself.

ANOREXIC: Yes. I don't remember things. I have to keep asking.

HELPER: It wasn't like that a few weeks ago . . .

ANOREXIC: No.

HELPER: So as your weight is going down, you can't work as well as you did.

ANOREXIC [grudgingly]: Mmm. I suppose so.

Such an intervention can be risky unless the helper is sure she has recognized the appropriate stage. A sufferer will be highly offended at the idea that she cannot concentrate if she feels she can. Yet, when she is blandly denying any problem at all, an appropriately judged intervention that homes in on a specific deficit may reach her.

The helper may find it useful to imagine polarized or altered thinking as a template that is set on every aspect of the anorexic's experience and that can help make sense of her holier-than-thou attitude at one time (i.e. when she feels organized and in control) and her total self-hatred and self-disgust at another time (i.e. when she loses her absolute control). It is a template with no intermediate positions. Hence her swings from one extreme to the other can result from her unplanned eating of an amount of food that to anyone else will seem insignificant, such as a few grapes, or a bite of a sandwich, or her failure to get to the fitness centre at 12.45 *exactly*.

Such a template also gives coherence to her statements about weight, such as 'It's all right if I'm 5 stone, 13. Then I'm thin. But I couldn't possibly be 6 stone. That's fat!' And to every other statement concerning quantity and measurement: 'In that exam? I only got 99 per cent. So what if the pass mark's 70. That's not what I ought to have got. Of course I've failed! I should have got it *all* right.'

Again these are statements that, when the hearer lacks the necessary informed understanding, can be dismissed as nonsense or madness. But to those who are aware of the changes starvation creates the meaning is clear and informative about where the sufferer is.

The perceptual changes that take place, that have the effect of making the anorexic feel fatter than she actually is, are in fact an example of a quite normal psychological process that occurs whenever a particular distinction acquires a great significance for any person.[2] This process (perceptual shift) is exploited every day by price tags advertising £6.99 rather than £7, or £18,950 rather than £19,000. It works by exaggerating the difference between two points on any scale that are in fact quite near each other so that they seem importantly different and far apart from each other. Because of the effects of starvation such perceptual shifts are very much more exaggerated at low weight.

Adjusting for low self-esteem

The sufferer's extremely low self-esteem may not be in the least apparent. Whether she comes across as confident and superior, however, or as depressed and self-effacing will also always be closely related to how she is feeling about being in control of eating and weight.

Whether or not her low self-esteem is evident, the helper will assist a great deal by allowing for its presence, by adjusting for this from the first moments of meeting her, by actively engaging with her in ways likely to promote in her a sense of her own self-worth.

Simple measures such as acknowledging her presence by greeting her by name, giving eye contact in so far as she seems able to cope with this, talking *to* her rather than *about* her, listening to and acknowledging what she says, and giving her plenty of time to express her position, are all helpful in this respect.

A particular adjustment that will need to be made is for the way her low self-esteem colours the way she relates to others, ensuring a pattern of either finding every possible fault with other people and dismissing them as worthless and inferior, or finding every possible fault with herself and so dismissing herself.

Either way her low self-esteem serves to protect and defend her from the burden of engaging with anyone at all, including the helper (see Chapter Nine).

A sufferer who has tried to express her feelings of inadequacy and worthlessness will have been used to having her feelings dismissed. She will be accustomed to others seeing her as being very talented, confident, poised, well qualified, as having great social advantages. So she will expect the helper to see her in the same way.

If the helper does take this view, she will create an impasse, for the sufferer will feel consequently obliged to sustain her 'false front'. If, on the other hand, the helper can gently demonstrate that she/he is aware of the mismatch that exists between the way the world sees her and the way the sufferer sees herself, this again can provide the point of surprise, of genuine meeting and understanding, that might stir the possibility of developing a helping relationship, or assist in keeping a fragile or incipient relationship alive.

It is important to be aware how easily the sufferer can take fright at being 'really known', or 'found out'; her underlying message being: 'This person might really find out how awful I am, and that'll be the end of it. So I'd better stop coming here, before that happens.'

So the helper should avoid carelessly triggering the sufferer's defences. Any hint of criticism or judgemental comment at this point is fatal to the development of any therapeutic relationship. In this intervention the helper must not laugh or snigger or joke. The sufferer is so readily humiliated. Total seriousness is essential.

HELPER [at a first meeting with a sufferer who appears resentful, silent and withdrawn]: . . . and your parents seemed proud to tell me you've just got your degree. . . . I guess most people see you as very successful. . . . I suspect that's not quite the way you feel yourself . . . (Watching the girl's face colour slightly) . . . even though you got a first.

SUFFERER [rapidly]: I didn't deserve it.

HELPER: You don't believe you deserved it. . . . You feel a fraud?

SUFFERER [quietly]: Mmm . . .

Though she will be afraid at being 'so transparent', it can, even so, be a great relief for the sufferer to meet someone who seems to know just how worthless and ineffectual she feels, and how much she hates herself, yet who does not blame her for feeling like this, in fact, seems, bewilderingly, to accept her, though she cannot see why.

Even when she is low weight and successfully starving, a sufferer will be terrified of losing control. So, though she may dismiss the helper's 'inferior' attempts to communicate with her, it is on the issue of losing control that the helper is likely to find a chink in her armour of 'superiority'. However, while aiming to help her bring this greatest fear into the open, it is also appropriate to acknowledge and accept her superior or dismissive attitude quite straightforwardly as her current feeling and/or way of seeing the helper. Thus a helper may say:

> From here it seems clear you think I'm pretty stupid and misguided to go on believing you need help when you've made it quite plain you think it's

unnecessary. You seem sure you've got your life organized. And I'm not going to deny that [Pause] but my guess is that a lot of your organization hangs on keeping a tight watch on what you let yourself eat . . . and trying not to eat . . . which is usually very hard work . . . [Noting a slight, inadvertent nod]. I wonder whether you always feel so sure about yourself? Like when it gets difficult to avoid food. Or you seem to find yourself eating by accident [Noting she is looking panicky] You look a bit scared . . . [Gently] Has that happened? Or is it that you're afraid it might?

Like any other human being the anorexia nervosa/bulimia sufferer is utterly ordinary and normal in wanting and needing attention, acknowledgement and respect. Indeed these are essential if she is to begin to create a self that does not depend on food control. But her low self-esteem effectively prevents her from taking the attention and the acknowledgement she needs. She does not feel she deserves them. She also sees them as creating obligations and responsibilities in the sense that she must prove she is worth acknowledgement and respect, and she is afraid of failing to fulfil these obligations. Thus her dilemma is that she both wants and does not want the helper's attention. However, where the helper accurately empathizes with her and gives attention that appropriately acknowledges her, even in recognizing the tangle of her ambivalence, then communication can become effective.

Adjusting for different physical experiences

The helper will need to be aware of and adjust for the many physical sensations the anorexic has in her starved state that are outside the experience of the adequately fed person. The detail of these was described in Chapter Two. It is also essential to appreciate the very distinct contrast that exists, when she is at low weight, between the physical feeling of being empty and the way this feeling changes when she eats even quite small quantities of food. Larger amounts eaten regularly will leave her feeling 'like one great big digestive tract'.

Failure to appreciate that the low-weight anorexic is speaking from a place that is physiologically different from that of those who are adequately fed has vitiated many medical research projects and investigations, and there is no progress to be made in terms of therapy by making the same mistake. Where the helper allows for her different physical sensations, then statements she makes about 'feeling disgustingly full', or 'being swollen and bloated', when she has eaten as little as half an orange become quite coherent and intelligible. The helper who understands them as accurate expressions of her physical experiences at low weight is more likely to be able to keep communication open.

ANOREXIC: I couldn't eat at lunchtime. I never eat till evening. That's my rule.

HELPER: You'd feel swollen up, even if you ate say an apple and a biscuit . . . You feel much better not eating at all.

ANOREXIC [looking suddenly relieved, as if discovering 'Here's someone who knows; someone I don't have to pretend to!']: Yes . . . It's always much easier not to eat.

HELPER: If you don't eat, then you don't get that terrible depressed feeling afterwards.

ANOREXIC: Yes.

HELPER: Like a kind of 'mood crash'? Does that describe it for you?

ANOREXIC [more alert]: Yes. That *is* how it feels . . . [Opening up] I got really upset I felt so awful yesterday after supper [This sufferer's only small food intake in the day] I'd been really cold and I knew I had to eat – but I felt terrible about it. My brother found me crying in my room, and my parents just thought I was being stupid. But it does make you feel so disgusting and really low when you eat. No one understands that.

HELPER: No. They don't. [Pause] The trouble is . . . till you've eaten a little bit more and put up with having these terrible feelings afterwards for quite a few more times, there is no way you can get on top of these feelings. At the moment slight shifts in your blood sugar are going to change your mood catastrophically.

The experienced helper knows that this, or something very like this will have to be said to the anorexic *over and over again.*

Adjusting for different implicit values

The helper's difficulty in communicating with the anorexic about the way she experiences her bodily states does not arise only because at low weight she is making statements about her physical experiences from a different physiological baseline. Like everyone else the anorexic uses her mental faculties to understand and creatively interpret her bodily sensations in terms of her values and her beliefs about herself. So she interprets all the physical experiences she associates with non-eating as morally positive, and all those associated with eating as morally negative (see Chapter Nine).

When the anorexic is obviously too thin and still rigidly refusing food, there is the greater temptation for the helper to assume that the sufferer 'must be able to realize that she cannot go on like this.' It can be useful, as with polarized thinking, for the helper to imagine a template set on the sufferer's values that completely reverses the ideas of good and bad, safe and unsafe. This helps adjust for the fact that the sufferer is using these ideas in a topsy-turvy way.

Nurturing a sense of self

No helper can work with anyone, anorexic/bulimic or otherwise, without their being willing to come to the next appointment. This most minimal co-operation is more likely to be given to the helper who, by making the appropriate adjustments, conveys an accurate and genuine understanding of the way the sufferer feels. There is a balance to be achieved between creating the appropriate safety and engaging her curiosity, which may occur initially as a result of the unusual responses she receives from a helper who is informed, even though these responses open up risk for her. Either provides a point from which minimal co-operation can be negotiated, such as coming for a next appointment.

Acknowledging the sufferer's need for control and thus at first not breaking down the little self-esteem she has is, in the long term, far more conducive to recovery. *The person who dismisses what the sufferer says is dismissing the person she currently is.* Interventions that attack her control destroy the only thing she really wants, and in so doing destroy her. They ensure she will continue to feel hopeless, despairing, a confused failure and 'something less than a human being'.

Whatever her current weight, the sufferer needs to find out for herself in quite practical ways how destructive her style of thinking is. When she begins to discover this, she will then need support and practical information about how she might begin to change. Such information will be the most valuable and enduring where it is learnt gradually through her own, first-hand experience. Meanwhile the kind of beginning that can be made in setting this process in train will always depend on her physical state, her current weight and pattern of food and body control, the circumstances in which she is living and the speed at which her weight is falling. Given that the natural progression of the illness is for weight to drop, an assessment of the amount of time there is available before an anorexic's weight becomes dangerously low is crucial to the helper's decision about what, at any point, should be the immediate focus of help.

References

1 Slade, R. (1984). *The Anorexia Nervosa Reference Book*, London, Harper and Row, 10.
2 Slade, R. (1984). Ibid., 97–100, 113–14.

· ELEVEN ·

Good medicine

We have said the single most important piece of information a helper can have about an anorexia nervosa/bulimia sufferer is her current weight, for it is this that gives a ready guide to the kind of communication that is possible, and that gives information about how urgent her need is for better nutrition. Different weight bands – and we will identify four of these – typically present a different cluster of problems. Identifying which band applies to a particular sufferer is an essential first step in adjusting help to individual needs.

While these four weight bands or stages reflect the most commonly occurring patterns within the condition, the time at which some symptoms occur varies. Although some chronic anorexics keep themselves at dangerously low weight levels by vomiting everything they eat, and others regularly take large amounts of laxatives, and some do both at once, this persistent simultaneous use of all the possible forms of weight and body control is usually only arrived at after a chronic condition lasting several years. For the sake of clarity problems associated with vomiting and laxative abuse will be discussed in Chapter Thirteen where issues that usually arise at higher weight bands will be considered. The point to note here is that the combination of binge eating and vomiting, together with habitual misuse of laxatives, provides the greatest threat to survival when the sufferer resorts to these at low weight.

The lower her weight is, the more constrained communication will be, and conversely the more pressing the concerns aroused by the anorexic's debilitated physical condition. How her physical needs in this lowest band of weights can most constructively be met, given her anorexic style of thinking, is the subject of this chapter. As weight increases, and as long as care is taken to sustain as far as possible her sense of physical and psychological safety in relation to food and weight, the focus of therapy will gradually widen to include other aspects of her experience. This widening of focus will be reflected in the content of each subsequent chapter.

50–65-per-cent AEBW: emaciation and medical help

As we have said, there is strictly speaking no medical cure for anorexia nervosa. The medicine required is food, and the problem is how to provide this in a way the sufferer can accept. There are techniques for refeeding an emaciated anorexic that are available to those who are medically trained that are not available to other helpers. But the medical options for refeeding are much more limited than many people believe or indeed hope, particularly when the more inappropriate and/or destructive approaches have been discarded.

It is not just because some refeeding must be achieved that hospital is the best place for the very low-weight or emaciated sufferer. Emaciation can bring about medical crises that only a hospital has the facilities to cope with. But, once such hazards have been successfully avoided, the techniques for refeeding in a way that reduces the threat that food presents to the sufferer can in principle be used inside or outside hospital. Which context is the more appropriate is a pragmatic decision and can go either way, depending on the circumstances in each individual case.

It should not be assumed, on the one hand, that using these techniques at home is necessarily easier or more humane if, in practice, this means giving extra tasks and responsibilities to a family that is already reeling from years of coping with an anorexic. Likewise the sufferer herself may find it easier to make some initial changes in a different situation, away from home. On the other hand, it is easy to exaggerate the competence of hospitals, as institutions, in providing food in the consistent and non-threatening way that the anorexic needs.

How much time do we have?

The helper's priorities must change as the sufferer's weight falls, and in the 65–50-per-cent weight band the thresholds of physical change become critical. It is not possible to do psychotherapy with a corpse.

An anorexic who is controlling her food intake by starvation alone, and whose weight is falling slowly (around 1 lb. a week) is usually medically safe until the point where her weight reaches 60-per-cent AEBW, *provided that no other factor is influencing her health*. Injury or illness rapidly alters the picture for the worse (see Chapter Three). However determined or content with herself the sufferer sounds when she is severely emaciated, it will be necessary to admit her to hospital at or below this point. Should her weight fall as low as 50-per-cent AEBW she may die within days. (These levels can be calculated, as shown in the Introduction to this book, from the tables in the Appendix.)

There are important qualifications to these thresholds however. If she is losing weight at a more rapid rate (i.e. 3–4 lb. a week), then 65 per cent is the level at which her condition must be considered medically dangerous. All of these percentage weight levels must be calculated from the original body weight, rather than the average expected body weight (AEBW), if the sufferer's rapid weight loss began from a point where she was substantially over weight (see Chapter Five for examples).

If food intake is markedly reduced and vomiting is occurring (either self-induced or, more sinisterly, spontaneous vomiting), then hospital admission at once is the only safe measure. Electrolyte imbalance and dehydration, in addition to malnutrition, are a lethal mixture. Dehydration and constipation can lead to gastric or bowel perforations due to gas pressure occluding blood flow in the wall of the gut, and so producing gangrenous patches in the gut wall. Infections in severely malnourished patients do not produce the same signs, such as feverishness and raised white cell count, as they would in a normal person. If patients cannot spare the resources to make the protein antibodies in response to an invading bacterium, they may have fewer symptoms, but they are the more gravely ill. An observer's impression that a patient is ill, and more ill and listless than she was the day before, should overrule laboratory results and thermometer readings.

It is essential that the helper should keep a close check on the degree of emaciation from the point where a sufferer's weight falls to around the 70-per-cent level. Between 69- and 65-per-cent AEBW the probability is that, unless she soon comes to the point where she can decide to attempt the task of refeeding herself with her therapist's help, she will need medical help to be re-fed. This will be all the more probable where the emaciated sufferer has no previous relationship with the helper she has been brought to see.

An unpractised helper, or one without ready access to medical support, will need to prepare at this level of just below 70 per cent for the possibility that medical care will be necessary and be aware of the time referrals, through a general practitioner, can take.

The helper must not assume either that, even if weight loss has been slow but steady before, it will continue at a steady rate. The anorexic's preoccupation with food and non-eating increases the lower weight she is. All other matters fade into the periphery of consciousness or are expressed only in terms of food/body control. With a very reduced range of ideas left to work with there is the tendency for food restriction to intensify just when its consequences become serious. Her weight may plummet suddenly. This must be responded to urgently. If a 1-lb.-per-week loss suddenly becomes a 3–4-lb. loss in the most recent week, then the helper should act immediately by calling in medical help. Any changes in behaviour at this point, such as moving from solid foods to liquids only or losing interest in a beloved pet must be taken seriously. At this stage she may well stop eating or drinking altogether. If she does, it is an emergency. For there are only ten days or so in which to get eating restarted. If she stops taking all fluids as well, then a critical point is reached in only 36–48 hours.

50–65-per-cent AEBW: communication

Sometimes life-saving measures must be the first consideration but, handled with appropriate care, these measures need not entirely alienate the sufferer from those providing the needed medical help. However emaciated she may be, she is not just a body.

ANOREXIC: They don't believe me when I say I feel better when I don't eat. But I do.

HELPER: Yes, that's right. You do feel better when you don't eat.

ANOREXIC: The more I tell them about how I feel, the less they believe me. The less they trust that I'm telling the truth. It's difficult if they don't believe me.

HELPER: You want to be believed. [The girl nods] And the truth is you feel really bad when you eat.

ANOREXIC: Yes . . . but *why* can't they believe me?

HELPER: They see you now as so starved you could die from starvation any time. And they're treating that as more important than you feeling better when you don't eat.

It is crucially important to meet the sufferer where she is, even when she is very emaciated; to acknowledge genuinely what she says and appreciate that her extreme statements are accurate for her because she is speaking from a position where her perspectives are extreme. Anything else here is to oppose her and, as we have shown, such confrontation works in a curious way to confirm the validity of her extreme thinking. When this happens, the helper becomes as stuck as she is.

The task, certainly when the sufferer's thinking is so constrained, is to hold the intermediate position that she cannot. While demonstrating genuine understanding and acceptance of her position, the helper can encourage very limited moves away from this extreme, which at this stage will focus on moving in the direction of eating a little more food. This for the helper means getting the information across that, while she/he understands and accepts the sufferer's way of thinking and feeling and believes the truth *for her* of what she is saying, she does not share her anorexic view of the position she is in. The message the helper needs to get through to the sufferer is, 'I understand; but I don't agree.' The helper who demonstrates that she/he genuinely understands and also genuinely disagrees will not fit conveniently in either of the sufferer's categories. This different experience can, as we have said, arouse her curiosity, and spur a helping relationship.

The lower the anorexic's body weight the greater difficulty she will have in following even quite simple conversations. Any verbal communication at this stage must be direct, clear, repeated and repeated often. Anything complicated will merely confuse her or make her frightened and/or angry about losing control over eating. She will often look far away and rather blank, and will easily be overwhelmed by attempts to communicate with her because she is unable to cope intellectually with the ideas that others are trying to get through to her. Everything has to be repeated because she rapidly forgets. Her preoccupation with not eating will be so extreme at this stage that it will be difficult for her to keep any other thought in focus.

Not only the way of talking to her but also the content of conversation must be simple; acknowledging her feelings, giving facts truthfully, dealing with *one* item of any topic at a time, and dealing with food because this is her central concern. It is vital that only one person engages her in conversation at any one time – unless the purpose is to overwhelm her on a particular topic. A statement such as 'You cannot leave hospital tonight. The last bus has gone. It's raining. It's cold. You are too thin to walk home, and it isn't safe anyway,' will be more effectively made by two or three staff together.

Whatever the message it will be conveyed as much by the helper's attitude and bearing as by what she/he says. Body language and tone of voice will support or deny the helper's verbal statements. If there is a mismatch between these, if helper does not believe what she is saying to the anorexic, then the anorexic will sense this and become dismissive or confused, even when she is very emaciated. Where a helper does get through and obtains even minimal co-operation, the task of caring for the sufferer's physical need for food will, to the same degree, be less fraught.

Refeeding the anorexic in hospital

Essential nourishment can be given by intravenous drip, or using a nasogastric tube (a tube that goes from the nose through the gullet to the stomach), or a liquid diet, or eventually a mixture of normal meals and additional fortified drinks, or normal meals and a bedtime drink. Obviously the first two of these methods are possible only in hospital. The procedure that is appropriate will differ in each individual case and will depend on the extent of the anorexic's emaciation and her physical condition.

Whatever a sufferer's weight, it is psychologically more beneficial to start the process of refeeding slowly and increase nourishment by small steps. The lower her weight, the more essential this will also be from a physiological point of view. Thus the total daily calorie intake will also vary from individual to individual and will depend on the amount of nourishment required for the task in hand. The first step is to work out what the particular sufferer will need to take to gain weight – for example, 3000 calories per day – and then (given there is one calorie per ml for most proprietary tube feeds) to start with one sixth of that amount (500 calories) at half strength (plus 500 ml water) the first day, increasing to one third at half strength the next day and so on till the full volume of fluid (i.e. 3000 ml) which at this point consists of 2000 ml tube-feed plus 1000 ml water, has been reached. Then from here, and by exactly the same steps, increase the strength of the feed but keep the volume the same. If the patient is not sick and normal bowel sounds can be heard, then the whole process can be accomplished over four to six days. But the iller she is, the lower the initial amount of nourishment that must be given and so the longer it will take to work up to giving the full amount the refeeding process requires.

Intravenous feeding

Intravenous feeding carries risks so it is usually only employed when a severely ill patient has developed a condition, such as gastric dilatation or paralytic ileus, in which her digestive system cannot absorb food. These are two conditions which are unfortunately likely to be produced by refeeding a sufferer who has a low serum potassium level and who has stopped eating altogether for a few days. Sometimes the intravenous route has to be used because the anorexic's emaciation has reached the point where there is not enough time left to reach an adequate intake any other way. The risks arise because food substances in solution are an irritant. This means a large-calibre vein has to be used to introduce them, and any infection inadvertently introduced will therefore spread very rapidly, a serious hazard, especially in a severely emaciated patient.

Nasogastric-tube feeding

Nasogastric-tube feeding is a procedure which has become easier to implement since proprietary brands of sterile tube-feeds and thin, supple, silastic tubes with flexible weighted ends have become available. These are so much easier both for the patient and for the staff and block so much less often that this method is no longer a feared last resort.

A co-operative patient will find that, once the tube has been gently introduced into the nostril and pushed until its tip is at the back of the throat, she has to swallow only a large mouthful of water and the end of the tube will curve and slip down into the oesophagus almost under its own weight. A gentle nudge from the doctor's or nurse's hand and a few more swallows of water will have the tube in place down the oesophagus into the stomach. This may be used for the patient to be fed with the entire amount of the necessary food.

Alternatively, because of the ease, speed and relative comfort with which a nasogastric tube can now be introduced, it is possible to encourage the anorexic, who is even marginally willing to make the attempt, to try for herself to drink either the whole, or some part of her prescribed liquid diet during the day. This can be done in the knowledge that, if she does not manage this by bed-time, a nurse can put down a nasogastric tube and let the amount that remains to be taken infuse overnight. With the aid of a pump this can go down at a slow, steady trickle and also avoids the abdominal discomfort created by the arrival of a 'bolus' of liquid in the stomach, as used to happen when liquid food was pushed down a tube at hourly intervals by the syringeful.

Nasogastric-tube feeding ties the patient to a drip stand, so its use effectively means bed rest. In our view the extra effort involved in letting the patient have a bath when one container of tube feed has gone through, and before the next one is started, is well worthwhile in terms of maintaining her morale. But it would be foolish and unkind to let her bathe with nutrient liquid still going down the tube. The temptation to disconnect and let the fluid food run into towels or dirty bath water would be too hard for her to resist.

Much less nursing time is needed in using this method, which is significant where ward staffing levels are less than generous. It also permits a flexible approach to feeding that gives scope, where there is the necessary psychological support, for the patient to attempt to feed herself and therefore retain some sense of autonomy, even in this situation. It can be used permanently or intermittently until she has achieved a weight level that is medically safe.

Liquid diet

The next level is where the sufferer takes a wholly liquid diet consisting of prescribed amounts of fortified drinks, such as Build-Up, Caloreen, Polycal, or a protein powder such as Maxipro for those who cannot tolerate milk because of lactose allergy or firmly held vegan principles. The problem here is that a great deal of nursing time and effort will be taken up at this stage, but this is a point we will return to.

Ordinary food, with or without liquid supplements

It is unwise, if not impossible, for an anorexic to switch in one step from a wholly liquid diet to three normal meals per day, and certainly it is a move that is inconsistent with the process of gradual change at all stages that, in the long term, is more beneficial.

The introduction of one meal at a time is the change that is most appropriate to start with. The sufferer herself will usually know which meal to pick to begin with, and the dietician's expertise can be used to reduce the patient's liquid diet by an equivalent amount of calories. The aim will be for her to graduate slowly to three ordinary meals and three snacks or fortified drinks per day. A pattern of meals which will maintain weight, plus drinks between these meals to provide extra calories needed for weight gain, has the advantage of teaching the sufferer to eat the kind of meals she can safely go on eating after discharge from hospital.

Moderate aims for weight increase

It is, as we have said, both unrealistic and misguided to bring an anorexic's weight up swiftly to a near normal level and then to expect she will feel better or be cured. Weight gain by itself is not a cure. Recovery depends on change of mind, and change in a total way of being. Necessarily this is a lengthy process. As a treatment on its own, rapid weight gain gives her neither the time nor the inclination to alter her fundamental beliefs about herself.

An aim that is more appropriate to the nature of the illness, and one that can be more straightforwardly justified to the sufferer, is to bring her up to a weight that is medically safe and which gives her a margin of a few pounds which she can lose without immediately being a medical risk. Where she has the support of an informed helper, and her circumstances generally are likely to enable her to maintain her recovered weight, or at least not to lose it again rapidly, then weight gain to 70-per-cent AEBW can be enough for the time being. Where she has little emotional support, refeeding to 75 per cent will give an extra margin weight she can lose without hospital admission having to be repeated at once.

While increasing her weight to this level draws the anorexic away from the extreme of life-endangering emaciation, it does not enforce upon her the real extreme of bringing her rapidly to a normal or near normal weight level and bringing about more emotional change than she is ready or able to cope with. As such it is both a demonstration of the possibility of middle positions, and an intermediate solution to the practical problem of her emaciation having reached the point of endangering her life.

From the perspective of the adequately fed non-anorexic person this can readily be seen as a moderate approach. But the helper must bear in mind that for the anorexic an increase of a single pound is her 'other extreme'. She will still be highly disturbed by the minimal weight increase involved in bringing her to a level where she is temporarily physically safe. Nor will this intermediate step remove her state of starvation. It will, however, bring her to a point where those around her will be able to relax a little, simply because they know she is not in immediate danger of dying of starvation.

No one who has been involved in helping an anorexia nervosa or bulimia sufferer has not at some time wished for an instant cure, and for all anxiety to be over. But it is important that parents, doctors and others concerned to help are moderate too, and realistic rather than polarized in their expectations. A sufferer cannot 'get better all at once'. But, when she is at least physically safe, there is a margin of time gained in which important steps can be made in continuing to assist her towards a degree of psychological change which will match the enforced physical change she has just undergone. Where her relatives are less anxious, the likelihood is that such help will be the more productive.

Helping the anorexic feel safe

Since her thinking is extremely simple, it is generally helpful to keep the context in which the anorexic is to be re-fed simple too. Hence there are advantages in admitting her to a medical rather than a psychiatric ward. The more predictable order and routine of the medical ward are more appropriate to her rigid thinking. The psychiatric ward or unit is by comparison a much more complicated environment; there is a wider range of unpredictable behaviour among patients and this, along with the less formal organization and less easily perceived routine, can overwhelm an anorexic. It can feel like the chaos and confusion that so terrifies her. If an anorexic loses her sense of routine, she will cling all the more rigidly to her food control.

As a patient in an ordinary medical ward the consequences of her non-eating and her body's need for food can be presented to her at a simple and straightforward physical level, as encapsulated in the following statement made to a newly admitted anorexic patient (at 4 st. 10 lb. – 57-per-cent AEBW) by her medical consultant.

> I am Dr X, your consultant. It's clear to me that you are very malnourished and at risk of dying. I don't understand too much about why you are not eating. But it's my job to see you receive enough nourishment to stay alive. We won't give you too much. It'll be hard for you to trust us, I know. But on my ward we don't let people die of starvation.

Where the actual task of refeeding is concerned, there are clear advantages in carrying out this procedure in a medical rather than a psychiatric ward, for in this context refeeding can be handled by hospital staff as another of the relatively matter-of-fact medical treatments that are carried out at prescribed times. In a medical ward her refeeding will seem ordinary because, for all the patients here, the emphasis is more specifically on bodily needs. The kind of help that can easily be given using a nasogastric tube is also an unremarkable procedure on a medical ward, and so the more comfortable psychologically for the anorexic. On a psychiatric ward it would be unusual and therefore conspicuous. It is also the case that actually getting hold of the necessary tube, giving set, drip stand and pump would be difficult as nowadays psychiatric hospitals do not hold stocks of these pieces of equipment.

Admitting the anorexic to a medical ward makes it much easier to convey the message to her that it is her physical safety that the hospital staff and her family are worried about. An anorexic who is being admitted to hospital for the first time is likely to be strongly resistant and possibly confused about why this is necessary at all, particularly if she is initially admitted to a psychiatric ward. For she believes there is nothing wrong with her actions. She has been praised and admired for being self-controlled in the past, and she feels better for being in control of food now. Nor will she be unaware of the stigma that is attached to being admitted as a psychiatric patient. This, together with the confusion of experiencing her good behaviour being labelled as bad and/or mad, can undermine her even further. It is proof again that, however hard she tries to get things right, she always ends up getting everything wrong.

When an anorexic's weight is at say 57-per-cent of her AEBW her doctor can tell her genuinely that the refeeding programme being organized is to prevent her from collapsing, or collapsing again, and from soon dying of starvation. Although she may still violently reject the idea of being re-fed, the message may get across, again particularly if the necessity for refeeding can be related to a specific deficit that the sufferer herself is aware of. 'I knew I was weak when I was down that low [In this case 61 per cent AEBW]. I remember when Martin [the speaker's husband] brought me up to the clinic, I could hardly put one foot in front of the other to climb the stairs. But I still thought I was all right.' This relating is easier when a sufferer has already fallen off her bike or is bruised from tripping over the kerb as a result of her starved state.

Where a sufferer's physical state is not immediately endangering her life, it is helpful if her doctor is genuinely honest about this too and provides her with the actual reason why she is being admitted to hospital to be re-fed at say 69-per-cent AEBW.

> At this moment you're not immediately in danger of dying. The danger point will come if you carry on doing what you are doing without increasing the amount of food you eat each day. Right now your parents are so desperately worried, I feel I have to admit you to hospital because they can't cope. I want to see that for a while you take more nourishment. And I think it'll be helpful to you if your parents become less anxious, knowing you're here and having more food. Would you agree with that?

Though the sufferer will not be overjoyed at the prospect of having no escape from eating enough, she will characteristically be aware of the anxiety she is causing those close to her and will dislike herself intensely for giving them so much worry. Reducing their anxiety will make sense to her in terms of her being sensitive to others' feelings. She does not get what she wants in terms of maintaining absolute control over her food intake, but she is nevertheless pleasing others.

This is an example of the way in which it may be possible to help her by bringing into focus some of her other cherished values that starvation effects will have pushed further and further to the periphery of her consciousness. It is an example of working with her by working with her own conflict, rather than setting up a situation that is totally against her. Her response will always depend on how emaciated she is, the previous experiences she has had of being treated in hospital, and how realistically she feels she can trust the helper.

Where the situation she finds herself in is to some degree understandable to her, in terms of her own values, there is the possibility of her maintaining some minimal self-respect. Where, on the other hand, the situation she finds herself in is incomprehensible to her, she will feel the more confused, frightened, angry, and will be very much more resistant. This happens when she senses she is being lied to (as when a person denies being angry with her, and she senses the anger) or when she feels that in some way she is lacking information that is important to her (as when those around her fail to tell her why they have arranged for her to be admitted to a psychiatric hospital). Low weight though she may be, the anorexic is no different from any other human being in these respects.

Refeeding and the need for predictability

Whatever her feelings about hospital treatment, the anorexic's need to feel in control of what is happening to her in relation to food and eating is absolutely paramount. Here too a great deal can be gained by working with her rather than against her, by acknowledging and acting upon her need to know exactly what food she is being given, how much, how frequently, and why. She will feel safer and more understood if as much as possible in her life can be made utterly predictable. So whatever information nursing staff can get through to her about what is happening is helpful, particularly if they can at the same time acknowledge her real panic at the increase in the amount of food she is being required to take.

Her need for predictability has a very practical side to it. For instance, she will always feel safer when her menu is organized around complete sachets or containers of the prescribed fortified drinks. To bring her a sachet that is twice the size of the prescribed amount, that she or a nurse has to divide in half, is to introduce uncertainty. She will not trust that the amount she is having to take is *exact*. Likewise, where ordinary meals are her prescribed food, these must be delivered as named, pre-arranged, standard portions. The anorexic must *know* that if a 4-oz. portion of cottage cheese and one medium-size jacket potato with salad is what is on the list for a specific meal, then that is what she will get. It is useless to present her with 3 oz. of curd cheese and three small boiled potatoes and tell her it amounts to the same thing (which is roughly true) because for her it is not *safe*. More than this, it demonstrates to her that the hospital staff are not to be trusted, because they do not understand. Her feeling is: 'If they understood how I felt they *couldn't* bring me the wrong food.' Meanwhile it has been found to be helpful for the nurses on the ward, the dietician, the doctor and the patient herself each to have a copy of a previously agreed and mutually signed menu so that misunderstanding can be prevented.

Reliability and exactness are essential support for the anorexic to eat, and this also includes having her prescribed food presented to her at the pre-arranged time.

If hospital staff can grasp this, they will make the extra effort needed to bring the anorexic her fortified drinks exactly on time and not keep her waiting for something she does not want. Nurses who forget the 2 p.m. drink until 3 p.m. and then say 'Why didn't you ask for it?' add insult to injury. As one sufferer said, 'They know I don't want it. Why the hell should I have to beg for it! It's not as though they're doing me a favour when they bring it.'

Where minimal co-operation has been enlisted and a sufferer has agreed to take pre-arranged amounts of liquid food if they are presented to her, this minimal co-operation must be recognized for what it is. More will be achieved by appreciating just how much she has agreed to in this, rather than by stretching her willingness to co-operate beyond its current limits. Her attitude is exemplified by the sufferer who said: 'No. I haven't had anything all day. No one brought it. I'll drink the stuff if you give it to me. I won't ask for it. I never said I'd do that. I only said I'd have what the staff gave me.'

To achieve the kind of security or containment she needs it is appropriate and often quite explicitly helpful for her pre-arranged food to be entirely 'boring'. It does not matter if, as a balanced menu, she eats exactly the same items of food every day. If she is feeling even minimally safe about food, she will to the same extent be less anxious and more able to give whatever degree of attention she can, in her low-weight state, to therapeutic help of a slightly wider nature – if this is offered or possible in the context she is in. But where anxiety overwhelms her, as easily it will, there will be absolutely no room for any other thoughts but those concerning food and body control. She will feel absolutely threatened and totally panicked.

Food as medicine

Whatever the context in which her food intake is increasing, whether in hospital or at home, it can be helpful for all concerned if food is seen and treated as medicine. For the anorexic it is helpful not only from the point of view of her emaciation, but also for her ease of mind. This is a conventionally understood way of saying, 'I appreciate you don't like it; but your body needs it.' Nor is it only a useful first step. In relation to the anorexic's need for complete predictability where food is concerned the analogy can be followed through.

To present anyone with a green pill one day, a blue pill the next and a yellow pill the day after, while insisting there is no difference between these pills and they are 'all just as good for you', would be a very effective way of inducing extreme anxiety in any individual: a sense of not knowing what he or she was being given or having done to him or her and of having no control over his or her own body, or own safety, or indeed over his or her own life. Yet this is precisely the anorexic's experience in relation to the food she is required by others to eat.

Likewise where, for example, the stated and agreed prescription has been two red pills three times a day, it is equally anxiety inducing for a person who is afraid these two red pills really *are* bad for her to find that suddenly, and with no previous negotiation or agreement, she is expected to take three red pills, or two red pills and a blue one. Hence the anorexic's resistance to much of her treatment. One girl's ability to confide in her doctor during a ward visit shows how this applies.

ANOREXIC: I said I would drink half a pint of fruit juice and 50 grams of Caloreen. But I'm sure they're giving me more than that.

DOCTOR: What gives you that feeling?

ANOREXIC: I never know how much it is. The first day they gave it to me in a glass. But the nurse brought it in a cup last night, and the one on duty this morning gave me a bigger mug . . . [Then as one uncertainty has arisen, further doubts are stirred] . . . and I'm sure they're putting in more Caloreen each time. It's thicker today than yesterday. [This doubt was in fact unfounded, but clearly the sufferer would have been less likely to have been anxious about viscosity, had the volume been always visibly the same.]

An unhelpful but all too frequent response here is, 'Don't be so silly. Of course it's the same amount. It just looks different because it's in a different container.' But knowing an anorexic's need to be absolutely sure that she is being given no more and no less than the agreed, pre-arranged amounts of liquid food, this doctor was able to respond in a more helpful way.

DOCTOR: Sometimes it looks as though they've given you more than we agreed, and sometimes less. [The girl nods] And you'd feel more comfortable if it always came in the same thing, wouldn't you?

ANOREXIC: It wouldn't make me so panicky if I could be sure how much liquid they were giving me.

DOCTOR: Does the glass feel safest?

ANOREXIC: Mmm. I'd rather have the glass. That's what it came in first.

DOCTOR: OK. I'll write it on the menu. Your drink should always be given in a standard hospital glass. So it's there for everyone to see.

The increments and alterations necessary to gain weight must also be made in gradual stages, and the patient will need to be consulted over these so that she is assured of knowing what is going on. She will also feel more comfortable with increases in the food that she is already agreeing to take, rather than having to cope with items of food that are different. For instance, increasing her two slices of bread to three slices, rather than introducing a small potato at this stage, to go with the two slices of bread she has been eating. Her menu may seem unexciting in the extreme. But as we have said the task is not to give her a varied and exciting diet. It is to enable her to eat increased amounts of essentially balanced food. Sameness and predictability equally create the necessary security early in therapy at higher-weight stages.

Avoid offering choices

Since it is in the nature of the condition that the sufferer cannot easily make choices and decisions over the most minor matters, it is not helpful for hospital staff or others to persist in presenting her with choices about food, either in an unthinking way, or from the mistaken assumption that it is 'kind' to offer her the freedom of choosing. The need for any spontaneous decisions, however small, will catapult her into the very confusion that is the core of her problem and which she will always resolve by not eating. 'A nurse came up out of the kitchen and said, "What do you want with your salad? Cheese or egg?" And I was gone. I ran away. It was too much. I didn't come back, not for hours.' A more helpful approach in this instance would have been for the nurse merely to have said to the anorexic patient in question: 'Here's your salad, like you agreed with Dr Y. You said egg or cheese was OK. You had cheese yesterday, so I ordered you egg today.'

Discovering preferences and making decisions are part of the therapy (see Chapter Fourteen), but the primary task of the nursing staff on a medical ward is to contain the anorexic in such a way as optimizes the possibility of her taking in food and minimizes her panic and confusion. Even without being given food choices, her level of panic will be very high in a situation where she is being made to eat. There are many ways in which this will become evident. Some were illustrated in Chapter Four. She may staunchly refuse to take her prescribed liquid food, and switch off the pump attached to the nasogastric tube. But her resistance by day and the number of times she turns off the switch during the night are a measure of her terror at losing control, and/or her anger that her control is being violated. Her actions need to be understood this way, rather than ignored or used as a cue for blame.

Making hospital staff comfortable

Doctors in a general hospital are usually more comfortable when refeeding an anorexic patient can be handled as a straightforward medical procedure. Nurses too work better where they know what is required of them, where their task is clearly defined. Where ward staff are comfortable and informed, it is easier for them to give the anorexic patient the support and reassurance she needs, and which is as important for her eventual well-being as implementing her increased food intake.

In the course of their duties, nursing and other hospital staff quite normally talk to the patients in their care. The least that is required for the low-weight anorexic over and above this is that they should talk to her in a way that demonstrates some understanding of what her feelings are likely to be, and so create some chance of relating to her rather than alienating her. For example, the nurse who is helping her, routinely, to suck an ice cube or swallow some water so the nasogastric tube can slip down, and so she can be fed whatever part of her planned intake she has not been able to take by herself during the day, is making an important contribution if she makes a small effort of imagination to see the situation the way her patient is seeing it. Thus she may say:

> You look terrified (angry/upset). I appreciate you'd rather not have it at all, but really it's your medicine that's going down this tube. Can you think of it as medicine? You'll die you see, if you don't have it. Look, all you need tonight is these two cans of Clinifeed, as we arranged. I'm *not* going to give you any more than you need. I promise you I won't. [This is, of course, a promise that must be kept!]

If it is borne in mind that an increase of even half a pound in weight, however it comes about, humiliates and destroys an anorexic, communicating with her along the above lines is more appropriate and more wholly nurturant than communicating in such a way that strips every remaining vestige of self-esteem from her by accusing her of 'stupidity' and 'unreasonableness'. A nurse is not being helpful who says or implies by her attitude, 'This is unnecessary stubbornness. I'd have thought you could have managed to drink this during the day.' Even saying 'Try a bit more' can seem to the sufferer to be an accusation that she has not really tried at all so far. Saying 'Well done' when she has drunk everything is even worse. The more emphatic and enthusiastic the praise, the greater the anorexic's certainty that she has had too much. Her reasoning will be, 'If they didn't expect me to have it all it must have been too much.'

The level of psychological support an anorexic needs while she takes the required nourishment is another reason why it is both practical and appropriate to refeed the sufferer on a medical ward to approximately 70-per-cent AEBW, and after this move her to a psychiatric ward to continue with an entirely liquid diet, and eventually a mixed diet of fortified drinks and ordinary meals. It is quite commonplace for an anorexic to find it totally unbearable even to pour her prescribed liquid food from its container into a cup. Most anorexic patients need 'specialling', that is, having a nurse sitting with them and attending to them until all of their 'food' is taken, and for half an hour afterwards to see they do not go and vomit. Doing this five or six times a day, which is the frequency with which a very emaciated patient will need to be fed, can monopolize one nurse for 9–12 hours. Nurses on medical wards follow laid-down procedures; they carry out tasks for patients, giving injections, changing dressings and so on. They are not allowed just to be with patients for long stretches of time. But nurses on psychiatric wards on the other hand have to be able to 'special' certain patients.

Considerable emotional resources are needed for a nurse to sit with a frightened, angry and unwilling girl of her own age or just above and without getting angry or blaming her firmly sustain the certainty that the 'food' will be taken because it is vital. Few registered general nurses (RGN) possess such resources. Most nurses without psychiatric training, and alas some with, resort to the cajoling, critical, judgemental approaches which others have already proved useless and harmful.

Generally any moral qualms about 'persecuting' the patient that may arise from unexamined beliefs that food intake should be a voluntary, and/or pleasurable activity make it impossible for a nurse or any other helper who holds such beliefs to succeed in feeding a convinced anorexic. Food has to be seen as essential medicine, and the helping task as supporting the patient to face and manage her fear of taking it.

The importance of psychological support cannot be underestimated. Nor should this support be conditional on whether or not she eats. Such an experience is nothing new to an anorexic. Likewise deferring her own wants and needs until she considers them to have been earned is the sufferer's own pattern. She will learn nothing from helpers who behave in the same withholding way. On the other hand, enabling her to feel she is worth talking to whether she eats or not is to provide her with a different experience, and one that may instigate change.

Problems of hierarchy and organization

There are certain practical difficulties in implementing the above strategies for refeeding the low-weight anorexic in hospital. Though she may need to see food as medicine, food does not have the same importance as medicine in the hospital setting. Nor do those who serve food have the same status as those who give injections and hand out 'real' medicines. It is hard to get those hospital staff who do not see the patient yet supply, cook and serve her food to realize just how important these matters are. If one-and-a-half small slices of wholemeal bread are put on an anorexic's supper tray instead of the pre-arranged single large slice, weeks of painstaking confidence building can be undone. Yet the limited communication possible between doctors and kitchen staff make it very difficult to ensure that those who provide the anorexic patient's meals understand the importance of their actions.

Other organizational factors also have to be accounted for. Where her menu is adjusted to increase her food intake, at least two days need to be left between each adjustment in order to prevent chaos in the supply line between hospital kitchen and ward trolley. The low level of literacy of some night-time ward cleaners employed by contract cleaning organizations has resulted in the cleaner, who had been given the instruction that no food should remain in a ward fridge overnight and who could not read the label which said: 'Use on Saturday', emptying the fridge at midnight on Friday, throwing away all of Saturday's fortified drinks for the ward's anorexic patient. This angered and frustrated the dietician and unhelpfully threw the patient into panic. In general the more direct contact there is between staff, and the shorter the lines of communication, the more smoothly the refeeding process is likely to run.

The use of sedatives in hospital

The anorexic can become extremely upset at being admitted to hospital for refeeding. She can be highly recalcitrant in her refusal to eat, and her behaviour can become very distressing and alarming, particularly where in her desperation she resorts to self-harm. Doctors may consider it appropriate therefore, as part of their responsibility in caring for her, to sedate an anorexic patient.

Some doctors might consider medication to be necessary in order to save her life. It can be useful while tube feeding is in progress to counter her alarm. But where such measures are employed, communication will be hampered. Drugs such as chlorpromazine tend to hinder progress. The larger doses make psychotherapy impossible. Certainly if she is sedated she will be a 'safer' and less distressing patient. This may be useful to those nursing her, and other patients need to be considered.

In the context of staff shortage it may also occur that there are not enough staff available for anyone to have time to talk her through her panic. Temporary medication may be better than leaving her alone and terrified. But the question is, how long should such emergency strategies be persevered with without some attempt being made to address the important task of attending to the anorexic as a human being.

It is characteristic of the condition that sufferers become more disturbed as their weight rises. But as a result, where they are treated on an in-patient basis, their medication is often adjusted accordingly. Thus, as they 'get better' physically and become more aware mentally and emotionally, their prescribed doses of antidepressants and tranquillizers tend to be increased. So they are shut down again, but by prescribed drugs rather than starvation. If drugs are used for anxiety, the *minimum* effective dose is always the best choice.

Problems of communication are difficult where a person's thinking and feelings are affected by drugs, just as they are when they are affected by starvation, and the more so where both effects are combined. There also seems little point in increasing an anorexic's weight at such a rate, and to such an extent as necessitates having to resort to drugging her in order that she can 'manage' emotionally at the achieved higher weight. A prolonged need for such measures would usually indicate that weight gain is proceeding too fast. Even in this lowest 50–65-per-cent weight band, once she is not actually dying of malnutrition, the anorexic needs to be helped to catch up psychologically with the enforced physical change and to be given the necessary time for this. It is communicating with her even at this stage, allowing her to begin to express rather than suppress her still anorexic self, that is important for securing the bottom rungs of the stepladder that will eventually enable her to climb out of her anorexic lifestyle.

We have indicated the possible necessity, and some of the drawbacks of sedating the anorexic while she gains the minimum amount of weight that will bring her part of the way, or even all of the way up to the level where she is medically safe. There need be no obligation on her to suffer the extreme emotional discomfort that is involved in eating and gaining weight. It may be more comfortable for her in some ways if her feelings of panic and terror can be temporarily suppressed, for instance, over a period such as a bank holiday weekend when 'her' doctor or nurse will be off duty, or there are fewer staff available than usual. However, there is a great difference in the experience of the anorexic patient who is sedated against her will and re-fed, and the experience of the patient who feels she has had at least some say in her treatment. Sedation will always be the more useful, therapeutically, where the sufferer gives her own genuine consent, where she is helped to feel that she has some control over what is done to her, and how long it is continued. Whether this can be achieved will, particularly in the case of the new and very frightened patient, depend on the helper's ability to get through to her.

DOCTOR: You found it difficult last night, lying here with all this food going into you.

ANOREXIC [silent]

DOCTOR: Look, I know it's terrifying. Sister told me you managed to switch the pump off five times during the night.

ANOREXIC [sullen, but also scared]: I don't want to get fat.

DOCTOR: No. I appreciate you don't. That makes you really panicky. [Pause] You must have the food. That's to keep you alive. But panic is very frightening. I don't think your fright is helping you at the moment. How about having something to help you have some sleep?

ANOREXIC [looks dubious, but says nothing]

DOCTOR [anticipating a possible fear]: No more food. Only as much as we arranged before. . . . But how about a night's rest from the panic, and all the other feelings? Try it just for tonight? And I'll come and see how you feel tomorrow?

ANOREXIC: I'm scared about the weight.

DOCTOR: Yes.

ANOREXIC [quietly, and after a long silence]: OK . . . because I am terrified . . . but I do need sleep. [Pause] Just for one night though.

An 'experienced' self-starver who has become familiar with her pattern of weight loss and the emotional turmoil that refeeding creates may, particularly if she has an adequately long-standing and trusting relationship with her helper, feel able to negotiate 'not feeling' for a period during the required refeeding process. Thus:

DOCTOR: Your weight's drifting down. It's 64 per cent now, and with all the pressure you're under you're not going to be able to eat more yourself, are you? And you seem so much more exhausted. How about coming into hospital for a while? We'll take you back up to 70 per cent, and then see how you go from there. Maybe things will have settled down a bit . . . elsewhere in life. . . . And we can refresh the plan for your menu as well while you are in. You may be ready to move on from baked beans on toast for supper by now?

ANOREXIC: I don't want to, but. . . . Well. I suppose so. Oh, I can't bear it. If I did come in on Friday could I have something . . . something so I can pretend it's not happening, just for the first weekend. I don't really want to be too awake the first couple of days – till I get used to hospital again.

Though this situation has happened, it does not happen very often, but it is worth bearing in mind as a possibility where there is a genuine relationship between sufferer and helper.

Dividing the task of help

An anorexic can be very unwilling to enter into a therapeutic relationship with those who are, or have been actually involved in refeeding her and making her put on weight. This is another reason why it can be useful for this particular task to be undertaken, when she is very low weight or severely emaciated, by those whose concern is clearly medical, and for emotional support to be provided by someone else, such as a psychiatrist, psychologist, community psychiatric nurse or psychiatric social worker. Ideally such a relationship with her non-medical helper or therapist would be fostered from the beginning of the refeeding process and continued through to the point where, having reached a medically safe weight, either the sufferer is transferred to a psychiatric ward or she then continues to receive help on an outpatient basis or in individual therapy. For what is needed is a constant helping relationship, usually lasting over several years. But such an arrangement is difficult to obtain in the hospital context. A large proportion of therapy in hospitals is conducted by junior staff whose careers move them at six-month or shorter intervals. Furthermore, many psychiatric units cultivate an ethos that suggests the procuring of rapid results through sophisticated techniques of intervention. This is an ethos in which a patient who has shown no change or only limited change over a year-long period – which is commonplace where a person has been anorexic for a number of years – is likely to be considered a failure. Hospitals are therefore generally better geared to the provision of intense short-term care in an emergency or crisis than they are to providing the continuous, long-term therapeutic support necessary to an anorexic.

· TWELVE ·

Turning around

This chapter deals with the tasks of helping when the sufferer's weight level is within the band of weights between 65- and 75-per-cent AEBW.

Where the sufferer's weight is falling, her weight loss by the time she is 75-per-cent AEBW must no longer be ignored. The trend is a real cause for anxiety, yet there is still some way to go before her weight reaches a level at which life-saving medical help becomes urgently necessary. Personality changes will certainly have taken place. She is hooked and will respond to any adversity by tightening her control.

However hopeless they may feel, at this stage relatives and friends are not without the means to gain some leverage on the problem. In this band of weights there are real deficits in performance, and these can be used to initiate action. Others should *not* make allowances for her diminished concentration, for the longer time it takes her to perform her usual tasks, for her tell-tale accidents. If they do, they simply enable her to get worse. As we have said, it is helpful to insist on the legitimate expectations that accompany the relationship they have with her, and it is usually possible to insist she sees somebody for an opinion on her health at least.

It is always worthwhile informing a sufferer about the nature of the path she is on but, however carefully and repeatedly she is told about the dangers of her lifestyle, it is unrealistic to expect that this will bring about an immediate change in her attitude. The anorexic's disbelief is often one of the helper's first problems.

> Everyone kept saying I'd have to go into hospital, but I knew they were wrong. I was sent to see a counsellor. She said the same thing. But I thought I was OK. I stopped going. My parents were still getting at me. It went on nearly a year like that. Then in the end they made me go into hospital, but I didn't believe I was ill.

Though helpers may know it can take a long time for an anorexic to acknowledge there is a problem, her disbelief can still be startling. A woman who has been severely restricting her food intake for at least ten years, who has been admitted to hospital several times during this period to be re-fed, can still say, 'I don't believe I'm anorexic. I was reading an article about it. I don't think I'm like that.' However, by the time her weight has fallen to 70 per cent or below, her belief in food control will have taken on a rather desperate air. Any alternative but to continue just as she is will seem the more unacceptable and terrifying. She dare not believe her control is a problem.

How to begin working together?

Where there is both refusal to accept that there is a problem and such great terror of change, it is difficult for help to get started. Substantive areas of agreement are needed so that both parties can begin to talk about the same thing. At the beginning the helper may have very little to work with except her/his ability to demonstrate an understanding of how the sufferer feels (see Chapter Ten). From any point of agreement the helper must build outwards until more and more aspects of the condition become shared knowledge between helper and sufferer. This usually takes time, months at least. It also requires close attention to the detail of her experiences and how these relate to her weight and her eating. This will be a genuine two-way learning process, and particularly so for the helper with limited experience with anorexia nervosa/bulimia sufferers. For there are many subtleties in the way in which a sufferer's feelings and sensations will vary with changes in her intake and ingestion or otherwise of food, and each individual will be a little different in these respects. The helper must aim throughout to provide the sufferer with an adequate feeling of safety. She will easily be overwhelmed and terrified of going out of control, and terrified people do not change. They usually deal with their fear by tightening their defences and so fail to take in and assimilate information.

Working with rather than against control

As the previous chapter showed, a greater sense of safety can be provided by working with the sufferer's need for control. This is not mere strategy but a responsible approach from the helper who is aware of the ease with which loss of control and desperation to regain it can move the sufferer from square to square on the board described in Chapter Three, and who recognizes the more complicated dangers that follow from food control by means other than self-starvation and exercise.

The nature of the anorexic's control is the first thing the sufferer and helper must come to agree about. For while the helper knows the natural course of anorexia nervosa is for weight to fall and knows the sufferer is trapped, the anorexic believes she is regulating food appropriately, doing so entirely of her own volition, and making continual effort to do so.

Offering an experiment

The way to build common ground over what is actually happening is for the helper to suggest that the sufferer tries to hold her weight stable at exactly the level it currently is, to aim for the time being not to increase it, but not to let it drop any lower either. To suggest this as a first step is equally appropriate at weight levels above the 65–75-per-cent band of weights. But where an anorexic is within this band it is a particularly relevant exercise in terms of enabling her to avoid the need for being re-fed in hospital, if this is what she wants to avoid. It also allows other crucial therapeutic issues concerning choice and decision making to arise.

Whether her weight is falling, has risen from a lower level or is swinging up and down, it is within this band of weights that it is still or again becomes possible to suggest she engages on the experimental task of holding her weight stable. For at this stage the necessary degree of communication can be achieved despite her low weight. Within the 65–75-per-cent weight band there is a narrower band at 71–69-per-cent AEBW where the sufferer tends to notice changes herself. If she has previously been more emaciated, she will find, as she comes up to this threshold, that she is more generally aware, but also that she feels more disturbed and uncomfortable. Where her weight has previously been a pound or two higher she will sense herself as more distant and psychologically more comfortable from 71 per cent downwards. The practised helper meanwhile will find it slightly easier to get through to her, compared with when she was more emaciated, or find it necessary to be even more simple, direct and repetitive than previously when she was a few pounds heavier.

Suggesting an experiment helps sufferers grasp a working understanding of what it is they are being asked to undertake jointly with the helper. This is something that tends to elude them, particularly when weight has been very low. The idea of a scientific experiment provides a familiar structure that is not too complex to cope with, and a framework that clearly maintains her position of being in control. Experiments by their nature run for a limited time span. This is also useful because, where there is no setting of this kind, sufferers feel compelled as a result of their polarized thinking to hold for ever and ever to any change they do introduce. Effectively an experiment can also be free of ideas of success and failure, for whatever happens during it or afterwards there will be something to be learnt.

HELPER: My idea is that you try to have an extra 200 calories a day, just for this week. As an experiment. For you to see whether this amount of extra food stops your weight falling quite so fast. We can talk about exactly what the 200 calories can consist of in a minute. What do you feel about the idea of doing this experiment?

ANOREXIC [shrinks back and says nothing]

HELPER: It's awful even to think about, isn't it? And it won't be comfortable to do. But how about trying it, just for this week? You may not be able to manage it all; or you may. But whatever you do, or don't manage, it'll be part of the experiment. Will you try it?

Others' anxieties may be reduced if they understand she is engaging at least to this extent with her problem, and the helper may encourage her by indicating this possibility. It can also be directly supportive if the helper, with the sufferer's permission, intercedes to stop relatives and others pressuring her while she attempts to keep her weight stable. The suggestion to experiment, if adopted, will not only enable a sufferer to find out more about herself but also allow her, and the helper, to discover how much control she actually has at this present time.

Discovering anorexia is in control

It can be startling for the anorexic to discover that, in spite of her belief that she could maintain her current weight at a stable level, it still continues to drop. It can shake her to find self-starvation does not give her the total secure control she thought it did. For example, Anya had been low weight for nine years, had been re-fed in hospital twice in this time and was enduringly convinced she would not need to go into hospital again, even though her non-eating was clearly leading to the point where her emaciation would soon become physically dangerous. But, after being routinely weighed by her therapist at each meeting over the previous seven months, it was possible to show her in good time how, in spite of her beliefs, her weight had gradually fallen by rather more than half a stone to 71-per-cent AEBW.

HELPER: What do you feel, about this graph, looking now at what's happening to you?

ANYA: Well . . . Shocked. Yes. When you see it like that . . . I've gone into hospital before when I've weighed more than this, because everyone got worried. It was when you [MD] said, just now, it doesn't seem to be in control. That's what really shocked me. [Looking puzzled] I can see that. It doesn't.

The inescapability of choice

In such a case, where the sufferer's weight is falling relatively slowly and a relationship has already been built between her and her helper, there is still time (a length of time that could be roughly calculated) during which it would be possible to go on supporting her while she gradually increases her food intake by small amounts to hold her weight stable at the new level, or while she continues on her slow downward path which would lead to a fairly predictable point in the not-too-distant future when she would need to be re-fed in hospital.

To start this process from scratch with a new client at this low-weight point would be more difficult. But it is not impossible.

Once she has begun to discover that her food restriction does not give her the control she previously believed it did, the anorexic is faced with an acute problem. Either she has to struggle to make some alteration to her pattern of extreme food restriction, with all this means in terms of her terror of losing control, or she can carry on as she is, knowing it will lead to her control being taken from her. She has to decide whether or not to change course and, if so, how. Not only is this exactly where she is paralysed (see Chapter Eight), it is also a very highly charged decision point, for she is a person whose core means of conflict resolution is prolonged not-eating.

Though she will be very resistant and find it very hard to move from the habitual safety of non-eating and to risk suggested change, it is helpful to make it very clear to her that this *is* a choice point, and a choice point that is inescapable. It needs to be held in focus that whatever she does or does not do, she is effectively making a choice either way. To do nothing, that is to make no change in her pattern of non-eating, is still to choose, but to choose by default.

> My responsibility, as your therapist, is to see you have the care that you want and need. We both know your weight's gone down again this week, by another pound. I appreciate you really felt it wouldn't. . . . If you lose x more pounds though (that'll bring you to a level of 65 per cent), then we'll need the help of your GP to take care of you. From looking at you, and seeing how very thin you are, my guess is that he'll be afraid of you dying of starvation. He won't want that. (I don't want that either.) But at 65 per cent he'll see it as his responsibility to get you admitted to hospital at once because of you're so emaciated. . . . That's the way you are going. Do you want that?

Focusing on the fact that this is a decision point, and reminding her repeatedly of the unavoidable implications of her choosing by default, the helper is persistently drawing the anorexic's attention to the true position she is in. This is a very uncomfortable position. Either option will seem equally intolerable to her. It is important therefore that she is given adequate emotional support in being led to this point, and that she is enabled to work through it.

It is not helpful to bring her to this point and then adopt the attitude that 'This choice is entirely yours. Whatever you decide to do is your own responsibility.' This is to abandon her, and to do so in a way that gives dangerous and misleading confirmation to her strongly held principle that she ought to be totally responsible for everything and ought to manage entirely on her own. It is also to fail to take into account the critical changes that starvation creates in the process of decision making. Rather at this point she needs continued support and encouragement in undertaking the enormous task of reclaiming real autonomy in her decision making. She also needs help to assimilate the idea that she does not have to be entirely on her own in experimenting with how to resolve this situation. She can be helped, particularly in being shown in practical ways how she might gradually move from her point of polarization to a more intermediate position.

Since the task is to encourage the sufferer towards making her own real choices, it is essential that the helper makes it clear too that she does not have to do as is being suggested, there are no 'shoulds' or 'oughts' involved. Thus a helper may tell her:

> You only need experiment if you want to. My suggestion is that you make a small change for this week. Then when you come next week, we'll look at how you've felt, and at what's happened. But you don't have to make any change. I don't mind. Whatever you do, either way I'm still prepared to give you the support you need. But this *is* a choice here for you, though it might not feel like it. . . . So I'm concerned that *you* know fully which way you are going.

The helper must also make clear exactly what the small experimental change is that she/he is suggesting, as we will show.

While the helper may say that there are no 'shoulds' or 'oughts' involved in experimenting with change, she may sense nevertheless that the sufferer is feeling coerced, and it is helpful to check with the sufferer to find out whether she does. It is safe to push, or coerce, providing the sufferer knows and accepts that the helper is pushing, and knows that the helper knows (see also Chapter Fourteen). While there need be no obligation to make any experimental change, the facts of her particular situation *must* continually be brought into focus. The lower her weight, the more frequently the consequences of her actions remaining unchanged will need to be reiterated. For the more emaciated she becomes, the more she will see food restriction as her only option, and the more closed she will become to altering course.

HELPER: It's difficult for you, I know. And you might feel it's easier to let the hospital take over. You can do that if you like. That's OK by me and, because your weight's dropping steadily, it's going to be necessary soon. . . . Can you feel what your reaction is when I talk about you letting the hospital take over? Is that what you want? . . . It may be that it is . . . [Gently] What are your feelings about this? Do you feel a 'Yes' or a 'No' inside you?

Though obligations may be genuinely removed, the anorexic will still find it very difficult to make any decision. It is her pattern to let others make her choices. So the helper, often through her/his own unclear dithering or anxiety, may be drawn into making the decision to hospitalize her, thus taking responsibility for her, but with neither helper nor sufferer being aware that this is actually what is happening because the issue is so delicate, or so fraught. So this possibility needs to be brought into the open, with the helper making clear statements about her own position, and what she perceives is afoot.

HELPER: I don't want to make your choice for you. But I wouldn't be doing my job if I didn't say that you are coming to the point where *I* will have to make a decision to refer you for medical help. This point will come only if you decide to make no changes. Because then I will reach that moment when I consider it's no longer physically safe for you to go on eating as little as you are now. . . . So you will be choosing, all the time, even by doing nothing. Choosing to reach the point where I make that decision. D'you see?

This will need to be said softly, gently and slowly. Body language must be free of all threat. This will be helped if eyes are at the same level and helper and sufferer are both sitting at the same height.

Allowing the necessary time to choose

It can take months in therapy for the anorexic to accept that she is stuck, and to pluck up the necessary courage to act differently. Possibly the helper will need to stand by her as her weight continues to drop, while she learns about the inevitability of her falling weight.

At all stages of the condition, however, and particularly when her weight is very low, parents and others will be inclined to define weight alone as the problem and want to know why quicker progress is not being made in dealing with such an obvious symptom. They will also expect the sufferer's emaciation to be magicked away and her standards and values left intact, and they nurture the hope that, if her emaciation is treated 'directly' by making her eat and gain weight, the sufferer will be able to continue at school or with her proposed career, and life will return to 'normal'. There may be difficulty therefore in getting relatives to accept that an approach that involves the sufferer gaining weight at a pace that matches psychological change is legitimate or useful, even though it is in fact more conducive to long-term recovery. There are rare occasions when psychological change proceeds by leaps and bounds; then rapid weight gain can be welcomed and encouraged. But usually the pace is tentative and slow.

During this process crises will occur: crises of lost jobs, disappointed careers, difficulties with relationships, increased anxiety and impatience in members of her family and other key people in her life, and the crisis of falling weight. It is these very crises, however, that bring the anorexic to a point where she may begin to see the need, and eventually the possibility, of taking a different kind of action. These are the crises that give her the impetus to experiment with change, and it takes practice and skill on the helper's part to 'hold' an anorexic whilst allowing the crises to happen so she can constructively learn from them.

Yet while the constructive use of crisis can have a key part to play in the therapeutic process, the helper must not lose sight of the fact that anorexia nervosa is a life-threatening condition. Complacency is dangerous.

Calculating safety: recognizing danger

When an anorexic's weight is around 70-per-cent AEBW and falling, the helper must be alert to the possibility of her condition becoming physically dangerous, and an accurate weight is the most simple yardstick for judging the extent of concern that is needed.

A sufferer may resist being weighed. She may also try to protect her anorexic lifestyle by contriving to appear heavier on the scales than she actually is, by, for instance, drinking quantities of water before her appointment with the helper, or carrying coins in her pockets, or even, as one girl did, going to the lengths of sewing fishermen's lead weights into the hems of her clothing. Like switching off pumps and pouring liquid food into empty drink cans in the hospital ward, she is not so much cheating or lying by using these ploys as indicating the extent of her fear/anger/resentment at what is being 'done to her'.

A practised helper who uses regular weighing as a structure for sharing information, and as a focus for helping the sufferer relate the minutiae of her experience to these facts, may learn to sense when there is a mismatch between the sufferer's measured weight and her appearance, or how she makes the helper feel. There are the obvious signs of increasing physical danger to be noted: her hollower cheeks and more sunken eyes, the bluish-mauve colour of her hands and other extremities, sometimes extending to the lower parts of her legs and forearms, the tell-tale 'wire coat hanger' look that her clothing has, and since, as her weight falls her day-to-day life becomes the more hazardous, bruises may provide evidence of her increasing accident proneness. The development of puffy swelling in the ankles and legs (oedema) is a serious sign, and talking with her may reveal that she is experiencing dizziness when she changes posture quickly, because of increasingly severe postural hypotension. The inability to sustain physical effort is a clear indication that the sufferer's condition has become dangerous. Although such weakness increases as emaciation progresses, the point where it becomes evident happens suddenly. *Its absence is no proof that the sufferer's condition is not serious.*

There are other important factors in addition to physical deterioration which are relevant to a helper's calculation of how much time is available before medical help with nutritional first aid becomes necessary. Any change or potential change of routine, such as is created by a holiday, Christmas or other celebrations, by guests staying with the family and so on is a threat to the anorexic, and she will always respond to such threats by reducing her food intake. Alterations in the weather must also be taken into consideration. She will be at risk of losing weight more rapidly if there is a sudden cold spell. Examinations and journeys are also danger periods which disrupt precariously balanced eating routines. The kind of support or otherwise the sufferer has from relatives and friends specifically during these events, and generally, will also be significant in relation to losing further weight.

The helper must become closely attuned to each individual sufferer, even if her low weight is not yet near crisis point. Patterns vary in each individual case. Depending on how few calories per day she is allowing herself, how much she is exercising, and the rate at which she is already losing weight, one may temporarily hold her weight stable on less than 800 calories a day; another on the same intake of food will lose weight steadily at the rate of two pounds per week.

Anxiety in the helper

Encouraging the anorexic to be her own scientist and allowing weight change at a pace that goes hand in hand with psychological change are slow processes and can be nerve-wracking for the helper. However, like any other relevant factor, the helper's own anxiety can play an important part in helping the anorexic to change, particularly where some trust has already developed in the relationship between them. The informed helper can create a context in which the sufferer feels safe. But the extent to which this context should be anxiety-free must be based on reasonable and informed judgement of her physical condition, and the helper's own feelings of anxiety. It is neither realistic nor appropriate for a helper to remain unconcerned, and it is actually dangerous for a helper to give an appearance which *looks* free of anxiety, where the sufferer's weight is around 65-per-cent AEBW and falling rapidly, and if there are signs that she is cutting down still further on food.

On this evidence it is entirely appropriate for the helper to present her own anxiety as a fact relating directly to the sufferer's deteriorating condition. It is a fact that needs to be expressed straightforwardly, repeatedly, and in a manner that shows awareness of the anorexic's feelings, but at the same time makes it clear that the helper's feelings and consequent judgements are based on different information from her own about what is going on. For example:

> HELPER: I know you feel all right as you are. But I'm anxious. I'm worried because you've found it too difficult to start eating a slice of toast at breakfast time [the suggested small change]; you're looking more pinched; you've said yourself you're slower, taking longer to get things done. Right now I think we've reached the point where we should soon arrange for you to have some help. Looking at how your weight's falling, my view is we can only go on like this for two more weeks at the most. How do you feel yourself reacting to that?

The helper should wait for, listen to and clearly acknowledge any response the sufferer may give to such a question and restate, if it seems appropriate, that she is causing anxiety. The helper should not be afraid of being boring, but be gentle, firm and very repetitive. It takes a long time for information to be taken in. Hence:

> I'm anxious about you because of the way anorexia goes. It doesn't stop by itself. You *will* keep on losing weight till it's dangerously low. Your present weight is on the edge of the 'danger zone'. Losing any more will tip you right into it, and then we'll need emergency action. That's what I'm worried about. How about you?

The helper's own informed anxiety can be a constructive element in the crisis that low weight presents but must be informed and well grounded. Where the helper is jittery and begins to be inconsistent or variable or is swept into unreflecting panic, this will not help at all. It will wipe out any trust there might have been, and the anorexic will then certainly not risk any change. She will feel guilty at being the cause of this anxiety and/or disappointed and utterly betrayed by the helper's apparent inadequacy. Either way she will end up immobilized by the helper's being, in her experience, yet another person who is unable to cope with her – and she will cling to her food control.

Choosing to change

A sufferer may not necessarily prefer or be able to make the enormous effort to refeed herself. Nor should it be assumed that, if she feels at one point that she can make this effort, she will consistently feel this way; or that, if she does attempt to refeed herself, she will manage to take the necessary steps to increase her intake enough to prevent her weight from continuing to fall. This road is a hard one. The sufferer will be reassured to know that the helper is aware of how hard it is. Nor is it failure still to need medical help when she is in the position of having tried to go against the grain of the illness, but without effect. The helper must let her know this.

> HELPER: It can be too much of a struggle to eat enough. You get panicky, compensate by not eating at all, swim 80 lengths instead of 60. That's how anorexia goes – and so you keep losing weight. I don't see you as a failure

if you can't manage the change to your eating that you need to make to stop losing weight, and so it happens you need help in hospital. It's a hard pattern to alter.

ANOREXIC: Mmm. [Thoughtfully] I've got to resist the resistance.

HELPER: You're right. And that's hard.

Where she continues on her path downwards until refeeding in hospital becomes necessary, she will need continued support. Anorexics do not have the existential stamina to withstand too many changes of helper. Continued contact with the person with whom she already has a therapeutic relationship can enable her to feel, even though she has been admitted to hospital, that she has not been totally abandoned to strangers who have no understanding of her needs.

Where, on the other hand, she expresses even the most minimal willingness to experiment, she will need to be shown step by detailed step what she needs to do, either to keep her weight stable or, where it is falling fast, to level off gradually the downwards curve.

Practical planning for experiment

A sufferer whose daily intake has been 300 calories would need to begin by trying to increase that intake from 300 to 900 calories per day by 200-calorie steps. So the first week she would attempt 500 calories per day, the next week 700 calories per day and so on. The suggestion should be that she attempts four small meals per day, adding the initial 50 calories per meal to the small amounts she is currently eating, and spacing meals regularly through the day, with the last meal near bedtime to assist sleep. Being unable to sleep, the anorexic will usually see the point of this.

Discussing together and noting down what is to be the precise content of each small meal are essential parts of the experiment. Absolutely clear aims are helpful, and she can be encouraged to build towards a balanced diet initially on the kind of foods she is already eating, and that she likes. If she has reduced herself to half a slice of toast for breakfast, she will generally feel safer about increasing this to one slice, with a quantified amount of butter and marmalade, than about eating something quite different like a bowl of cereal. If she is only taking liquids, then a first move would be to work out four meals consisting of soups that are not low-calorie soups, and of fortified milk drinks. Proprietary brands of dietary supplement can be useful in this instance, such as the carbohydrate powders Caloreen and Polycal, and the high-protein drinks such as Build-Up and Complan. These can all be obtained from chemists. Different food items, most helpfully the ones she likes but currently is not allowing herself to eat, can gradually be introduced after she has got over the hurdle of the first experimental change. She will also cope better where the quantity or calorific value of food is easily calculable. Two digestive biscuits are always safer than one small homemade cake.

As in Chapter Eleven it is useful to use the idea that food is her medicine. Rather than the helper listing the agreed meals and their exact contents, and each week's adjustments, it is more helpful for the sufferer to take charge and write her own 'food prescription' with the helper alongside her. This may seem a small point, but this arrangement will give the sufferer a greater sense of control, a greater feeling of the possibility of taking real responsibility for herself than where the helper writes out her 'food prescription' for her experiment.

Routine and predictability will be absolutely essential, as ever. So she will need help not only to plan her eating, but also her routines of work, exercise and indeed leisure. The more secure she is in these respects, the more she will be able to cope with making changes in her eating. Empty or unstructured time is a great danger to an anorexia nervosa/bulimia sufferer, and work will have acted for her as a defence against eating. Because she is so terrified that she will never be able to stop eating if once she starts, the helper can usefully suggest to her that she can create her own safety net by using her known ability to stick to allotted periods of work, and other specific activities that she enjoys, in a positive way to protect her from her fear of her refeeding going out of hand.

It is also helpful if relatives and others can support her at each stage in not eating more than the pre-arranged menu. If she is worried or frightened because after her prescribed meal she still feels hungry, which will usually happen when she begins to increase her food intake, it will help if she and the helper discuss and organize a way for her to manage this potential danger-point safely, for instance, arranging a planned top-up amount – a single item of extra food that she will know she is allowed to eat, like a piece of fruit or a carton of yogurt – that will be there for her to have if necessary.

In view of her emaciated appearance, such minimal increases may seem ridiculous to the onlooker. But small incremental steps of the order we have described are changes that the anorexic is more likely to be prepared to try, particularly where her helper is clearly prepared to accompany her through the many feelings that even the prospect of these changes create, and through the many experiences that even small increases in weight awaken in her. Where there is continuing help and support, any gain in weight is more likely to be permanent. Permanent weight gain is also likely to be the result of regular meals. Weight gained by chaotic eating feels so guilt-laden and wrong that it is nearly always lost again.

It should also be appreciated that for a sufferer who has reduced her daily intake to 200–300 calories a day, which is by no means unusual, to suggest she begins by increasing this first by 200 calories to an initial 400–500 calories a day, is to suggest that she immediately doubles her daily intake, and to work towards 800–900 calories a day is to work towards eating three or four times as much food as she has become accustomed to. Apart from her fear of instant obesity and chaos, even these small steps will usually cause her a great deal of physical discomfort as her digestive system readjusts to this greater amount of food. Each goal needs to be realistic. Only when she is securely eating 800–900 calories a day, will she feel safe to experiment with the next step of adding a necessary extra 200 calories to her daily intake to bring it to 1000–1100 per day. Expectations of the likelihood of her achieving these goals must be realistic too. For the first week or so she may well not manage to increase her intake to the level suggested, or even to make any change at all. She may increase her intake from 300 to 500 calories the first two days, then return to the safety of her previous routine and lower intake. But within the framework of the scientific experiment this need not be seen as failure so much as a discovery of how risky change is, or how frightening, or how little courage she seems to have, or whatever has been her experience.

Information relating to food, body functioning and alterations of mood can usefully be provided as it becomes relevant to the feelings and experiences she is currently struggling with. Where she begins to feel that the frightening changes involved in eating more do not take her into a territory that is total unmanageable chaos, but that her helper can give her a predictable 'map reference' of the many different feelings, moods and uncomfortable physical sensations she is experiencing, so her sense of safety will increase. Where she begins to have the confidence that her helper can find her if she gets lost, panicky and confused as she makes small moves to explore change and begins to experience the feeling that she can be helped to get her bearings again, then she is more likely to begin the attempt to eat and slowly to gain weight.

As with her need to please others, the strong moral attitudes that have taken the sufferer into anorexia nervosa can be openly engaged to initiate the process of her moving out of the starvation whirlpool, as this ex-sufferer describes:

> I knew I was very independent, and stubborn, and I used that stubbornness to start eating. I was only drinking fruit juice and I started with one slice of toast. I was terrified. I was so terrified my stomach would stretch. I knew I didn't want to go into hospital, I was terrified of that too. But I was in such a panic that I'd eat and eat and never stop. But I didn't. Mum knew I was terrified, because my therapist had told her I would be, and that helped.
>
> My first proper meal was lasagne, and afterwards I nearly died. I went hot, and cold, and shook terribly. This happened after each meal for two to three months, but I was determined to do it.

Where she is at risk of losing her job because she is slow and cannot concentrate, the helper may usefully point out the mismatch that exists between her expressed preference for being independent and efficient and the likelihood of her losing her job, and so losing her independence. Similarly, where an anorexic cannot easily complete her examination papers because she is slowed down by the chilblains on her hands as a result of her poor circulation, the mismatch between the reality that she is crippling herself and her desire to do well in her exam needs to be brought into focus, again to find out what she really wants. If she drives a car, she must be told that, if she continues to lose weight, it will be unsafe for her to drive any more. This again is a restriction on her independence. Though her low self-esteem will ensure she ignores warnings about her own safety, she will be reached by worry about acting in such a way as might cause others harm.

The helper must not be afraid of pointing out these obvious connections. They are often news to the anorexic. Indeed they may be the only route by which information can get through to her that her position is untenable and she needs to make some change, but it will be blocked if the information is given with even the slightest admixture of blame.

Learning points

A range of learning points emerges as the low-weight anorexic begins to engage in the process of experimenting, and it will be helpful to focus her attention towards these as they arise.

She does not realize how much more she needs to eat just to keep her weight stable. This learning takes time. In terms of her own subjective experience, if she begins to eat the minimal amount to begin to maintain herself at a stable weight, she will feel she is 'eating like a disgusting fat pig'. There is a mismatch again here that can be drawn out between her experience and her actual measured weight.

She needs to be shown that there is not the simple one-to-one relationship between eating and weight gain she thinks there is. An increase of 500 calories per day for a sufferer who is 70 per cent of her AEBW and who has previously been taking 300 calories per day will not necessarily produce weight gain. Indeed this increase may barely slow the rate at which her weight is falling. But an increase of this order in calorie intake will increase her metabolic rate. Her heart will beat faster. She will feel a little warmer, and these are changes that she may notice for herself.

She is likely to be terrified at what appears to be an instant gain of a quite enormous amount of weight when she first begins to eat a little more, so it will be helpful to let her know that this 'carbohydrate effect'[1] may occur, and what actually happens when it does. When a starved person begins to eat, even a small increase in carbohydrate intake allows the body immediately to retain more water. This effect can result in the scales recording an increase of as much as 6–7 lb. in weight, although 3–4 lb. is the more usual range. This change is temporary. Within a short time most of the apparent gain disappears and the sufferer's weight falls again to almost its former level. But the anorexic or bulimic who experiences this weight shift invariably panics and immediately reduces her food intake even further. She finds it hard to accept that this carbohydrate effect is the ordinary and quite normal response of a carbohydrate-deprived body to a sudden, and even quite small increase in bread, biscuits, potato, or other starchy food. This effect can occur at any body weight after a few days' near-total starvation, or a diet of lettuce leaves and cottage cheese only. Even if sufferers are given the information that this will happen, they will still find it very hard to let it happen without subsequently cutting down or trying to cut down their food intake in the following days.

> Then there was the week my weight didn't drop. The first time for six months. I was so pleased, because I had been trying, because I didn't want to go into hospital. But I was frightened. What would happen if I put on loads of weight? And by the end of the following week, when I'd been eating extra bread and a potato with my supper I put on 5 lb. in two days. That sent me into a terrible panic. My therapist said try another week on exactly the same menu. Don't change a thing! I was *terrified*, but the week after when I saw her it had gone down, just like she said it would. Dropped right back. All I'd really gained was half a pound!

A sufferer needs to learn that her feelings and bodily sensations are directly influenced by her food intake, or lack of it. She also needs to learn that these feelings and sensations are not immediate indicators of her moral worth. She needs to become aware that there is an ordinary physiological component to her experience that results, for instance, in a predictable lethargy after eating, and a predictable loss of euphoria or mood crash. Having an accurate and testable account of her body processes will enable her gradually to disengage her judgements about her own moral worth from these feelings and sensations. Being informed beforehand about their likely occurrence can help her to stop judging and blaming herself for ordinary predictable experiences. It is important too for her to realize that feelings are temporary.

Starving and low weight or locked into the repetitive cycles of stuffing/vomiting/starving, sufferers are continually preoccupied with thoughts of food but, through experimenting, both the low-weight anorexic and the bulimic will discover that, after they have eaten enough, regularly, they will, in the end, be less preoccupied with food and be able to concentrate better on other things. With the low-weight sufferer this will be an intermittent effect at first but, as her weight rises, her general ability to concentrate will improve. She will be able to read for longer periods. Where she was previously able only to flick through the pages of a magazine, as she moves towards 75–80-per-cent AEBW, she will be able to follow the whole storyline of a novel, or watch the whole of a television programme.

It is important not to dismiss the sufferer's physical discomforts after eating, or even at the prospect of eating, as irrational or silly. She can feel choked, she can have a grossly stretched stomach, she can feel heavy or bloated or puffy. These may also be expressions of her panic at going out of control, or expressions of other feelings. But when she is very thin, and when she is beginning to take an increasing bulk of food that her body is not accustomed to, she will feel these physical changes very acutely. If she is able to talk about how she feels, physically and emotionally, and experience herself as making sense to the helper, then her fear and mistrust of herself, and of her relating to others, will slowly diminish. The helper can warn, even promise, her meanwhile that she will feel terrible in every way after eating a meal and promise her too that the feelings will pass. Each time the helper accompanies her through a turmoil of change that even these first steps create and stands by her, without criticism and without blame, each time the sufferer discovers the information the helper has given her is an accurate reflection of her experience, her confidence will increase, and the effects of this will gradually become evident in all other areas of her life.

Reference

1 Slade, R. (1984). *The Anorexia Nervosa Reference Book*, London, Harper and Row, 102.

· THIRTEEN ·
Transition

This chapter deals with the band of weights between 75- and 85-per-cent AEBW. This is a transitional stage.

At the lower end of this band the starvation effects that we have described will be present. They recede as weight reaches 80–83-per-cent AEBW, so significant changes take place around 80-per-cent AEBW. But this is only one of a number of important thresholds. Its existence, as we have said, does not constitute a reason that justifies rapid refeeding to this level. At the higher end of this 75–85-per-cent range of weights the sufferer will have regained most of her mental and physical potential. This is the stage at which there will be few traces of her problem in her appearance or behaviour, but the sufferer will find herself confused and unable to act effectively except when she achieves food/body control. Extreme confusion and ineffective action are the problems that up to this stage will have largely been hidden by the effects of low weight. But they are the problems underlying the need for food/body control.

How the helper can assist the sufferer in coping with her confusion and indecisiveness will be considered in Chapter Fourteen which will focus on the band of weights from 85–100-per-cent AEBW and over where these experiences are most present. The transition stage meanwhile creates difficulties of its own.

In this band of weights between 75- and 85-per-cent AEBW the helper will meet a very much wider range of behaviour. The uniformity that starvation creates fades away and the individual's personality begins to emerge. The possibility increases for conversations to become deeper and more complex, and for their content to include a wider range of experience. But this greater variability also reflects the sufferer's dithering confusion. Bombarded by myriad possibilities for action, and having no sense of her own direction, the sufferer shifts abruptly, and in extreme ways, between her various possibilities. Hence her vulnerability to bingeing and other forms of uncontrolled or compulsive eating. Feeling like a cork tossed in a sea of chaos can produce impulsive behaviour of all kinds. She may turn to alcohol and/or other drugs and/or become involved in sexually promiscuous relationships and/or shoplift and/or resort to varieties of self-harm (see Chapter Three).

Here we will consider some aspects of the help that is needed where the sufferer is on the switchback between control and chaos, when her inability to cope is manifesting itself in these more extreme and desperate ways. These considerations also apply when a sufferer's weight is in the 85–100-per-cent AEBW range and over, when she has reached that higher-weight stage without being given the time or help to adjust her attitude in step with her gain in weight. But they will begin equally to be relevant as she moves through this transition stage: from a low weight to a viable weight, or from not eating to eating.

During this transition help becomes more necessary rather than less so, and in principle it should be easier to provide. For, as we have said, this is the stage at which it becomes markedly easier to reach the sufferer. But in practice the matter is not quite so straightforward. There are many problems and pitfalls.

Catching the sufferer on the way down

A sufferer may have entered this stage because her weight is rising from a previously lower weight, or because her weight is falling from a previously higher weight. Her attitude will differ according to the route she has taken in arriving within this band of weights. She will be more content if she has been successfully restricting her eating, and more depressed and anxious if her eating has been out of control. Where her weight is falling for the first time she will be adamant that she needs no help. The helper should be ready to adjust to the sufferer's style of thinking as outlined in Chapter Ten. This will certainly be necessary where her weight is below 79-per-cent AEBW and can still be useful at weights as high as 83–85-per-cent AEBW.

The helper may note that, during this 75–85-per-cent AEBW transition stage, the sufferer looks 'model thin'. Even as she drifts towards the lower end of this band of weights her appearance will raise few questions and much admiration in a society that places a high value on thinness. It can be difficult to appreciate the extent to which her visible organization is functioning to keep her away from food, and her mind away from thoughts of food. As with the social drinker whose behaviour is seen as fairly unremarkable, yet who is biochemically dependent on alcohol and therefore 'feels better for a drink', the self-starver at this stage is already hooked. It is very difficult to issue warnings to a person who confidently dismisses these with self-assured offhand comments such as: 'I'm all right. You don't have to worry about me. I eat what I want if I feel hungry. I'm perfectly happy. In fact I've never been so happy. There's no harm in that, is there?'

At this stage there is only very subtle evidence that the way of life she has chosen is addictive and constraining, such as her spending more time alone, her need to know precisely what is going to happen, her panic or aggression when things do not go precisely as arranged; the sense others have of being controlled by her, of feeling that somehow she is holding all the cards; but these changes can warn that the individual concerned has become control-dependent. It is by focusing on these aspects of her behaviour that she may be led to realize there is a mismatch between what she thinks she is achieving and what she is actually achieving.

Holding the sufferer on the way up

Where a sufferer is emerging from low weight, having had the kind of help described in the preceding chapter, she may by this time begin to have a sense of being alive and real that is grounded in the experience of autonomy she has gained so far. This is particularly possible where she has reached this stage as a result making her own decision to alter her attitude, perhaps at a crisis point at a lower weight. Providing her personal growth has paralleled her weight gain thus far, then she is likely by this time to have developed just a little faith in herself. She is likely to have at least a germinal ability to like and trust herself rather than hate herself totally. She will no longer feel so desperately that she must keep up her false front. She may feel that she can show more of herself. Yet though her confidence may be growing, it will still be tentative and fluctuating. At this stage she will still be discovering or rediscovering how confused and indecisive she is. She will still be very afraid of going out of control. She may still need help and guidance over the detail of what she eats. She will also still be highly sensitive to demands, pressures and obligations, and uncertain of her ability to assert, let alone maintain her real self in the face of them. She does not know whether she can cope in this new way. She has not yet had enough practice to believe that she can. So she is still very vulnerable to being overwhelmed by fright and confusion about relating with others, about handling situations differently and weathering events as they arise. Although physically she may look as though she has recovered from anorexia nervosa, food/body control is still her easiest refuge and will be her haven when she has the slightest sense of not being able to cope.

Recovery involves continuing practice at being her non-anorexic self in the hurly-burly of day-to-day life. A less protected environment will provide her with more experience to learn from and so increase her chances of recovering. A chronic anorexic who has achieved an isolated, static, sealed-off lifestyle does not have enough happening to her to learn from. This learning and practice requires time.

The early results of her new ways of behaving need to be affirmed by the helper she trusts, if she is to persevere in these new ways. At this stage she still needs that same helper who has learned to empathize accurately with her, who will still listen and respond to her openly, honestly and as an equal, who will still be her guide and continue to provide signposts without intruding her/his own moral rules and obligations on every suggestion, who will not add judgement and criticism to the sufferer's own judgements and criticisms of herself, who will not tell her she is stupid, ridiculous or inadequate to feel so fragile still, or that her feelings are unnecessary and/or exaggerated, who does not secretly believe 'she ought to be able to manage on her own by now'.

It is usually easier to achieve this quality of help if the helper is not a relative, work-mate or landlady. Where one person has different roles, these can become difficult to keep separate.

Getting better feels like getting worse

To feel her way through enormous confusion and uncertainty towards a way of being that is new and untried takes a great deal of courage on the sufferer's part.

The helper's open appreciation of this courage will be needed, for there are many points at this or any other weight or stage when getting better feels like getting worse.

This is not an unusual experience for anyone undergoing personal change during therapy, but it is an experience that is particularly frightening for anorexia nervosa/bulimia sufferers. They are already too well acquainted with feelings of confusion and chaos, and such feelings trip them into instant panic. It was experiences like these that made reliance on the ritual organization of food and body control so attractive in the first place. The sufferer must re-experience the original difficulties to some extent, however, if she is to have the opportunity to respond differently. Looking back over the previous five years during which she had substantially recovered, one woman described her experiences this way:

> When you're just becoming unfrozen, it's terrifying. You can go back to freezing up, but the further away you get from it, the harder it is to get back, and that's appalling – the uncertainty of it all. And living with that uncertainty. No one knows how terrifying it is. You die a thousand deaths on the way up.

A sufferer will not easily *be* convinced that re-experiencing some chaos is necessary for some progress to be made. However, even the sense of getting worse can be marginally more tolerable if it can be seen as something to be expected, if warning is given in advance that this is part of the pattern of recovery. Again she will have a greater chance of coping with the process of change if she knows her helper is aware of the kind of feelings and experiences she is going through, if she knows there is someone with whom she can share the panic and the terror, someone who will not themselves become panicked, terrified or unhappy because of her state when she becomes chaotic and confused, or critical when alterations in her behaviour reflect this. Hence helpers must take their own need for support seriously.

Giving the sufferer the appreciation she needs

Once a sufferer, at any stage, begins to move away from her totally anorexic lifestyle, she will begin to perceive many small and promising changes in herself and can become quite upset when her family and/or friends appear not to appreciate what enormous steps these are for her. Indeed feeling she deserves some appreciation is in itself an indicator of her growing self esteem.

> What's really upsetting me is the way they don't seem to notice how I've changed. I'm eating a bowl of cereal for breakfast. I know evenings are still sticky. I get so edgy, and I still hide in the kitchen and hate anyone coming in while I try to make myself something, and eat it without taking a bite and throwing the rest away. But *I* had to point out that at least we don't have blazing rows in the morning now, and Dad can get off to work peacefully. That seems a real achievement to me, and it really makes me angry when they accuse me of not trying. They've *just no idea* what a struggle it's been to get even this far.

The kind of support she needs, or would like from her family and/or friends, may not be forthcoming however. Her family in particular will usually have been very stressed for a long time by their anorexic or bulimic member. Even if the significance of each small change is pointed out to them, there may still be a deep well of antagonism, resentment and despair about the way they see her as having wrecked the family's life. Whatever she does, and however she changes, there is the possibility that for them she will not be getting better fast enough, or that this improvement is too little too late.

To some extent the situation can be helped by providing her family with information about the kind of problem anorexia nervosa/bulimia is. Understanding that it is possible for any person to become drawn into the whirlpool of self-starvation, without realizing this is happening, can help lift a great deal of self-imposed blame from the sufferer and from her family. Yet even so, her family may not recognize the signs of recovery for what they are. When this happens, it is the more essential that at least her helper recognizes and appreciates the effort the sufferer is making and appreciates the courage it takes by acknowledging her steps, however small.

Changes in the sufferer's attitudes towards herself, particularly those that lead her to reveal feelings that have previously been carefully hidden, may be experienced by her parents and others close to her as difficult, unreasonable or disappointing behaviour. It will often be seen as an affront to their standards. Since more bouts of arguing, crying or expressions of despair do not look like progress, her family will almost certainly see her as getting worse as therapy progresses, so it can help if they too are forewarned that this is likely and usual, if uncomfortable. They may find this idea difficult to accept, in which case the sufferer's recovery may highlight certain areas of inflexibility in those close to her. Changes in their own values and attitudes may be a price of her recovering from anorexia nervosa or bulimia that they may be unable or unwilling to pay. Even her teachers may meet some of her changes with a certain wistfulness, or ambiguity. As a professor of psychiatry said of a recovering fourth-year medical student who was no longer working fourteen hours a day to get A grades all the time, 'It's very nice she's getting better. But it's a pity she's only getting B grades now. She was always top before.'

The sufferer who begins to leave anorexia nervosa behind may sometimes find it genuinely difficult to behave in the way others see as appropriate for a person 'of her age and intelligence.' But recognizing that where addiction begins development ends, her helper (usually more readily than her family) can allow a twenty-four-year-old recovering anorexic to be more like, say, an eighteen-year-old, or a twelve-year-old when she needs to be, and allow her to explore the feelings that go with this experience, rather than erroneously assume that since she happens to be twenty-four 'one has a right to expect that she should behave like a young woman of twenty-four.'

The constructive use of crisis

In relation to situations that arise at lower weights we described how crises can be used constructively (see Chapter Twelve), and during the transition stage too

Hurt	*Hungry*
Anxious	*Angry*
Lonely	*Listless/bored*
Tense	*Tired*
Excited	*Edgy*
Disappointed	*Depressed*

Figure 4: Checklist for feelings

crises will occur. There will be crises of panic at unforeseen events, crises of impatience with herself for not coping well enough, and so on, and she will respond to these by tightening her food control or slipping into a bulimic cycle. But learning to value herself in ways that do not centre on food and body control is a matter of two steps forward, one step back, and there may be a plateau every now and again where no progress appears to be made at all. Where both the sufferer and her family know these stages are only to be expected, it can save a great deal of disappointment and help prevent false hopes and unrealistic expectations.

When a crisis occurs, it is not failure. It is quite normal and ordinary for people to revert to old patterns of behaving when they are stressed, and it is essential that the helper lets the sufferer know this quite explicitly. Furthermore, much that is valuable can be learnt from these isolated relapses. Indeed she can learn far more from these slips than she ever could from long stretches of extreme behaviour (anorexic or bulimic), for triggering factors can be seen more clearly. One exercise that can be helpful is for the sufferer to note for herself the kind of events and situations to which she as an individual is particularly vulnerable. For instance, by ticking a checklist for feelings (see Figure 4), whenever they find themselves withdrawing from food or slipping into a bingeing episode, most sufferers find after several episodes have occurred that there are one or two feelings that receive significantly more ticks than the others. In this way they become more aware of their chief areas of vulnerability and become the more swiftly alerted to the possibility of falling into their own particular, or current, non-eating or compulsive-eating trap. It then becomes possible to formulate alternative strategies: 'non-food' activities or obtaining support, instead of bingeing or starving when these situations next arise.

Self-knowledge of this kind tends to increase confidence and, with this, self-respect. Learning to respect herself and see the value of those feelings that render her vulnerable, rather than despising herself for them and/or feeling guilty about having them, can be an important step towards finding other ways of satisfactorily expressing or constructively containing those feelings, instead of immediately 'taking them out on food'.

Because she will still be very uncertain of herself, she will be prone to see, in any crisis, incipient or actual failure. So it is helpful not to let her lose sight of the steps forward she has made, but to bring them into focus, so she can keep in perspective the fact that she is a person who can enjoy or allow her feelings and/or who can be self-directed and autonomous in matters other than those related to food.

Likewise, if the sufferer seems to have reached a plateau, it needs to be made explicit that in therapy there is no rule to say that she should continually and unremittingly progress. Should she need or want to, she is entitled just to stand still and rest. She is entitled to take the time to integrate her understanding of how far she has come.

Further learning points

There is straightforward practical information a recovering anorexic or bulimic needs from her helper that relates to bodily changes that take place as weight increases. One quite alarming but normal occurrence is that hair thins, sometimes very obviously, as any emaciated person gains weight. The anorexic who is already frightened enough by the pounds she is putting on, who finds her hairbrush or the bathroom sink full of hair each time she brushes or washes it, will need to be reassured that this is usual and to be told that new stronger hair will grow.

Likewise, as her weight increases to around 85–87-per-cent AEBW, it is helpful for her to know that, even though she has reached the level where it is high enough for there to be the possibility of menstruating again, in practice this will not usually happen until she has held this weight consistently for about 9–10 months. Menstruation can be confidently expected only if she holds her weight at 90-per-cent AEBW or higher, for fat cells are thought to produce minute amounts of a hormone that is essential to the reproductive cycle, and it takes 9–10 months for that hormone to have its effect on the functioning of the ovaries.[1]

At low weight she will generally have avoided the colds and other minor infections that other members of her family, or friends, have suffered, but as her weight increases she will 'seem to catch anything going'. So it usually reassures her to know this too is a normal and predictable, if uncomfortable, consequence of her increasing weight, and that it happens when anyone who has been very thin regains weight. It is what the body's defence system manufactures in the process of responding to the infection that causes the symptoms, not the illnesses themselves. At low weight the body cannot spare the raw materials to make the antibodies to the invading organism, so, although infection may be present, symptoms such as a fever or a streaming nose are missing.

Withdrawing from therapy too soon

At 85-per-cent AEBW the anorexic is still underweight but, because she looks better, the whole world assumes that she must be and feel better (see Chapter Six). Not only may she get little credit for the effort she is making in taking steps to change, but she is likely to find everyone around her encouraging her to act as if she is fully recovered. Since there appears to be nothing obviously wrong with her, all the usual expectations and obligations flood in: expectations that she will now be able to get back down to her school work, or complete her training, gain her degree, fulfil all kinds of social obligations, make friends and/or find a partner, take up a challenging job that is appropriate for a person with her intelligence and qualifications, have children. In general, the expectation is that she will climb back on the relentlessly rolling bandwagon of success in whatever way others see as being appropriate for her. Since she appears to be so much better, it is also assumed that she needs no further help.

The sufferer meanwhile is only too likely to accept these assumptions as valid and 'right', even though she feels swamped by them. This is the stage at which she typically tells herself she ought to be able to manage by this stage without support; she does not look as though she needs help, so she is a liar and a fraud to continue having help; she ought not to take up any more time or resources, she has taken enough, she does not deserve any more; she ought to keep her family happy and they will be happy if she is better, so she ought to do her best to seem better, and so on. Thus she will put up her old appearance of coping, whilst actually still feeling she is failing and inadequate.

It is at this stage, or at any similar point where she feels such pressures, that the sufferer may withdraw or be withdrawn from therapy, that is, unless her helper is agile enough to help side-step this development. Not yet secure or confident enough in herself, not yet liking herself enough to be sufficiently self-directed to avoid getting caught up again in the same conflicts and the same confusion, she will be unable and/or unwilling to say that she feels swamped and unable to cope, she will find it impossible to say she still needs help, or to say so loudly enough, and she will sink.

Where she clings to control, her sinking will be obvious because her weight will fall again. Depending on how long she has been anorexic and on her history during the illness, she may be unaware that she is sinking, or she may be fully aware and openly admit: 'I feel such a mess. I know I still need support, but if I get fat I won't get it. So I can't get fat.'

Far from being deceitful, sufferers are usually as honest about themselves as those around them will allow them to be. What is so painful and causes them so much despair is that, however honest they may be, they still feel helpless and powerless to change.

Alternatively the fact that a sufferer is sinking may not be obvious, because she is taking cover behind her false front in different ways, and with equally unhappy consequences.

> They thought I was better, so I thought I'd better be better. But I got worse. I had this continual feeling of being totally out of control. I ate and ate and ate, then made myself sick. Vowed I wouldn't eat and did. Felt dreadful and guilty. So I'd vomit again, or clean the chemist out of laxatives. But it wasn't just over eating. I was out of control over everything. Everything was total chaos. A never-ending nightmare. I'd run anywhere, constantly running, do anything, sleep with anybody to get away from it. Anything to block it out.

Acting out the chaos

Despite her higher weight the sufferer's involvement in food and body control will be every bit as strong, so she will continue to think in stark black-and-white, all-or-nothing terms. Hence dramatic changes in behaviour are the common pattern when a sufferer is in the transition between starvation and near normal weight, and when she is around her average expected body weight or overweight.

Because her sense of chaos is the greater, her swings into her 'absolutely bad' category are likely to be bigger, more violent; her feelings and her behaviour are in every respect more impassioned and can result in actions which are humiliating to the sufferer and alarming to others. These dramatic changes are a consequence of the way the sufferer thinks and feels at this stage. They are part of the illness and not to be considered a sudden deterioration or some new kind of problem. This perspective may enable the helper to be steady and to accept the sufferer as she is in the face of events that will be traumatic to the sufferer and devastating to her family.

Where her behaviour serves as a focus for others' disapproval, her conviction that she is utterly worthless can become the harder to bear, so she may punish herself the more stringently and/or try more determinedly to keep her mask intact. It is where these strategies fail that she may perhaps come for help for the first time, after years of being at a regained higher weight and hiding her disordered eating.

Help and care at viable weight

Just because a sufferer's weight is above or around her average expected body weight, it should not be assumed that it is no longer necessary to check her physical position. As we have indicated, the possible range of problems is greater at this stage than when she is lower weight and successfully starving, and evidence of them can be more difficult to detect. So the following is a useful checklist that the helper may bear in mind.

Patterns of food and body control
Here the task is to ascertain:

– the sufferer's current weight and whether it is stable or not. If not, at what rate is it rising or falling?

– her current pattern of restricting her food intake. Is this constant or does her control break down. If so how often? How much food does she consume in one episode? How much does she spend? Can she afford it?

– whether and with what frequency this includes vomiting and/or purging and/or using diuretics. Whether she is taking purgatives or diuretics, in what quantities and combinations is she taking them?

– what forms of exercise she is routinely undertaking and how much.

Seeking oblivion
The helper should check with her whether and to what extent she resorts to alcohol and/or other drugs, prescribed or otherwise, to escape from unbearable feelings. It is also helpful to check whether, and how often she has felt so despairing as to have actually overdosed to escape into temporary oblivion or if she has more seriously explicitly wanted or tried to commit suicide.

Self harm
Since sufferers may try to limit the overwhelming effect of their feelings by cutting or burning themselves, scratching the skin, hair pulling, banging their head against a wall or otherwise deliberately bruising themselves, visible marks should be taken seriously. It is helpful to ask her how any such hurt occurred and give her the opportunity to talk about her need to resort to self-harm, and how this relates to her feelings and their intensity.

'Deviant' behaviour
The helper should be open to the possibility that a sufferer may be desperately sleeping around, this promiscuity being an escape from her own company and/or a protection against night-time eating; also that she may have found herself stealing money or food from members of her household, or shoplifting.

Alternative ways of restricting food and obliterating feelings can occur at lower weights, but such behaviour is the more likely at higher weights. Meanwhile, for the sufferer to be provided with the care she needs, it will be necessary for the helper to be the kind of person who can be told these things.

Practical responses to the consequences of chaos

It will usually be a relief for her to find a helper who is aware that she can feel so hopeless and be so desperately out of control, who knows and accepts that this is the pattern of the illness. She also needs a helper who can give her, or direct her towards, any further practical help, information or advice she may need, as, for instance, from a general practitioner.

Since it is not possible, simply by looking at her, to tell what degree of biochemical disturbance a sufferer has created by her regular vomiting, purging or use of diuretics, it is essential that this is medically checked. As we have said, a routine blood test of her electrolytes can be requested from her doctor.

Just as it is important to increase food intake by gradual degrees at very low weight so her body has time to adjust, so it is equally important that a sufferer who is limiting the absorption of food reduces her use of laxatives by small steps, thus modifying her body chemistry gradually and the more safely. It is useful if both helper and sufferer understand in general terms how the body progressively adapts to laxatives and the hazards that sudden change can bring.[2]

A sufferer may experience a welcome release of tension as a result of gorging herself, then making herself vomit, and so achieve a sense of 'at least resolving something'. But as well as the profound guilt and self-disgust she subsequently feels, a binge–vomiting session is usually followed by lethargy, fatigue and patchy concentration. This is the result of switching on the parasympathetic nervous system, along with activating normal digestion processes. Severe and prolonged fatigue and muscle weakness can also build up, if frequent vomiting leads to a drop in the body's potassium levels.

These experiences are no more evidence of a sufferer's fundamental worthlessness than the effects of starvation are evidence of her virtuousness. But the bulimic will blame herself for her ineffectiveness, for her inability to be lively, active, clearheaded and able to concentrate, and for not doing all the things she feels she ought to be doing. So here the helper's task again is to assist her in disentangling the physical basis of her feelings from her interpretations of them, and from the implications these interpretations have for her self-esteem. The task here is more complicated than when she is simply restricting food intake, because biochemical changes are intermittent, depending on what the sufferer is doing to herself, and their effects are less predictable although her generally higher weight level will result in her being more able to listen and to talk.

A helper can begin by providing information, because the sufferer will probably be unaware of the effect that her vomiting and her purging are having on her moods and feelings. It is also useful for a person who binges and/or vomits and/or purges to find this out for herself in practical ways like again noting her feelings before, during and after these episodes. The effects may also be apparent in her diet. Talking with her may reveal that a sufferer has been drinking orange juice or taking other potassium-rich foods after vomiting or purging; thus she may learn that, without realizing it, she has, in this way, been compensating for the imbalance she has created in her body chemistry.[3]

Coming to know that her feelings and emotions are affected by her vomiting and purging can give the bulimic a new perspective on her habitual devaluation of herself. As at low weight, it can help the sufferer learn to separate her actual feelings from her moral judging. Information alone is unlikely to 'cure' the anorexic/bulimic's very low opinion of herself, but providing her with this information may enable her to peel off at least a first layer of self-recrimination, and thus take a step forward.

Mixed addictions

Where a sufferer is using or abusing alcohol and/or other drugs, the physical picture becomes even more complex and there is the danger of further addiction. These extra substances tend to create swift and frightening mood changes which exacerbate tthe sufferer's sense of confusion, confirm her ineffectiveness, reinforce her feelings of self-hatred and self-disgust and easily justify further self-harm.

Priority must be given to reducing the complexity of her situation generally. This is the first step on a path towards more productive conversations. Communication is easier when there is only one 'layer' of altered thinking to get through, that is, where there are only the changes brought about by starvation instead of unaccountable possible variables in mood and experience as a result of the biochemical changes brought about by the elimination of body fluids and/or the ingestion of various kinds of psychotropic substance in any combination. So many variables acting together produce a picture which is beyond a helper's ability to assess, let alone adjust for in communicating with the sufferer. Meanwhile the sufferer is the more likely to remain hopelessly locked in her resultant chaos because its roots are too many and too complex for her to sort out by herself.

Giving the sufferer back her control

Where a sufferer has a pattern of bingeing and vomiting and/or using laxatives, or total stuffing followed by total starving, or using alcohol and/or other drug substances, then a useful strategy is for the helper to provide such direct practical assistance as will enable the sufferer to regulate her food and eating, best of all in quantities that will at least keep her weight stable. Helping a sufferer to establish or re-establish a routine of eating and exercising, appropriately modified to fit her current individual needs, has the advantage of reducing the complexity of her physiological picture. For some multi-substance abusers this process can be started only in a residential setting.

The approaches outlined in Chapters Eleven and Twelve for creating appropriate measures of safety and predictability will still be needed. Establishing a routine breakfast of agreed amounts of prearranged food is still a useful first experimental step towards achieving a sense of organization. Likewise three days on liquid food can break cycles of stuffing and starving, or bingeing and vomiting. A sufferer will usually feel better about herself where she can begin to alleviate such recurrent degrading and humiliating episodes. By giving her practical help with regulating her food and eating, it is possible to enable the sufferer gradually to re-establish for herself the control she has lost. She needs to regain her sense of autonomy first in this albeit very limited sphere because food/body control is central to her. Where she is helped towards more safe self-regulation in this sphere, she is likely, over time, to resort less to bingeing, vomiting and laxative abuse as a way of feeling in control, or to drugs or alcohol as a way of obtaining oblivion and getting out of 'the whole confusing mess'.

Tackling every problem at once does not usually yield progress. Thus it may be useful to encourage a sufferer to concentrate first on stopping drug use absolutely, whilst not changing anything else. Any measure of autonomy that the sufferer sees herself as achieving can found confidence and create the faith in her that change is possible. The success of giving up heroin by heroic 'cold turkey' tactics has strengthened the resolve of at least four addicted anorexic/bulimics in such a way as enabled them to go on to free themselves from their original eating problem. Their attitude, as expressed by one of them was, 'If I can get off heroin, I'm not going to be beaten by anorexia.'

Overdosing and potential suicide

There is no point in the helper assuming, or pretending, that the sufferer will not already have resorted to calculated oblivion, or that she will not have brooded on or attempted suicide as a way of solving her problems. The helper who hides from these possibilities, because they are disconcerting and because they make the helper uneasy, is falling into the same trap as the anorexia nervosa/bulimia sufferer and will certainly be the less helpful to her. The expression of self-destructive thoughts needs to be allowed and the feelings that give rise to them acknowledged without judging, criticizing or blaming. It is as important to the development of a person's sense of self to acknowledge their suicidal feelings as it is to acknowledge any other aspect of their being.

Enabling the sufferer to allow suicidal feelings into the open is not only therapeutic in itself, it also enables the helper to work with the sufferer on the content of her experience. Unlike the global despair of some potential suicides, the anorexic/bulimic's anguish will tend to focus around a particular instance of losing control over food. In her panic she will see *all* as lost. Here, as at lower-weight stages, it is helpful to bring into focus the progress the sufferer has acknowledged herself as having made at other points in time, and the less despairing moments she has experienced, thus reintroducing the more intermediate positions that the sufferer has temporarily lost sight of.

Open expression of suicidal feelings also enables the helper to judge the level of the sufferer's desperation, how committed she seems to be to the intention of dying, how specific the plans are that she has made for killing herself, and to respond accordingly. It is appropriate to increase the frequency of appointments. Explicit instructions or invitations to phone the helper to maintain contact between sessions are also helpful. A sufferer may not take up the invitation but can find it supportive to know the helper is available, should she need the contact. A helper can encourage the sufferer to alert sympathetic others who are close to or responsible for her; or it may be necessary for the helper to alert them her/himself, preferably with the sufferer's prior knowledge and agreement; otherwise this is the only time when breaches of confidentiality can be contemplated. If the risk of suicide is immediate and detailed, it is in the sufferer's interest for the helper to mobilize more help.

Knowing overdoses are possible, it is sensible to assess what is available to the sufferer at home or at work to overdose with, act to remove the drugs that are most dangerous, and keep other drugs in smaller quantities. Anti-depressants can be helpful for a time, possibly to give the sufferer some respite from her feelings, and hospitalization may be necessary in some cases.

Anti-depressants and tranquillizers are not only useful for their pharmacological effect, but also for the way they influence the form an overdose may take. A sufferer who plunges into her extreme 'bad' category may well, as a result of her extreme thinking, swallow all the pills she has got, but be prevented by her inability to make decisions from taking any more action at this instant. Providing he is adequately informed, a sufferer's GP could take the precaution of not prescribing the more risky kinds of drugs and will take care not to supply quantities large enough to be lethal, while ensuring his patient still has something she can take to deaden the despair. In some cases this strategy may be adequate to 'hold' a sufferer through a suicidal period. The alternative, as chaos and desperation increase, is that the sufferer might resort to the more dangerous of the pain-killing drugs that are obtainable over the chemist's counter, so it is always appropriate to watch discreetly. Time can be crucial when it comes to caring for a person who has overdosed. Should hospital treatment be necessary, ward staff should bear in mind that the patient is anorexic/bulimic. Though she has needed a stomach pump, she will also need to be fed.

Stealing

For the starving anorexic who shoplifts, or the bulimic who takes food from a supermarket prior to a binge–vomit cycle, there is sometimes an effective defence to a charge of theft based on the absence of a prior dishonest intention. In lawyer's language many sufferers lack the necessary 'guilty mind' or *mens rea* because of their biochemically altered state.[4] A sufferer needs to know that in law taking goods by itself does not establish that a theft has occurred.

Her very low self-esteem ensures that she feels bad and deeply guilty anyway, so she will assume that, having taken the goods, she is therefore proved guilty. These preconceptions thus render her the more vulnerable to a verdict that will provide her, and her family, with yet further evidence of how low she has sunk. Her attitude is likely to be similar to that of the bulimic university student who automatically pleaded guilty, having been found taking food from a department store. When she came before the court, she was asked by the magistrate whether she knew what her guilty plea meant.

STUDENT: It means I took the food. I must've done. It was in my bag when I was stopped. Nobody else could've put it in there.

JP: No, it means you set out from home intending to steal. That you went to the store thinking how to take goods without being seen.

STUDENT: Oh, no! I had no idea I'd even gone into the shop. I meant to go swimming, but the fitness centre was closed.

The magistrate in this case refused the student's plea and referred her to the duty solicitor. He advised her to plead not guilty, arranged for an informed medical report from a psychiatrist experienced in working with patients with eating disorders and, once the court had the full facts, a verdict of not guilty was returned.

References

1 Slade, R. (1984). *The Anorexia Nervosa Reference Book*, London, Harper and Row, 36–7.
2 Slade, R. (1984). ibid., 55–9, 64–6.
3 Slade, R. (1984). ibid., 65–6.
4 Welbourne, J., 'Do bulimics really steal?', (in press).
Slade, R. (1984). ibid., 70.

· FOURTEEN ·

Moving towards a real sense of self

At weights around 85-per-cent AEBW and above it is possible to reach the sufferer most easily and work with the existential malaise that lies at the root of anorexia nervosa/bulimia. This has, of course, been the aim throughout the preceding chapters where the suggested interventions have consistently been those calculated to enhance her sense of autonomy rather than destroy it. But within this top band of weights all her faculties will be present, so therapy can be more wide ranging and progress may be more rapid.

It is still appropriate to keep watch on patterns of eating, non-eating, vomiting, bingeing, etc., and, as part of the whole picture, to note fluctuations in weight. But the main task now is to deal with the underlying lack of a sense of self in a person who has been inadvertently drawn into the starvation whirlpool by the need to feel that at least in some way she is author of her own life; a path she took because it was compatible with the values and aspirations she grew up with.

With the problem thus identified, it might be assumed that therapy can now be a relatively straightforward matter of using techniques that have been found generally to be helpful in assisting personal growth and change, such as gestalt, psychodrama, encounter, assertiveness training and so on. It might seem that the experiences of self-discovery they engender will automatically be beneficial but, while these therapies are certainly a useful source of ideas, they are not applicable to anorexia nervosa/bulimia sufferers in any simple way.

The main difficulty in their use lies in the fact that, even when the effects of starvation have receded, the sufferer's sense of self remains one that has been formed around food and body control. She still believes that in this food-control self she has a solution to her problem of how to live. The helper may know it is an aberrant solution that can destroy her both physically and psychologically, but it is the only solution the sufferer knows. She may have no conviction that any alternative is necessary, or she may lack all faith that there can be any alternative and so cling to her belief that, if only she were totally controlled, all her difficulties would permanently be resolved.

We have been to some lengths to show that food/body control is far more efficient than most people realize at providing any person who lacks a sense of self with a feeling of self-directedness and autonomy. Thus while her control routines are in place, the anorexic/bulimic will still appear to the world as someone who seems to be strong and effective, and this will still create difficulties.

Therapists and counsellors who are new to the task of helping the anorexia nervosa/bulimia sufferer do not realize how very limited her sense of her own being is outside her food-control routines. Her apparent effectiveness encourages them to assume she can put together or integrate the experiences that therapy itself creates. Consequently they tend to engage their skills and techniques at too 'advanced' a level. But the reality is that the sufferer is so conflicted and fragmented, and so wound up in the anxiety and frustration this brings, that she cannot, and indeed dare not, use new experiences of any kind, including those she gains in therapy. Not only does she typically feel humiliated, indeed mortified, by would-be therapeutic experiences (see Chapter Six), but when therapies focus on parts of herself, or create more parts, there is a real danger that this will serve merely to increase her fragmentation. Where gestalt therapy is used, for example, she will hold on to parts of her perceptions and be unable to allow these parts of herself to flow together and connect as a whole. Or unless special care is taken to avoid this, she will merely integrate new experiences around her old, established pattern of food restriction and control. The exercise itself will merely reinforce her lack of experience of existing as a complete person beyond food and body control.

She is frustrated by techniques that involve her being asked to act out roles. This to her is an empty game. She already sees her life as an act, a meaningless pretence. This can merely seem to her to engage in more lies. Similar problems bedevil self-assertion therapy. It is difficult to assert a self that does not exist (see Chapter Eight), and her rigid food/body control self she is already well practised at asserting.

It is easy meanwhile for helpers to remain unaware that they are engaging the mechanisms of therapy without engaging the client, that they are meeting only the sufferer's well-practised performance or false front and not engaging with the underlying existential problem at all. But the sufferer will know something is wrong. She will know that the exercise of therapy is not really touching her, but she will be at a loss to know what to do about it. She will feel yet again she is a fraud, or a failure at therapy, and this will increase her hopelessness and her despair.

For the anorexia nervosa/bulimia sufferer help needs to begin at a much more fundamental level. The task is not to assist her in enhancing the self she has. It is the more delicate process of enabling her to create and define herself anew. This involves organizing basic experiences from which selfhood can grow, and eventually supplant, her need for food control. It is a process that involves the helper reaching through the sufferer's protective façades and sharing the frightening emptiness, the sense of nothingness and 'not being' that lies beyond them, and out of these experiences helping her generate a sense of being. By the time gestalt, self-assertion skills and other techniques of these kinds can be used to full effect, the sufferer will already have made considerable, and painful progress.

Choice, decision and defining self

A crucial part in the process of creating and defining self is choice and decision making. Without the ability to choose or decide for herself, the sufferer cannot act or achieve in a way that gives her a sense of existing in her own right.

Where the anorexic or bulimic is concerned, the helper will need to focus on the finest detail of her choosing and deciding. Again, few people without experience of helping anorexics/bulimics realize how very minute the choices and decision are that they have difficulty in resolving. Few realize the extent to which they rely on externally derived routines provided by work, study or other people's routines to get anything done. To many it seems highly implausible that, for instance, a successful psychology undergraduate, or an efficient staff nurse in a busy surgical ward should, when left to herself, be unable to make a decision to move from one point in the room to another, or take her coat off, or, having made a cup of black coffee, to drink it. Yet this is, as we have shown, the degree of her indecisiveness. It is at this minute and detailed level that her choosing is paralysed, that she loses both her sense of self and her traction on the world.

Where therapy attends to the minutiae of choosing and decision making and attends particularly to *who* is doing the choosing and *who* is doing the deciding, then the sufferer will usually begin to gain the traction she needs; she will gain a sense of herself as a person who can initiate action that springs from her own will, or volition – as distinct from will-power – and so gradually develop a feeling that she exists for herself. Effective choices, no matter how minute, are affirmations of self that can be built on.

Constituent parts of choosing and deciding

Feelings and sensations are important for making choices and decisions, for these are the source of the wishes and wants that are the basis of personal preferences. Without prior wishing or wanting that comes from within the person, choices and decisions cannot be made, especially when external demands conflict, which is the overwhelming experience of the anorexia nervosa/bulimia sufferer.

Equally important on the other hand is accurate knowledge of the world, of how the world *really* is rather than how it *ought* to be. Judgemental and non-accepting of themselves as they are, sufferers also characteristically deny themselves 'value free' information about their world. It *must* be 'positive', no matter what distortion of reality this entails. Yet access to and acceptance of information 'from outside' is essential if choices and decisions are to connect with people, events and situations in a way that is real and down to earth.

When wishes and wants are freely felt and are combined with an understanding of the world that is grounded in how that world really is on the evidence of current testing, then effective choice is the more likely. The actions that follow from such choice are satisfying and rewarding and so contribute to, rather than detract from, the person's sense of self. They enhance confidence and build self-esteem.

Learning to live in the present

Decisions and actions take place in the present. It is in the present that the feelings occur upon which preferences for action are based. From the present moment a great deal can be learned about what bears upon the person who is deciding. Thus the simple technique of helping the sufferer to focus on the minute detail of her moment-by-moment experience is a potent means of helping her gain leverage on her problem.

Staying in the present involves the sufferer allowing herself to be aware of, and possibly express, feelings, wishes and experiences that arise in the here and now as she relates with the helper within the limited and prescribed world of the therapy session. It involves exploring in this context how she chooses, and where her choosing becomes paralysed. Helping the client to focus on herself in this way is rather like encouraging her to place herself and the way she relates to the world under a microscope. Initially just a few minutes of this exercise will provide sufficient detail of experience for the helper and sufferer to work on. Each experience that occurs, each aspect of herself that she allows to surface and risks exploring – be it intellectual, emotional, physical or spiritual – can bear on and connect with every other aspect of her self. Thus, although she may not see herself in this way, she has the potential to be wholly present, 'connected' as a person, and to the world. Thus focusing on herself in the present will enable her to *real*ize her self.

In Chapter Twelve we illustrated how it is possible for a helper to direct the sufferer's attention, even when she is so starved and emaciated, towards her own personal wishes and wants in relation to her current situation, and, by continually bringing her alternatives for action into focus, help her to adjust her actions in accordance with her real wishes and so have a greater chance of realizing them. The anorexic at that stage was physically at risk and psychologically shut down, and the task of choosing was closely framed by the constraints these changes produced. The decision there was concerned with whether she would stay out of hospital and how to achieve this. In essence the task of helping her focus on the real choices and decisions she is making, and on what is involved in her making them, is no different at this point from the task as it was then. But, when her weight is in this topmost band, she will usually have ordinary access to her feelings, and the more ready potential to make connections and integrate her experiences.

Discovering personal rules and core beliefs

The very suggestion that she might stay in the here and now is one that will immediately bring to the surface the tangle of rules and beliefs she is living by, which will by now be familiar. For these are the rules and beliefs that reflect her moral, rule-bound nature, her extreme sensitivity to the needs of others and her sense of profound personal worthlessness (see Chapter Six). They are the 'shoulds', 'oughts' and 'musts' that are derived from, and continually reinforced by, the culture of which she and her particular family are so much a part (see Chapter Seven).

The exercise itself will conflict with her rule that she ought not to attend to herself, and with her belief that she is not worth attention. So it will immediately generate discomfort in her. The following is a typical response. 'I can't sit here and just talk about myself. Talking about me makes me feel guilty. There's no way I can avoid feeling selfish if we're talking about me.'

It will conflict with other rules that she has too, that fix her in a 'past or future' pattern, and so continually work to prevent her from focusing on her awareness of how she is in the here and now. One of these, for instance, may be: 'I have always been so bad [in the past] I must strive to be better [in the future]'; or, 'I am so negative. I must look to the future where there might be a chance I could be positive.' These rules will tie in with other equally fundamental rules and beliefs, such as 'I alone must take full responsibility for who and what I am. I *must* be right.' (See also Chapter Seven.)

As she is encouraged to explore her rules and beliefs, conflict between these will also emerge. While she believes she ought to strive to be better in future, she will also believe that she can only ever be worthless. This way the value and purpose of her striving are instantly negated, and her conviction that she is hopeless becomes the more profound. Similarly, while she must be sensitive to others' needs, she must also be the winner; she has to be the best, yet this creates hurtful failure for others (see Chapter Eight). The helper's attempt to acknowledge her may assist in bringing to light her rule that she must get everything absolutely right for others; she must be as the other person wants her to be. Hence she may say exasperatedly to her helper: 'Tell me what you want me to do! How d'you want me to be?' But, not believing she can get anything right *ever*, for *anyone*, there will be painful conflict here too.

Thus there is no especial need to delve with the sufferer into her past. For the rules and beliefs that will emerge from the exercise of staying in the present will illuminate the way the paralysing conflict that sustains anorexia nervosa/bulimia is continually being created in the present.

The variety of rules that emerges is actually quite limited, but all will reflect her characteristic lifestyle. So that she may become the more familiar with this aspect of herself and learn where she might risk change, the helper may encourage a sufferer to formulate her particular set of rules and beliefs in her own words, for example: 'I must never be wrong. I must always be absolutely right/good/perfect'; 'Only the best is good enough'; 'I should put others' needs/feelings before my own, otherwise I am selfish'; 'I must be pleasing/acceptable to/liked by everyone'; 'I should think the right/proper thoughts'; 'I must not have wants, I ought not to have needs of my own. I must give to others'; 'Emotional behaviour is wrong/disturbing to others and I ought not to upset anyone'; 'Feelings are unreasonable/self indulgent. I ought not to be unreasonable. I must not be self indulgent,' and so on.

Each sufferer's own particular rules or guiding convictions will present themselves in her responses to the helper. As they emerge, the helper may carefully draw her attention to the conflicts and mismatches and show her how they lead to her suppressing, or otherwise denying herself access to, the very information within herself that would enable her to know what her own wishes and wants are, how they prevent her connecting with her world as it currently is, and so how they stymie her choosing and decision making at every turn. By becoming aware of them as they emerge, the sufferer may be helped to gain insight into the ways they trap her in self-denying and self-defeating patterns of thinking that both maintain, and reinforce, her low self-esteem.

It would be mistaken to assume, however, that just because she does gain some insight here that she can, or will, alter her approach. Clear access to her feelings and greater confidence in her perceptions are also necessary to this, as is a great deal of practice in coping with the fine detail of moment-by-moment living. There is in fact a long and painful journey between insight and achieved change.

Acknowledging the rest of the iceberg

Attending to the fine detail of the decision-making process will eventually enable the sufferer to create her own change. But helpers will often find themselves attempting to communicate with someone who is markedly unresponsive. The sufferer will often describe herself as 'a very private person'. In line with this she will give away very little information about what she is currently thinking, feeling or experiencing, either spoken, or in terms of body language. In the early weeks and even months helpers will frequently have to rely on their knowledge of the condition to keep the therapy session alive.

The sufferer may, as we have said, reject the idea of attending to herself as being selfish. Or she might be very confused by the suggestion that she does something that she believes is neither right nor proper. Her confusion may be further complicated by guilt and anxiety at not doing as is being suggested to her. On top of these uncomfortable and unwanted feelings she is also likely to have a rule that she ought not to be confused. She ought to be clear, intelligent, she *ought* to know what to do. She *should* know the answers. She will be going round in endless circles, on a dizzy merry-go-round of feelings and obligations with no way of stopping, and no way of getting off. She may panic at this or end up feeling totally blank. But she will reveal nothing of this to the helper.

Rules such as 'I ought not to cause trouble' will stop her openly disagreeing with the helper's suggestion. She would rather not come back to another session than state her disagreement. Bad as she feels about herself, she cannot afford to be disliked by anybody. Discomforted as she is by disagreements, she cannot afford to make enemies or create situations in which she may have to assert any aspect of herself that may result in her feeling worse about herself than she does already. Saying nothing is also a way of considering the helper's feelings. It is this rule that can nullify the effectiveness of self-assertion exercises, as the sufferer demonstrated who dismissed a manual on assertiveness training with the comment 'I see what they mean. But I don't think people ought to behave like that. It just seems exceedingly self-centred and inconsiderate. It wouldn't be very pleasant to be like that.' Being assertive over righteous causes is more acceptable. This kind of assertion is justified because it is on behalf of other people or things. But the whole idea of taking a stand for her own sake she will believe to be morally wrong.

It is important to let the sufferer know that these ways of thinking, feeling and responding, are typical of the person who is anorexic or bulimic, and that they are by no means unusual for other people either. This can be particularly important where the sufferer is mute or recalcitrant. By indicating that these experiences are shared, and understandable, the helper may make it safe enough for the sufferer to bring her thoughts and feelings into the open. The less defended she becomes, the more she will learn about who she is and how she might change.

While encouraging the sufferer to become more expressive and more accurately aware of how she currently is, it is crucial for the helper to remain tuned to the fact that the sufferer's real self is so tentative and fragile she does not have the resources to cope with even the most minor intrusions. Even talking to her can leave her feeling invaded, exploited, controlled. So it must be made equally clear to her that it is entirely acceptable for her to keep her thoughts, feelings and experiences to herself. She does not have to share them with the helper, and it is important that the helper does not create an obligation, unspoken or otherwise, that she should. The 'very private person' she is needs to be explicitly respected.

Yet while clarifying the sufferer's right to say and do nothing, the helper may usefully suggest that the sufferer herself notices what stops her expressing herself; that she allows herself to become aware of the points at which she habitually censors herself. For this can tell her much about herself and her way of relating to the world, even though she may not yet be ready to let those aspects of herself out into the open.

Allowing feelings and emotions

In addition to becoming clearer about her deeply held rules and beliefs and how they bind her, the sufferer will need to allow herself freer access to her feelings and emotions if she is to come to make choices and decisions effectively. But again this is likely to be problematic. She will be afraid that, if she does focus on her feelings, the experience will be too painful, too terrifying, too upsetting, too unbearable. She will be very scared of being swamped by her own emotion. Her often unspoken fear is: 'If I do that I might cry, and if I let myself cry I'll never be able to stop'; or 'I'll get angry and then it'll get unreasonable and out of hand'; or 'I hate myself and I know I hate myself, so what's the point? Just hate, hate, hate – so it's not worth going on. I might just as well kill myself.'

Not only is she afraid of being overwhelmed and unable to cope with herself if she lets go of her feelings. She will also be afraid of the effect this will have on others, including the helper. Her specific fears may be that they will be unable to cope with her, or that as a result of expressing her feelings she will jeopardize what relationship she has with them and leave her more isolated and out of touch than she already feels. So the helper will find that the sufferer skids easily this way and that, diverting and distracting into anything, or anybody – especially anybody else who appears to need help – rather than focus on who *she* is, and how *she* feels in the here and now.

For instance, when she is asked about her own feelings or experiences, she will characteristically reply in terms of other people's feelings and experiences. Where the helper holds the focus for her, the sufferer may discover for herself how readily she 'disappears' or 'merges' with someone or something else.

VEE: I can see what I'm doing. I just go blank every time. I noticed I looked out of the window just then, when you asked me how *I* was feeling. I disappeared. Completely cut off.
HELPER: From?
VEE: [Pause] Attention.
HELPER: My paying attention to you?
VEE: I suppose so. [Pause] But that's silly. Because I always thought I wanted attention. But it seems I don't.
HELPER: I'm attending to you now. How does this make you feel?
VEE: [Pause] Scared.
HELPER: You're scared. Of?
VEE: What you might notice.
HELPER: What are you scared I might notice?
VEE: [Pause] How inconfident I am.

Sufferers typically find it very difficult to use the word 'I' in relation to their own feelings. They struggle to make statements that begin with 'I want' and 'I need' without adding 'oughts' and 'shoulds'. Experiments in making simple statements of this kind without adding 'oughts' and 'shoulds' can help a sufferer to stay in the here and now. They also enable her to practise expressing current feelings and current wishes and looking at what her feelings are rather than what they ought to be; then, in relation to these, eventually arriving at preferences, and making decisions on the basis of priorities that are her own.

A helper may enable the sufferer to flex her rules and beliefs just enough to ensure that she no longer dismisses therapy out of hand as self indulgent, or as something she does not deserve, or should not have because she *ought* to be able to manage on her own. But it can still take months of regular sessions before a tightly controlled anorexic will risk, as she sees it, humiliating herself by revealing her 'weakness', showing her vulnerability by crying in front of her helper, or will risk letting herself down by being irritated or angry. There are sufferers who may be more emotional, but they will usually be less ready to reveal or admit to feelings that one woman described as 'the more twisted and shameful ones', such as jealousy and resentment, or touch the more deeply painful disappointment and grief. 'It's when I think of what I've lost . . . the waste, ten years of my life [her face distorting with emotion] like this . . . I could cry . . . but somehow I can't. It feels too deep.'

While crying, anger, laughter can usefully relieve tension, catharsis alone will not result in the sufferer being able to move on from her conflicted and paralysed position. It does not by itself resolve conflict and may even provide a place to 'hide'. For it is possible to cry or rage, or indeed talk, whilst omitting to acknowledge other simultaneously occurring experiences, and so not connect at other levels. It is possible to be emotional and at the same time ignore an underlying statement that may run, 'I believe this is what this therapist wants me to do, so I'll express and get her/his approval.' On the other hand, as we pointed out in Chapter Six, being pushed into expressing more than she is ready for will merely add to her chaos by introducing yet more variables to the tangle of feelings and wishes and rules that she is already failing to cope with. A sufferer who is merely encouraged to express her feelings is in danger of being left with the same sense of wheelspin as she endured from endlessly analysing and criticizing herself, thinking herself round in circles. She will be left with the same sense of pointlessness and frustration but this time through 'making a noise and going nowhere'.

Relating to the world

Attention will also need to be given to achieving relatedness to the world; the other essential part of the process of choice and decision and resolving conflict.

The sufferer doubts the value of her emotions and, highly perceptive though she is of people and situations, she has little trust in her perceptions. Confused as she has become, she has lost all faith in herself and all confidence in her ability to make sense of her world and her relationships within it. Her lack of confidence is, in large part, rooted in her experience within a family that, for its own historic reasons and often from the highest motives, has covered up its painful or difficult past by 'making everything right', or 'making everything better', thus denying the facts and the experience that would have confirmed the sufferer's own sense that things were not as they were made out to be. Experiences at school and work and in relationships beyond her immediate family will often have confirmed her lack of confidence, and specific instances of loss and failure may also have shaken her; instances that, as we have said, may not always appear significant to others.

She needs encouragement, therefore, to allow herself to relate to what is going on around her, so she can test and assure herself of the accuracy of her own perceptions, and so gain confidence in these. As with matters concerning food, weight and eating, straightforward information given by the helper can be useful here too. But even more so is the affirmation of self that can be gained first hand.

HELPER: To me you looked angry, when I suggested you experimented with moving by moving physically – taking a few steps away from the chair.

MEL: [Silence]

HELPER: Are you feeling angry now?

MEL: [Silence]

HELPER: I'm wondering what it is you're not saying.

MEL: [Still silent and looking more tense]

HELPER: You don't have to tell me. I don't mind if you don't want to.

MEL: [Scowling]: I suppose I feel pushed.

HELPER: You feel pushed. By me, now?

MEL: [Tight-lipped]: Mmm.

HELPER: Yes. I am pushing you. My own feeling, as I sit here, is that I'm pushing you. Hard. [Mel looks up with an expression of surprise – and some relief] How do you feel at my saying that?

MEL: [Thoughtfully] Relieved, I think. . . . You didn't deny what I was feeling.

Thus in the immediate relationship between sufferer and helper there lies the foundation for the sufferer's establishing, or re-establishing, through her own experience her relatedness with the world.

To help the sufferer connect what is happening in the here and now to her experience of herself in the world outside, as well as to encourage her to experiment further, the above conversation might continue in the following way.

HELPER: I wonder if feeling pushed is a familiar experience for you?

MEL: Yes, and it always makes me angry.

HELPER: Try looking at me and saying, 'No! I don't want to move away from the chair.' [Pause] Try it as a way of pushing me back.

MEL: I can't. [Long pause] It's hard to look at you. I feel ashamed. [Pause] I ought to be able to move away from this chair. [Pause] I feel angry with myself. I do want to! I want to be able to move from here, but I feel stuck. I *ought* to be able to do such a silly little thing. But this is what happens when I'm on my own, when I've got time and space to myself, I just can't move!

HELPER: You can't move. [Affirming her statement] I'm wondering whether there's a thought or a feeling in you now that goes with that sense of 'I can't move!'

MEL: I mustn't get it wrong!

HELPER: You mustn't get it wrong. [Pause] Who for?

MEL: Me. It's got to be right. [Sounding irritated] Absolutely right. That's what I'm telling myself. Otherwise I won't do it. [Pause] If I move, it might not achieve anything.

HELPER: And you've got to achieve something?

MEL: Always. . . . And if I make any move I must know in advance what every little outcome will be.

HELPER [nodding, and pausing]: Are you comfortable standing as you are now?

MEL: No. I feel stiff.

HELPER: How about risking a move? Maybe see whether you can let yourself be a bit more comfortable?

MEL [silent at first, then annoyed]: I just caught myself then thinking, 'I don't deserve to be comfortable'. [Pause] That's how I put the stoppers on myself. Trap myself, all round!

In Chapter Twelve we suggested the sufferer might be encouraged by the idea of seeing herself as an experimental scientist in finding out about herself in relation to weight and eating. In the same way she may find it useful to see the exercises of focusing in the present moment, expressing her thoughts and feelings, and attending to how she is relating, as different kinds of scientific experiment, ones from which she may learn that she need neither cling to control, nor flip into chaos, but can choose to move from these extremes towards a more middle position.

It is important for the helper to assess a sufferer's readiness at any time for a particular exercise or experiment and make it clear, as we have said, that she does not have to do something just because the helper suggests it. Nor should the helper underestimate the degree of support a sufferer needs to be able to risk a move.

Characteristically the sufferer would like a magic wand or a miracle to make her better instantly, and she clings to the hope that there might be one. As one anorexic said, 'I thought if I kept on coming here, to these counselling sessions, I'd wake up one morning and it would all be all right.' Beneath this lies an example of extreme thinking: 'I want to (must) be better this instant! Otherwise I'll never be better at all.' Likewise they often cherish the belief that, if they were 'normal', there would be no failure, no unhappiness, no discomfort, that even if a problem did arise it would be instantly resolved.

It is a significant step forward when a sufferer begins to let go of these ideas and allow and accept that 'normality' is not so static; that there is no once-and-for-all, instantly achievable resolution of conflict; that to be alive is to be part of a fluid and changing process that continually produces new challenges. It is a move when she begins to accept that practical steps involving trial and error are steps she can take in response to these challenges, and to accept that these can be steps where 'you win a bit and you lose a bit'. She does not have to strive to win absolutely, all the time.

It can take months, both in therapy sessions and in the process of learning that continues to take place between times outside this prescribed context, for a sufferer to accept not only that there are such risks of trial and error to take, but that it is *she* who has to take them. Neither the helper nor anyone else can take her risks for her. They cannot make her decisions about expressing and exploring feelings, or about experimenting with different ways of relating with the world, any more than they can make for her a decision to eat (see Chapter Twelve). In other words she has to engage her real self, however little of this she may allow, in the therapeutic process.

Help can be given; indeed it is essential. But she will probably also need to learn to allow herself to take it, to amend her belief that 'I ought to achieve everything entirely on my own, otherwise it is not rightfully and deservedly my achievement.'

Nor are such lengths of time unusual. For any individual the process of learning to live and live effectively may be seen as a process of a lifetime, and at any point appropriate therapy can enhance this. But the person who has become trapped in an anorexic/bulimic style of thinking and who has undergone the experiences and changes in personality that this condition creates will need a longer time to let go of the familiar 'security' and the familiar 'certainties' it gives.

Integrating the experience of self

Working with anorexia nervosa/bulimia sufferers who neither trust nor want their own feelings is not only a long, slow process, but one in which help is often not so much a task of organizing access to feelings, for they already feel a great deal, nor of improving perceptions, for these are often highly accurate, though they have lost faith in them. It is more a task of encouraging them to allow their rigidly held rules and beliefs to give a little, so that they can acknowledge and accept their thoughts and feelings, and their perceptions, and use them more effectively.

Just as at the low-weight stages it is the helper who has to make the mental adjustments to get through and communicate with the anorexic, so it is the helper who has to take the initiative to direct and structure the sufferer's experience, even at this stage. The helper will also have to be a visible person in this process, to be experienced as real her/himself. The sufferer needs the security of being contained in this way, of 'knowing where she is' clearly in relation to the helper.

While the task for the sufferer is to define her self, to do so is to risk change, and this risking takes enormous courage. She will need to be allowed time to learn to believe and trust herself, and so to gain the confidence to choose to follow her *own* direction. But where the helper enables her to become more aware of the moments where she *is* choosing, more aware of the nature of her choices, and of alternative choices she might experiment with making; where she gradually allows herself to try out these alternative ways, her confidence in herself will gradually increase.

HELPER: Listening to you I have the impression you've got a rule for yourself that goes something like: I ought not to be happy. Does that sound like you?

KAY: Mmm.

HELPER: How about saying that statement for yourself. See if it really belongs to you.

KAY [pause]: I ought not to be happy. Yes. I believe that. It's true, I've no right to be happy. That's for other people.

HELPER: Happiness is for other people. So when you are happy, you *choose not* to have that feeling? You choose to follow your rule: 'I ought not to be happy.' And then make sure you're not? [Kay nods slightly] How about trying out something a bit different. See how you feel now saying 'I can be happy'?

KAY [tentatively]: I can be happy . . . [Pause] But I'm not! [Hunches herself up over her knees] I'm miserable feeling so stuck!

HELPER [gently]: No. OK. You're not happy right now. I can see that. [Pause] There are times when you can be though. I wonder, d'you remember you told me a few months ago you'd gone for a walk and you'd felt happy just sitting by a pool in the fields near you? [Pause] How about trying out the statement another way. 'I can be happy sometimes.'

KAY: I can be happy . . . [Anxiously] But then I think straightaway I ought to be happy all the time. Everyone will expect me to be happy all the time. And I know I'm not. I can't be.

HELPER: No. You can't be. [Affirming her statement] Because feelings are things that change. They come and they go, and they come again, if you let them. [Informing about the nature of feelings] Sometimes you feel hurt, angry, bored, guilty, disappointed . . . sometimes you feel happy.

KAY: It's too insecure, being happy. I'm scared something might happen to spoil it. So I rush on. Must keep going. Always on to the next thing.

An alternative movement might be suggested here; a change the sufferer might try out for herself, in her own time. For instance:

HELPER: How about experimenting? Allowing yourself a different choice: to feel whatever happens to be going on in you – happy when you're happy, disappointed when you're disappointed – without rushing away from those feelings. Without rushing into what might happen next. I'm not saying you'll feel comfortable that way. But those moments belong to you. They are your happiness, your disappointment, and bitterness perhaps. They're all part of you.

Since attention will need to be given to the process of integrating experience, to encouraging the sufferer to allow her experiences to connect, providing ways of doing this will usually be helpful. For example:

HELPER: As you let yourself sense what's going on in you, try letting yourself see each experience of you as a fragment of a stained-glass window. So maybe your experience is 'I sense myself as cold, and somehow edgy.' Study this fragment closely while it's in focus: 'Now my edginess is changing, to a restlessness . . . or perhaps another feeling, or thought. Stay with that part of you while it's there, in your awareness . . . and at the same time be aware that all these fragments are joined. Held together, like a stained-glass window, with lead: your complete picture. This is who you are. Every part needs to be present. Every fragment of you is essential for your picture of you to be whole . . .

KAY: I like the idea. But I don't know if I'd be able to do it.

HELPER: You like the idea. [Affirming her] You don't have to be able to do anything with it. Let liking it be enough for the moment? Allow yourself to focus it now. Gently let it in. This idea you like can nourish and strengthen you too. It belongs to you. Like your happy moments. It's part of you. No one can take it away from you. It'll be there in you when you want it.

KAY [very thoughtfully]: I've never looked at it like that before.

Confidence and relaxation are essential to being able to take in an idea or experience and then 'let go' of it without analysing its meaning, or taking it to pieces in a desperate attempt to 'make sense' of it. They are essential to being able to let go and at the same time to remain assured that this 'part' will be there to emerge from within, as a personal resource, as and when needed. This is the confidence illustrated by the former bulimic who found herself able to say as she contemplated the week ahead of her: 'I'll be all right. It'll come together. Nowadays I just wait and see. I don't analyse so much. The ideas just connect. It feels much better. *I know where I am*.'

Where the helper is careful to 'feed' the sufferer clear, constant affirmations and does so in such a way that she can assimilate these, then her ability to relax will increase and her confidence will grow. Indeed as she becomes more sure of who she is, the more readily she will be able to affirm herself. Nor need self-affirmations necessarily spring from conventionally 'pleasant' episodes. One recovering anorexic gained a great deal from a moment when she found herself able to tell her parents directly, face to face, that she was angry with them. Still openly anxious about her calorie intake, she had suggested the soup she had just eaten had been thickened. Simultaneously her grandmother, who had made the soup, said that it had, and her parents said that it had not.

> I was angry, and suddenly instead of keeping it all to myself I said: 'I despise you! I've told you I'm still scared, and you were prepared to lie! I despise you for that.' Don't know how I came to say it, but I did! I felt very hot and cold afterwards. OK, they're scared I'll slide back, but it doesn't help if they lie about food. I know I'm not as panicky as I was. But I still get anxious, and I still need to know what I'm eating, because it makes me feel safer.

Hence change can be difficult for those close to the sufferer. There are many ways in which her getting better can appear as 'getting worse'. As another substantially recovered twenty-year-old remarked: 'I think my family's surprised how selfish I've become. Before, if I said I didn't want to go out with them, I'd have felt really guilty for a week. Now I feel guilty for about ten minutes!'

Signs and sounds of recovery

Accustomed as she has been to feeling and telling herself she is bad, worthless and hopeless, the sufferer will easily dismiss and forget positive experiences. She will need time to alter this pattern and learn to accept and assimilate complements and expressions of caring, affection and love, rather than push these aside in favour of the criticisms, punishment and blame that are easier to take in because she has so long believed these are what she deserves. Being predictable and familiar they are much safer. Yet as she gains confidence in her own feelings and perceptions, as she allows herself to believe the positive affirmations her helper and others give her, her sense of 'nothingness' will diminish. She will begin to feel she is worthwhile.

There are often very minute shifts that indicate this change in attitude and in her growing sense of self is taking place. It is useful for helpers to be able to recognize the signs and sounds of these shifts, to keep them in focus for the sufferer, to hold her direction when she cannot, when she gets lost. It may well be appropriate too to point them out to her family as the steps towards recovery that they are.

An important sign is when the sufferer begins to be able to express straightforward statements about her personal wishes, needs and wants without becoming totally paralysed by guilt or shame or the feeling that she must placate. These will not be the global or absolute statements, such as 'I want to be normal' and 'I wish I could be better instantly'; nor the statements where the wish implies a 'must', such as 'I need to (must) know exactly what is happening and what everyone is doing all the time so I know where I am.' Rather they are statements that are grounded in what is actually possible, or likely, for her at the time, that express wishes and needs that, with or without help, she personally may have a reasonable expectation of fulfilling. At low weight a wish may revolve around food, or medical intervention. 'I don't want to go into hospital. I'm sure about that. So I need to try and do it for myself. I could try that drink you suggested at bedtime . . . just for a start. But I'm so petrified!' [68-per-cent AEBW] She may express needs that bear on her relationships with others. (The girl's weight here is around 78-per-cent AEBW and increasing.)

> I need a bit of encouragement sometimes. Not just with eating. Though I do want to get over this thing about I *must* eat on my own. It's when people drop in, and unexpected things like that happen. I need Mum and Dad to know how panicky it makes me when everything's not exactly as planned. . . . I need a bit of encouragement, because when it gets panicky I lose confidence and just run away.

A sufferer who originally believed she ought not to take up a helper's time is progressing, not regressing, when she asks for support, as one woman did, for instance, by asking for an earlier appointment in a week where her husband was going to be away. She was unsure about coping on her own and felt this would help her feel safer and avoid binges.

Often sufferers find they express themselves in terms of what they do not want or do not need. These expressions may be quite clear statements of their personal preferences. But so strong is their rule that they 'ought to be positive' or 'think positively', they dismiss them or judge them as invalid because they are negative statements. Yet there is a positive side to knowing and expressing what is not wanted or needed at the moment. For when these 'layers' are peeled off, the number of alternatives is diminished and it becomes easier to be clear about what she *does* want.

Signs of self-acceptance are a hopeful sign, and even more so when a sufferer comes to notice them in herself. The eighteen-year-old here had re-fed herself gradually, in the way we have described in the preceding chapters, from a low weight point of 68-per-cent AEBW. She made the following observation of herself when her weight was around 74 per cent and increasing slowly, and her meals were still carefully prearranged, but her attitude had significantly changed.

> I can let myself just slump in the armchair now when I've eaten my meal. I know I'm going to be exhausted, and I can let myself just flop and be lumpy. I know it won't last for ever. Before, when I felt the least bit tired like that, it would immediately be the signal to get up and go out for a long run. I'd got to do something about feeling like that, otherwise I was lazy pig.

Any changes in routine that indicate a shift in core rules and beliefs are also hopeful.

> I was going for my jog – I still need that – and I got to the crossroads and suddenly I thought, just because I turned left yesterday that doesn't mean I've got to turn left again today. So I went straight on and round, back home by a different route, and I didn't worry because it was a bit shorter.

Similarly a helper may notice the sufferer has tied her hair in a different way or happens to say: 'It was the first time I'd been out of jeans for months.' Such changes often coincide with changes in eating.

Greater flexibility and spontaneity are generally signs that a person is recovering. The less fearful she is that she might not be able to cope with the consequences, the more likely she is to be able both to initiate action herself and respond freely to others' suggestions for action and in a way that feels satisfactory and rewarding to her.

Further experiment, self-discovery and creativity

Once she has begun to learn that she can allow her needs and wants, and to learn she can order her priorities and effectively choose, then other specific therapeutic techniques become a valuable way of strengthening her feeling that she is somebody. Assertiveness training, used carefully, can be a way of allowing her to discover that she can still be sensitive and yet can say 'No', without ending up feeling completely guilty, despicable and inadequate, and say 'Yes', without feeling totally coerced, resentful and used. Providing care is taken that she does not become too overwhelmed by the feelings they stir up, psychodrama techniques and gestalt therapy may, through role play, give her a firmer grasp on the world. They may help her increase her confidence in herself as a real person who has a right to her feelings, who can mesh positively and constructively with the world, whilst still maintaining her sense of who she is. Likewise the use of dreams, images, guided fantasy, art therapy and so on can enable her to experience her imaginative and creative self in a way that can be exciting and enriching and help her reach and create herself in a deeper sense.[1]

There is, as we have said, a very high incidence of particular kinds of events in the histories of sufferers' families. These included the death of grandparents or great-grandparents occurring before the sufferer's parents or grandparents were fourteen years old. They also included rapid changes in social class, and actual or threatened changes in economic status (see Chapter Seven). But, having often happened before all the present family members were born, they are events for which none of them can really blame themselves, or indeed be blamed.

A sufferer may gain a more rooted idea of who she is by finding out about her family history and about the people who belong to her in her past. The longer perspective that this gives on the problem can also help to alleviate the burden of guilt and confusion, the paralysing sense of 'It's all my fault', that both the sufferer and members of her family feel about her having become anorexic/bulimic. To the extent that it explains and increases understanding, so this exercise may help defuse anger and increase self-acceptance.

It can also help the sufferer to integrate her experience further. To discover that certain events and situations, and the consequent rigorous adherence to a particular set of cultural values and beliefs, which she is likely to find in the history of her own family, are present so frequently in the backgrounds of all sufferers that they may be seen as constituting a reason for her having become ensnared by the illness in the first place can be very reassuring to a person who badly wants to know *why*. Such information can relax a sufferer who is typically clinging to the rational, analytical approach to all problems, including her own, and who will often ask in frustration and despair: 'But why should this have happened to *me*?' For it demonstrates that at a historical and cultural level too there is some order. Even here there is some predictability.

As a practical exercise many find discovering all that belongs to them in their past enjoyable for its own sake, and in addition it can strengthen a sufferer's relationship with her members of her family in the present. For it usually involves her inviting them, for better or worse – and often, as it turns out, for better – to talk about people, events and feelings that will usually have lain buried for years. 'It was a bit difficult at first. I wasn't sure mum wanted to talk about her family, but then in the end she seemed really pleased, and relieved. I think it's brought us much closer. I enjoyed it too.'

This cultural perspective is also relevant to the sufferer's being able to sustain her emerging sense of self. For as she becomes less isolated and makes more contact with the world, as she begins to explore the possibility of new friendships and relationships and needs to find peers, she invariably discovers that too many of the people she meets are stuck with the very beliefs and attitudes that have been so destructive to her, and that she has worked so hard to relinquish.

> I was glad when I got this job [at a garden centre]. But what's really hard is working with Betsy all day. She never eats. She has an apple at lunch. She might have a biscuit at five o'clock. She works late. Everyone says how committed she is and what a wonderful caring person, and what a way she has with plants. And I know what she's doing. She isn't stopping for meals, because she daren't.

The person who is recovering from anorexia nervosa or bulimia can thus experience a different kind of isolation at this stage, a loneliness that can make it easy, where she has no continuing support, to falter in her newly found certainty in herself and slip back into feelings of hopelessness and not believing there really can be a way through.

> I don't want to get back into anorexia again. I know I don't. But the awful thing is you begin to look around and everyone's into dieting, or being vegetarian, or aerobics, or running, or work-outs, or something, and you get to wondering, is there anything else?

Hence a helper's own self-accepting attitudes and secure sense of self are crucial anchors for the sufferer at this, as at any stage.

While a sufferer may become more able to express her own needs and preferences and create in herself her ability to choose and feel more effective in her relationship with the world, it is important that no one, neither the helper, nor her family or friends, assumes that she will always or consistently 'eat normally'. Her pattern of eating will alter. But change will be gradual and may be erratic. Relaxation over eating will tend to follow after, or happen at the same time as, she begins to change in other ways and feel more confidence and trust in herself, rather than precede these changes. It will take time before her fear of uncontrollable eating and weight gain entirely disappear, before she can say, as this woman did: 'Now when I hear that nagging little voice telling me not to eat I don't take any notice. I know it's not the *real* me.' Fears about food and weight are usually the very last to fade. But they will fade as self-confidence grows and other priorities emerge:

Of course, I don't want to be fat. But nowadays it's ordinary wanting. My life doesn't revolve around that. There are all sorts of other things I want as well that are more important. Like enjoying myself without feeling guilty, and deciding to do things on the spur of the moment. Yes, and being really able to laugh.

So she may go on experimenting and learning still, and allowing her self-acceptance to grow. She may continue to discover how she makes her choices and creates a balance between her own needs and wants and those of others, a balance between herself and the demands of external situations and events. From here she may go on learning that she can have fun, waste time, create enjoyment, that she can *be* in ways other than being in control, that she can be free to get things wrong.

Reference

1 Ernst, S. and Goodison, L. (1981). *In Our Own Hands: A Handbook of Self-help Therapy*, London, The Women's Press. (This book provides a good introduction to a variety of helping techniques and suggestions for further reading.)

Appendix

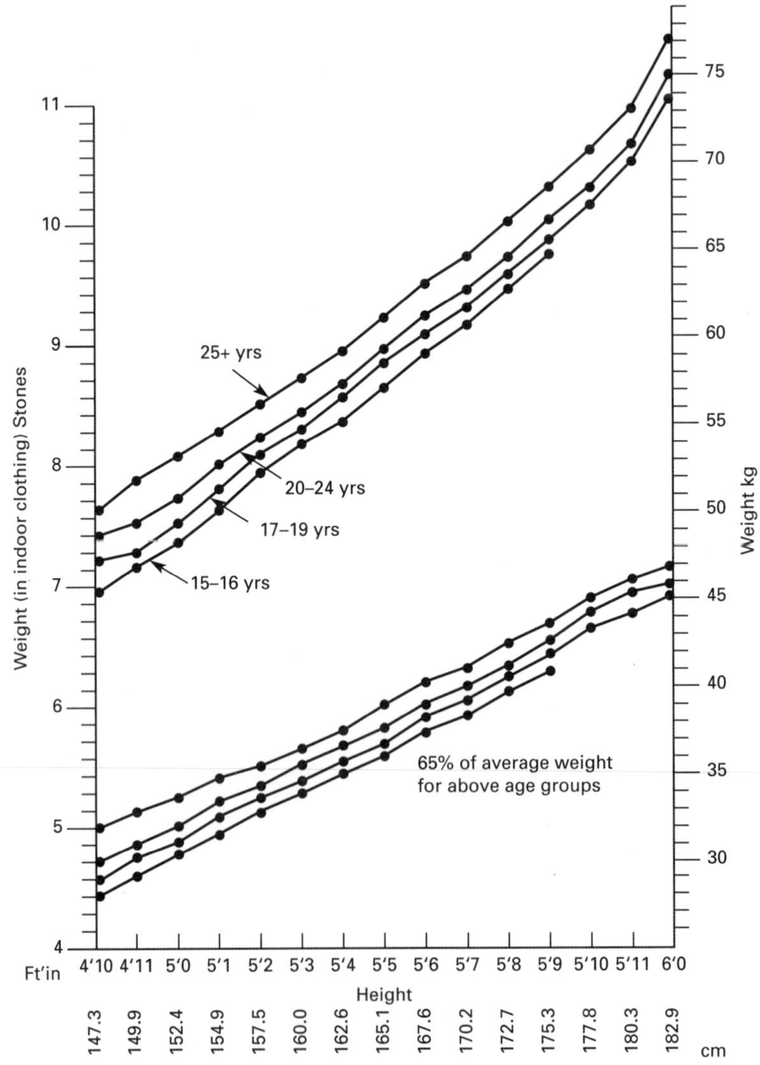

*Average weight for women. *Height was measured in indoor shoes; it is suggested that 1 in be added to normal height to read weight. Adapted from Scientific Tables from J.R. Geigy SA, Basle, Switzerland.*

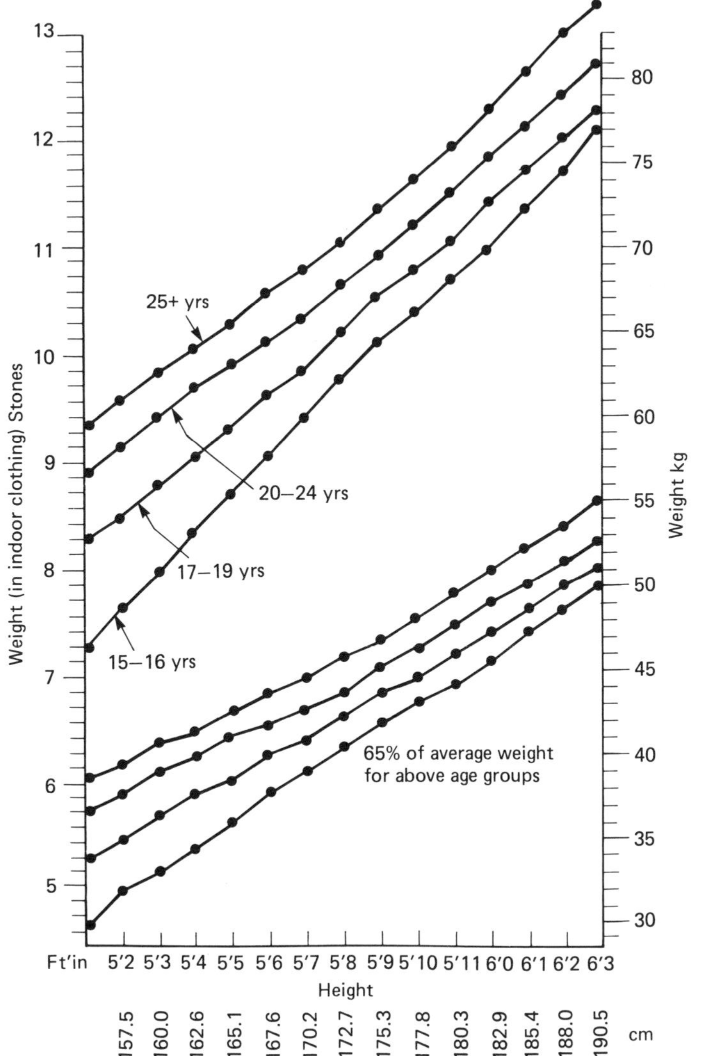

*Average weight for men. *Height was measured in indoor shoes; it is suggested that 1 in be added to normal height to read weight. Adapted from Scientific Tables from J.R. Geigy SA, Basle, Switzerland.*

Index